To Dave,

WITH MY BEST WISHES

Ray Gun

17TH JANUARY 2008

SAVE THE JUBILEE HALL !

The Jubilee Hall redevelopment on the Piazza, Covent Garden, completed 1987.
© CGHP.

SAVE THE JUBILEE HALL !

**The battle to preserve the three hundred year old
tradition of street market trading in the
Piazza of Covent Garden**

*Chuck Anderson
with Ray Green*

RANDOM THOUGHTS LIMITED
London

Anderson, Chuck with Green, Ray
SAVE THE JUBILEE HALL!
The battle to preserve the
three-hundred-year-old tradition
of street market trading in the
Piazza of Covent Garden

British Library Cataloguing-in-
Publication Data

A catalogue record for this book is
available from the British Library

ISBN 0 9513573 2 8

Published by
Random Thoughts Limited
46 Old Compton Street,
Soho, London W1V 5PB

Designed by
Jon Anderson

Edited by
Sarah Barrett

Printed in Great Britain by
The Bath Press, Avon

DEDICATION

 **To my dear wife *Ros*, for her encouragement and patience throughout the entire venture.**

My eternal gratitude to the following without whose support, guidance and expertise the dream would not have become a reality:

To *John Povey*, my friend and partner who managed to keep our own business going during my long absence from 'work'.

To *Charlie Rossi*, one of the key factors in the success of the project, for his vast knowledge of the political hurdles that had to be surmounted.

To *Derek Parkes*, a developer with a conscience who had the vision to see that the impossible could become a reality.

To the late *Malcolm Landaw*, who staunchly supported me throughout and who is remembered by all with great affection.

To *Grace Cook*, who was ever willing to help and who had a calming influence when things did not go smoothly.

To *Frank Ferris*, whose unflagging encouragement was much appreciated and whose expertise in financial and property matters eased some of the more intricate problems.

To *George Armstrong*, *Mick Aldridge* and *Jean Robson*, members of the original Committee all of whom are still committed to the success of the Jubilee Market Hall.

Finally, my sincere thanks to all the Jubilee Market Traders whose faith never faltered and who ultimately financed the project.

Ray Green

FOREWORD

FOREWORD - JUBILEE HALL PUBLICATION

I was pleased to be asked to write a short introduction to
this book. The twists and turns of the fight for the survival
of Jubilee Market Hall make fascinating reading. I am happy
to have played a small part during my first period as
Environment Secretary. The success of Jubilee Market Hall in
providing a focus for Londoners and tourists alike, is an
example of what can be achieved by the combination of the
community and private enterprise, and I am sure it will
progress from strength to strength.

MICHAEL HESELTINE

dti
the department for Enterprise

Recycled Paper

Contents

ABBREVIATIONS

Action Area Plan

Covent Garden Action Area Plan. The overall GLC plan for development of the area, published in 1978.

CGAT

Covent Garden Area Trust. Established in 1986 to protect uses of a few key Covent Garden buildings and to advise on planning matters affecting the general area.

CGCA

Covent Garden Community Association. Established by residents and other locals in 1971 to fight the GLC plan to redevelop the area, it has continued to press for community interests, particularly housing and essential services.

CGCAC

Covent Garden Conservation Area Committee.

CGHP

Covent Garden Housing Project. A local architectural practice founded in 1979.

CGJPC

Covent Garden Joint Planning Committee (GLC). Established by the GLC in 1965 as a joint planning group on which Camden and Westminster councils were represented.

CGJDC

Covent Garden Joint Development Committee (GLC). Replaced the CGJPC in 1970. Camden and Westminster councils were no longer represented.

CGPC

The Covent Garden Planning Committee (GLC). 1973 successor to the CGJDC as the subcommittee of the GLC Central Planning Committee with a specific planning brief for the area. In 1981 its role was taken over by the Covent Garden Panel.

CGMA

Covent Garden Market Authority. A government body which owned and controlled the Covent Garden Market area from 1962 to 1968.

DoE

Department of the Environment.

Forum

The Covent Garden Forum of Representatives. Established by the GLC 1974 as a body to reflect local opinion. It did not survive the GLC.

GLC

Greater London Council. Established in 1963 as an intermediate layer of government between local authorities and the national government, with overall responsibility for London. Abolished 1986.

GRE

Guardian Royal Exchange Properties Ltd., an arm of the Guardian Royal Exchange insurance company.

JCF

Jewish Cultural Foundation.

JHDC

Jubilee Hall Development Consortium. Formed by the CGCA, JHRC, JMTA and S&W to represent their joint interest in the Jubilee Hall site. Later joined by the SHA.

JHRC

Jubilee Hall Recreation Centre Ltd. A charity established in 1977 to provide recreation facilities for schools, residents and workers in Covent Garden, Soho, and Fitzrovia.

JMTA

Jubilee Market Traders Association. Formed in 1981 to represent the traders on the Jubilee Hall site.

JMHL

Jubilee Market Hall Ltd. A non-profitmaking company formed by the Jubilee Hall market traders in 1983.

Labour Group

See PCC.

LRB

London Residuary Body. Created by the DoE to dispose of the properties owned by the GLC after 1986.

Panel

The Covent Garden Panel (GLC). Successor to the Covent Garden Planning Committee after the GLC elections in the spring of 1981.

PCC

Policy Co-ordinating Committee (GLC). Colloquially known as Labour Group, its members determined Labour Party policy within the GLC.

PCPC

Planning and Communications Policy Committee (GLC). A central area planning body to which the committees set up specifically to deal with Covent Garden were subordinate.

ROH

Royal Opera House.

Team

The GLC Covent Garden Team, a multi-disciplinary group of professional officers – planners and surveyors – set up in 1965 to provide technical advice to the various GLC planning committees concerned with the area through the years.

SHA

Soho Housing Association.

S&W

Sherman & Waterman Associates.

WCC

Westminster City Council.

ACKNOWLEDGEMENTS

Many of the people who graciously gave their time and co-operation to this record of the Jubilee Hall and the long campaign to preserve it played a leading role in the crucial events of the 1970s and 1980s.

Robert Whytehead, formerly of the Museum of London and now with English Heritage, allowed us liberal access to the material he published about his exploration of the Jubilee Hall site, and Team Leader Michael Hutchinson of the Museum of London Archaeological Unit helpfully secured the relevant photographic material.

Tony Sherman of the market operators S&W contributed colourful memories of the early days of the Jubilee Market which he and his partner Cyril Waterman started.

Former vice-Chairman of the GLC, Charlie Rossi, provided insight into the cloudy political environment of the most critical period in the fight to save the Jubilee Hall.

Mike Pargiter, the last leader of the GLC's Covent Garden Team, generously allowed us to extract considerable material from his own personal written reminiscences of events and helped to correct the manuscript.

Martin Dyke-Coomes, the architect responsible for the redevelopment of the Jubilee Hall, consented to a lengthy interview and reviewed a draft of the book, as did his former partner Jim Monahan, who was instrumental in achieving so much in Covent Garden. Many of the illustrations in this book appear with the kind permission of the architectural practice they started together, Covent Garden Housing Project.

Grace Cook, former Chairwoman of the Covent Garden Community Association and the first deputy executive of the Covent Garden Area Trust, put matters into community perspective, while Tony Earle, a latecomer to the scene but now Secretary of the CGAT, helped bring our information up to date.

Derek Parkes, the property developer who had the singular vision to back this unconventional project, remains an enthusiastic supporter. Ray Green's close colleague Frank Ferris, of Covent Garden Estates, contributed continual ideas and advice. Keith Hudson, of Hudson Freeman Berg, also gave useful guidance, and David Bond, of Weatherall, Green & Smith, was another who dredged his memory to help us.

Illustrations came from many sources, but particular credit goes to photographers Sean Sullivan, for his evocative portraits of his fellow traders, Stan Strangeway, for his candid coverage of the visit of Her Majesty Queen Elizabeth II to officially open the Jubilee Hall in 1987, and Clive Boursnell, for permission to reproduce a few of his superb pictures which capture so well the lost, wistful mood of Covent Garden in the 1970s. Those illustrations not otherwise credited are from the private collection of Ray Green.

CHAPTER ONE

The Piazza looking north, before 1666.

Collection: The Earl of Pembroke, Wilton House, Nr. Salisbury, Wiltshire, England.

A Stroll around the Piazza

1992

RAY GREEN first came to the Piazza in 1976. After more than three centuries of day and night bustle, the oldest of London's great squares lay desolate and surrounded by empty warehouses. At first he sold his rolls of fabric from a stall out in the open in front of the old Jubilee Hall, on the south side of the boarded-up Central Market Building, where the wholesale fruit and vegetable market once flourished. Later he moved under the corrugated roof of the former potato shed tacked on to the Jubilee Hall, which was warmer and drier. At the time it was just a place to keep the rain off his head, but the Jubilee Hall became an obsession which was to inspire a new career.

Today the former tailor's cutter and Brixton market trader, now an administrator, still works on the same site, but a few feet higher up, on the first floor of a tiny, high-tech, steel and glass cube inserted into a modern block in one of the most enviable locations in any city. In the mean time the Piazza has revived and the heart of Covent Garden throbs once more. All around are the landmarks of four centuries of London's robust popular culture. Britain's oldest and most famous theatres are here, the Royal Opera House (ROH), backing on to the Piazza itself, and the Theatre Royal in Drury Lane. Licensed by Charles II following his restoration to the throne in 1660, they shared a duopoly of the performing arts in Britain for decades. London's oldest restaurant, *Rules*, and oldest pub site, the *White Hart*, are close by, too.

All of these institutions cluster near the focal point of Covent Garden, London's only Piazza. Constructed in 1633 by Inigo Jones, the name derives from the Italian influence of the design, in flamboyant contrast to the prosaic northern European square. Unusually for London, it was designed as a paved area without a garden, and for more than three-and-a-half centuries has clung to its role as a public space where people gather. Surrounding it, Inigo Jones constructed an early property development; his elegant porticoed buildings were intended to attract 'Persons of great Distinction', and among the the first residents were three earls and many other titled persons.

The dimensional frame of the Piazza is all that is left of the great architect's formal conception today. The colonnaded rectangle was never completed on the south side and the rest has been rebuilt piecemeal ever since. St Paul's Church on the western edge was twice burnt down and faithfully reconstructed, the last time in 1798 by Thomas Hardwick. The most impressive residential building in the Piazza, the former town mansion at No. 43, King Street, in the north-west corner, was not built until 1716.

Although not part of the original design, most of the buildings which surround the Covent Garden Piazza today are suitably grand. The most recently constructed is the Jubilee Hall redevelopment, where Ray Green works, on the south side. A modern red-brick, five-storey office building and seven-storey housing block, embellished with post-modernist flourishes, rises next to a restored Edwardian market warehouse. Like most of the important historic buildings in Covent Garden, the fact that it is there at all is thoroughly amazing. And in common with many of its more elegant neighbours, its survival was fought

Part of the 1987 addition to the Jubilee Market Hall, corner of Southampton Street, on the Piazza.
© CGHP.

for and achieved, not for aesthetic reasons, but because the building plays a vital role in the life of the community. Ordinary people wanted it to be there, and, overcoming a daunting series of obstacles, their will finally carried the day.

The Jubilee Hall is a unique and complex inner-city redevelopment. It contains commercial offices and studios, restaurants, public-sector housing, a community recreation centre, and a vigorous surviving remnant of a tradition of trading which has been associated with this particular patch of land for a millennium.

IT STANDS AMONGST ILLUSTRIOUS and historic neighbours. A clockwise tour of the Piazza begins with Lloyds Bank Chambers, on the corner of Henrietta and Southampton Streets. This is one of six neo-Renaissance stone and brick blocks erected in or near the Piazza between 1876 and 1890, to the design of Henry Clutton or influenced by his work. The white-framed glass gazebo at ground level is the entrance to *Le Boulestin*, a spacious subterranean restaurant founded in 1926. When Art Deco was new, this was one of London's most expensive dining places, and certainly the most stylish, with its modern murals,

Francis, fourth Earl of Bedford c. 1636, by Sir Anthony Van Dyck.

By kind permission of the Marquess of Tavistock and the Trustees of the Bedford Estates.

fabrics, and fittings. Chef Marcel Boulestin was the world's first television chef, appearing on the BBC in 1937. The site was previously occupied by an Edwardian hotel, the *Covent Garden*, and before that the *Bedford Head Hotel*.

Just around the corner is St Paul's Church. When Inigo Jones designed the rectangular enclosure of the Piazza in 1630, its centre was an open space designed to lead the eye to this building which dominated its western side. Modelled on an austere Tuscan temple, it inspired the entire architectural conception. The Earl of Bedford had requested a plain building "not much better than a barn", a preference owing less to an austerity of taste than to a shortage of cash. The architect replied, "Well, then, you shall have the handsomest barn in London."

The sealed portico facing the Piazza looks as though it should be the entrance, and indeed that was the intention. But this doorway was never used because, ecclesiastically speaking, the Church nave faced the wrong way around, so you have to enter through the gardens behind the church. Under the portico is a plaque which commemorates the first Punch and Judy show in England. It was here, near the present-day public lavatories, where Samuel Pepys recorded in his diary in 1662 that he had seen the Italian puppet-show of *Punchinello*, transmogrified into an Englishman called Punch with a wife named Judy and a dog, Toby. The shelter of the church porticoes made it a favoured venue for election speeches and so popular as a rendezvous that a coffee-house was erected beneath it. Eliza Doolittle meets Professor Higgins at this spot in Shaw's *Pygmalion*, the original for *My Fair Lady*, and the theatrical tradition is continued today by jugglers and street entertainers performing on the cobblestones before the elegant blank portico. Opposite, the terrace of the *Punch & Judy* pub on the upstairs floor of the restored Central Market Building furnishes a convenient outdoor balcony for spectators.

No. 43 King Street, now the oldest construction in the Piazza, is in the north-west corner. The history of its occupancy mirrors the changing economic fortunes of Covent Garden down through the decades. Originally, like so many of its neighbours, it was a substantial private mansion, the home of Lord Archer until 1756. Later it was rented to a peruke maker, before becoming the *Grand Hotel* in 1774. In part it stayed as such, serving song-and-supper entertainments; but from 1835 it was also the home of the new Royal Institute of British Architects. Exclusive gentlemen's clubs followed: the *Savage, Falstaff, New*, and *National Sporting*. Later, the building became the premises of *George Monro*, a wholesale fruiterer. In the 1980s Covent Garden attracted the communicators, and now, behind its pink and white wedding-cake frills, there is a public relations company.

The Italianate arcade it abuts, although not original, gives an idea of Inigo Jones's original conception. His grand scheme of an open garden surrounded by arcaded buildings was never realised; only the north and east sides were completed. They were framed with the tall and uniform fronts of four-storey houses, and the Piazza became the first of London's great sequence of residential squares. Over the centuries, however, the arcade was gradually destroyed, the last surviving group of houses on the north and east sides, now greatly altered,

Inigo Jones, the architect of the Piazza.

After Sir Anthony Van Dyck.
National Portrait Gallery.

succumbing as late as 1933. An impression of the measured order and dignity of the original design is preserved here in the north-west corner, in the Bedford Chambers, but this was built only in 1877, by Henry Clutton, as a recreation of the earlier harmonious arcaded style. Today the grand exterior conceals a labyrinth of small offices with a number of colourful eateries splaying out into the arcade beneath.

BEYOND JAMES STREET, which enters from the north, there is an unflattering rear view of the ROH. The first Opera House was constructed here in 1732; the present romanesque design by architect E.M. Barry dates from 1858, and is the third on this site. Today it houses the Royal Ballet and the Royal Opera Companies. Market forces have so far deferred the plans to restore this area with a grand Jonesian arcade extending around the elbow between James Street on the north and Russell Street on the east. Until it goes ahead, a busy outdoor market uses the space at the foot of the ROH extension, which was built along James Street in 1980, to display a colourful jumble of handbags, toys, china, anoraks, fabrics, prints, and ethnic handicrafts. This is an outdoor outpost of the Jubilee Market on the south side of the Piazza.

In the meanwhile, too, there is a forlorn view of the iron grillework and skylights of the Floral Hall, vestigal hints of the soaring barrel vault which was destroyed by fire in 1956. The original exuberance of this market building was perhaps due to the fact that it, too, was designed by E.M. Barry, for the manager of the ROH, and built two years later. It became the foreign-fruit section of the Covent Garden wholesale market, and now remains in the property portfolio of the ROH. Pending commencement of its postponed redevelopment scheme, the basement of the old Floral Hall provides temporary wardrobes and dressing-rooms for principals, and scenery is stored on the ground floor. When the expansion goes ahead, this florid glimpse will disappear as the building is submerged within the new design; its barrel vault will be restored, however, as well as the fine portico framing the entrance around the corner in Bow Street.

In the north-east elbow of the Piazza, *Judy's Pantry* occupies a squat little post-modernist temple first designed by Terry Farrell as a garden centre, a 1970s comment, perhaps, on St Paul's Tuscan edifice across the Piazza. Next to it is a little green space known as the Italian Garden. The homely *trompe-l'œil* mural above it in the style of Magritte on the blank side wall of *Maxwells* brasserie is a relic of the heady days of community action in the 1970s, when the locals created temporary parks in the wasteground of demolished buildings, expressing their attitudes creatively and wittily on strategically placed brick walls. In the 1980s the mural was repainted by local residents as a visual protest against the ROH expansion scheme, now approved but 'not in funds'. This will demolish the old buildings on the northern frontage of Russell Street; however, the ROH points out that all of these were refaced between 1850 and 1912 and contain only a few archaeological fragments of seventeenth-century work in the interiors.

Russell Street exits from the Piazza on the east, overlooked by the first-floor terrace of the Central Market Building, where a restaurant recreates the original conservatory which displayed indoor plants and flowers in the wholesale market. The street is named after Francis Russell, the fourth Earl of Bedford (hence Bedford Chambers and Bedford Street), who commissioned Inigo Jones to build the Piazza. You could have eavesdropped on the finely tuned conversations of some of the best-known English essayists and writers in the three well-known seventeenth- and eighteenth-century coffee-houses which stood here. Many of the patrons would have worn large, flowing flaxen periwigs, a fashion introduced in the reign of Charles II which persisted within the theatrical profession until about 1720. *Wills*, on the corner of Bow Street at No. 1, was the most famous of these meeting places, where noblemen in their stars and garters were wont to drink their tea and coffee on the balcony exposed to the common gaze. The poets John Dryden and Alexander Pope, the masters of Restoration comedy William Congreve and William Wycherley, and the satirist Jonathan Swift were regulars in the 'wits' room' on the first floor (though it was from the floor above that the proprietor, Thomas West, flung himself to his death in a delirium in 1722). Across the way, at No. 17, was *Tom's*, where you could have found the poet Oliver Goldsmith, the literary master Dr Samuel Johnson, and his former pupil, actor-manager David Garrick. A few doors down, at No. 10, was *Button's*, a haunt of the essayist and fiction writer Daniel Defoe and of the founders of the *Tatler* and the *Spectator*, Joseph Addison and Sir Richard Steele. The eponymous Daniel Button was a former servant of Addison's whom he acquired when he married Lady Warwick. At No. 8 you can drink a cup of coffee today in the very house, then a bookshop, where Dr Johnson first met his biographer, James Boswell.

The Flower Market, in the south-eastern corner, with its cast-iron columns and glazed roof, is a fine example of Victorian industrial architecture, erected in 1871 to the design of William Rogers. It now embraces the Theatre Museum (a branch of the Victoria and Albert) as well as the London Transport Museum, exhibiting the history of public transport in London; the latter now shares with the present-day *Tuttons* brasserie the site of *Hummums*, a notorious *bagnio* of the late seventeenth century.

Throughout its history famous people lived all around the Piazza, particularly actors and dramatists, whose unsocial hours demanded they reside close to their work. The playwrights Wycherley, Congreve, and Richard Sheridan, and the great thespians Garrick, Charles Macklin, John Kemble, and Edmund Kean, as well as Nell Gwynne, were all local residents, although hardly a trace of their homes has survived. An exception is 27 Southampton Street, just off the south side of the Piazza, where David Garrick found it convenient to live within a short stroll of the theatres from 1749 to 1772. He was manager of the Theatre Royal, Drury Lane, for nearly thirty years from 1747, and nearby Garrick Street and the *Garrick Club* are named after him. Theatre-goers were more passionate in those days, and from time to time his home was besieged by angry mobs enraged by his productions. The theatrical tradition of his former home survived well into this century. Until a few years ago the building was occupied by the famous play-

A letterbox sculpture designed as an antique Egyptian lion, "its face compounded of that of a lion and a wizard." It was put up at BUTTON'S coffee-house, No. 10 Russell Street, in July 1713 to receive communications posted through its jaws. It was removed to the SHAKESPEARE tavern about 1731.

The building that housed TOM'S coffee-house, No. 17 Russell Street, as it appeared in the mid-nineteenth century.

The OLD HUMMUMS hotel, as rebuilt 1888.

publisher and bookseller, *French's*, and still retained its original staircase, much of the original panelling, and a water-tank in the basement dated 1713. However, after recent renovation, only the original exterior facade now survives.

THIS CLOCKWISE JOURNEY has, of course, been circling the Covent Garden Central Market Building. Within 25 years of the completion of Inigo Jones's noble square, as early as 1656, market traders had established their stalls in its open centre. This building, designed by Charles Fowler, was put up to provide a covered hall in 1830, and until 1974 it remained the primary fruit and vegetable market for London. The whole of central Covent Garden was steeped in its atmosphere. In the early morning hours, lorries pregnant with ripe produce rumbled in from the countryside to crowd the narrow thoroughfares. Boxes of fruit and vegetables and flowers were piled high on the cobbles, and on the heads of the porters, both male and female, who fetched them to the stalls. Tea-shops did a brisk trade all night, and pubs opened at dawn for thirsty porters and drivers. You can still see the market regulations painted on large boards in the entrances to the Central Market Building.

Left empty in 1974, this structure was preserved and renovated by the Greater London Council (GLC), and reopened in 1980 as a complex of shops, boutiques, and open air restaurants. This redevelopment sparked the regeneration of the entire area. Today it is owned and managed by Guardian Royal Exchange Properties (GRE), the investment arm of an insurance company which bought a significant parcel of Covent Garden property formerly owned by the GLC after it expired in 1986.

The complex is strictly tourist-orientated. Street entertainments – musicians, clowns, dance and special exhibitions – are staged in the west Piazza and also under cover in the north hall. The retail shops generally observe extended opening hours, six days a week from 10 a.m. to 7 p.m. Depending on the season,

View of the nineteenth century Piazza from King Street, by William and Frederick J. Havel.

The Saturday crafts market in the Jubilee Market Hall, 1992.

Photograph by Ketan Patel.

up to one million people per week pass through or around this building in the centre of the Piazza.

It was all a little too smart for the market traders like Ray Green who had once again collected in the area in the 1970s during the renovation of the building; they were not invited to set up their pitches there. As the area became posh again, the traders were generally expected to push off. But today a busy traditional market flourishes in a covered space beneath the new building on the south side of the Piazza, and spills out onto the pavement underneath the glass portico of the adjacent baroque Jubilee Hall, built in 1904. On the floor above there is a community sports hall.

This is the story of how, against all the odds, that came about.

Covent Garden Piazza and Market, painted about 1726–30, looking east from St Paul's Church and showing the market stalls and the sundial.

By Joseph van Aken (c. 1669–1749),
© Museum of London.

This view from the opposite end of the Piazza, painted between 1761–80, shows the houses of Tavistock Row, now the Jubilee Hall site, on the extreme left.

By John Collett,
© Museum of London.

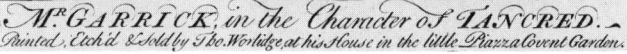

Clockwise from top left:

David Garrick, by Thomas Worlidge, who lived in the Little Piazza. Garrick lived around the corner at No. 27 Southampton Street, and in 1745 at the house of Mr Watts, a cabinet maker in King Street.

Actor-manager Charles Macklin, born in 1700, lived almost to the end of the century, dying in 1797 at his home in Southampton Street.

From a sculpture by Hopwood, published 1898.

The playwright William Wycherley lived on the west side of Bow Street, where he was visited by Charles II.

Drawn by J. Thurston in 1824.

The last likeness of the formal tragic actor, John Kemble, who lived in Covent Garden.

By T. Lawrence.

The painter John W.M. Turner, RAPP, a Covent Garden resident.

By George Dance.

Clockwise from top left:

William Hogarth found inspiration in the teeming alleys of Covent Garden.

Thomas Hardwick, who supervised the rebuilding of St Paul's Church.

By George Dance, 1795.

The painter John Zoffany, RA resided in the Piazza.

By George Dance, 1793.

The writer Charles Lamb lived at No. 20 Russell Street.

Drawing by Hancock, 1798.

CHAPTER TWO

The overcrowded market, looking west, c. 1812. The buildings on the extreme left are on the present site of the Jubilee Hall.

From an aquatint after a drawing by Pugin and Rowlandson, reproduced by kind permission of the Trustees of the British Museum.

A Millennium of Trading

AD 720–1974

*T*HE LOCATION of middle Saxon London in the seventh to ninth centuries had always been a mystery. This was the gap between the abandonment of the Roman colony and its subsequent reoccupation. As the Roman period petered out, Londinium became depopulated, but there was little evidence of Saxon occupation. The contemporary writings of the Venerable Bede suggest that Saxon Lundenwic, as it was called, was a large and thriving port; but despite extensive excavation, no hint of it had been discovered within the area of the older Roman city now buried beneath the City of London. Some archaeologists therefore concluded that the urban Saxon community did not come into being before the tenth century.

'Wic' in Saxon can mean a stream or a farmstead; 'wych', as in 'Aldwych', is the plural. In 1984 Professor Martin Biddle and Alan Vince independently conjectured that the ancient Saxon port of London might have been located about a kilometre upstream to the west, around the Aldwych, rather than inside the walls of the old Roman city, as conventional wisdom held. Though Saxon finds were dug up when the *Savoy Hotel* was being built in the 1930s, and a complete pot had been found in Drury Lane, it had previously been surmised that the dwelling-places here must have been isolated farmsteads supplying the city.

Just a year later, after a long and sometimes bitter civic controversy, construction work finally began on the Jubilee Hall site bounded by Tavistock and Southampton Streets and the Piazza. Despite its potential archaeological importance, Robert Whytehead of the Department of Greater London Archaeology at the Museum of London agreed with the developers to maintain only a watching brief. He knew that the intensive building of large eighteenth-century houses had driven deep basements down to the natural gravel, and the modern construction of large hotels, department stores, and offices around the Strand had long since obliterated all archaeological traces in the area. No basement was planned; there would be only limited piling and foundation-digging.

Soon after excavation began, in May 1985, the diggers' shovels broke through into deep vaults. The building plans were hastily revised to incorporate a basement, and Robert Whytehead now kept a constant watch on the site. The old vaults were full of loose backfill. All archaeological deposits had been removed long ago, apart from the bottoms of a few scattered pits. Then, unexpectedly, the north-east corner, under two former house plots, turned out to be only semi-basemented, and beneath these the mechanical shovel bit into a layer of 'dark-earth' deposits of original decayed organic matter. As it scraped into a lower level at the very edge of the excavation, a narrow rectangle of discoloured earth was uncovered. Centuries ago, someone had dug out and then replaced the soil and gravel. It was a shallow grave. Digging carefully by hand, the archaeological team uncovered the articulated vertebrae of a human skeleton, intact apart from the head. "That's probably what I just put on the spoil heap," chipped in the driver of the mechanical shovel, and he retrieved it, in three pieces.

Archaeologists from the Museum of London on the Jubilee Hall site in May 1985.

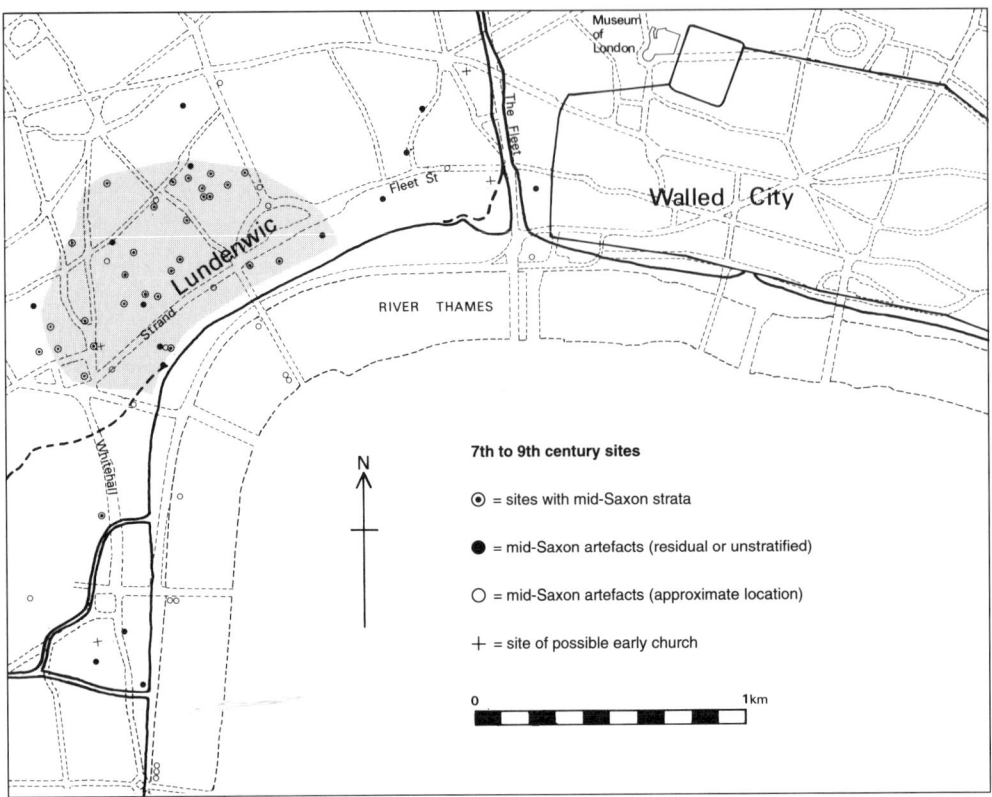

Lundenwic was centred on the area where the Jubilee Hall stands today, between the walled Roman city and Thorney Island, now the site of Westminster Cathedral.

Department of Greater London Archaeology, Museum of London.

It was an exciting discovery because it was the first to prove that the area had been occupied during the middle Saxon period. The excavations at the Jubilee Hall and later sites in Covent Garden solved the historical puzzle. It is now apparent that for about 300 years from AD 600, Saxon London lay, not within the Roman city, but along the Strand foreshore, between the River Fleet, now Farringdon Street, and Trafalgar Square.

This confirmed Professor Biddle's theory, which had been based on the evidence of three other Saxon villages uncovered outside the walls of Britain's ancient cities of Southampton (Hamwic), Canterbury (Fordwych), and York. In the fourth and fifth centuries the pestilence caused by overcrowding in settlements had ravaged the classical world. The people of the period saw culture die in cities, while in barbaric lands such as Germany the primitive tribes fared better. The seafaring middle Saxons described the deadly walled cities as "mausolea with nets" and perhaps because of this, as well as for economic reasons, preferred to establish themselves in open areas. It appears that they did not know how to build in stone. Like wandering survivors in a post-nuclear holocaust, they held the great cities of the earlier culture in awe, and thought they had been built by giants. They felt more comfortable in this broad area at the side of the Aldwych by the sloping gravel banks of the Thames, where they could beach their clinker-built longboats.

Robert Whytehead persuaded Derek Parkes, managing director of the developer Speyhawk, to allow him a week to excavate. He found archaeological deposits up to two metres deep and his report provided detailed insight into the way people lived then. There were several distinct layers to the site. At the bottom was a layer of brick-earth which the original settlers dug up and compacted into a hard floor of yellow clay. It contained traces of fossilised dung. Industrial use was suggested, too, by burnt areas and a crucible-shaped hearth scooped out of the brick-earth floor at the north-eastern corner, which had probably been a blacksmith's forge. Fireplaces and circular pits were discovered, filled with combustion byproducts – slags and horncores – as well as centuries of domestic rubbish. The presence of four possible middle Saxon buildings was betrayed by slots for beam-ends, and post-holes perhaps used to support internal partitions. Deep wells penetrated two metres beneath the occupation level (five metres below today's street level) to a water-bearing band of gravel.

Above the clay floor was a layer of decayed organic matter up to 0.75 of a metre thick. These were the remains of timber frames, of wattle, daub, and plaster stucco from walls, and of thatched roofs. They showed that the area had been occupied for a long period of time. A higher tier of the same thickness of 'dark-earth' was similar building debris reworked by natural action, indicating that the area had later been under the plough.

The human skeleton lay on an east–west axis at the most ancient layer, and may have been buried in an open field between 630 and 675 AD, before the town was built. It was an adult male, about 5' 8" in height, who had been placed lying face down with the hands pushed to the right side of the body. Possibly his wrists had been tied together. The body seemed to have been rolled into the grave, it lay awkwardly on its left side. The left ulna had sustained a 'parry' fracture, so called because it was a frequent result of fending off a blow with the forearm. A lone burial of this type in the prone position usually indicates that the deceased was an outcast, a stranger or criminal. Some were buried alive.

The presence of animal and cereal remains suggested considerable husbandry of cattle, pigs, sheep and goats. Bones of these animals, mingled with oyster shells, were found in great numbers at all depths. One layer contained a profusion of mussel shells. There was also evidence of trading in imported goods from Belgium, France, and Germany, so there must surely have been a major market in the vicinity of this thriving settlement.

Pottery was relatively sparse, and, apart from a few Roman potsherds, all of it was of middle Saxon date. There were examples of local handmade pots

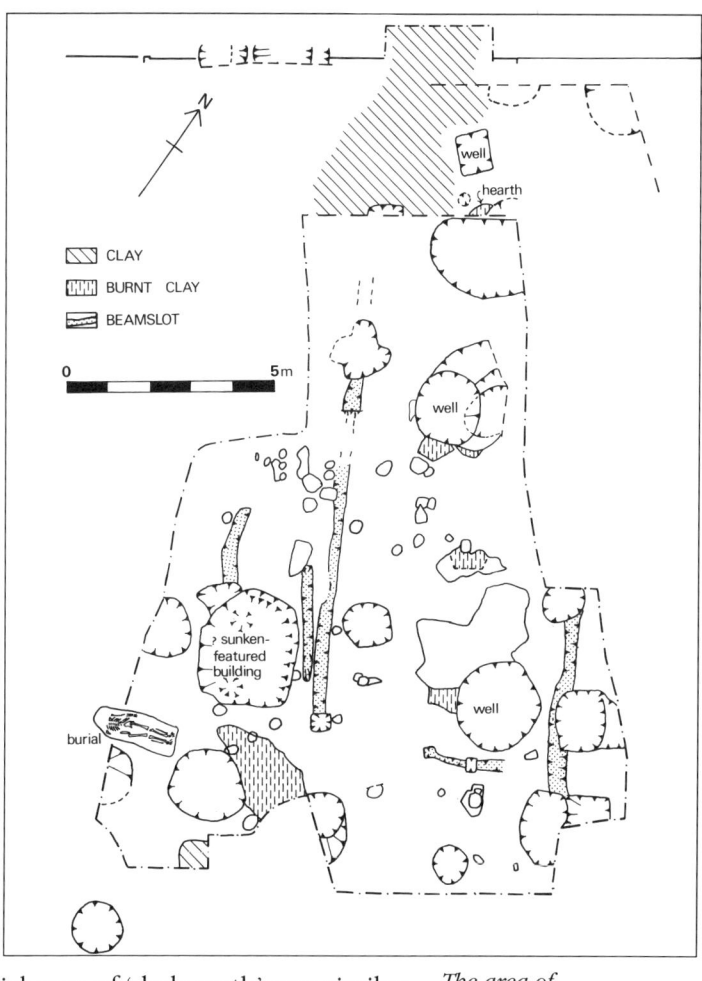

CLAY

BURNT CLAY

BEAMSLOT

0   5 m

well

hearth

well

sunken-featured building

well

burial

The area of archaeological excavation on the Jubilee Hall site.

By Robert Cowie, 'Archaeology Today', June 1987.

The headless Saxon skeleton found on the Jubilee Hall site in May 1985.

Department of Greater London Archaeology, Museum of London.

tempered by chaff, Ipswich wares, and also wheel-turned imported objects from the Rhineland, Belgium, and northern France. Fragments of circular, doughnut-shaped loomweights were common, and testify to cloth production. They were used to hold threads taut on a vertical loom during weaving. Chunks of quernstones used for grinding corn and probably imported from Germany were also found.

Small finds included a *sceatta*, a coin dated *c.* AD 710–30. It bears a bird-and-vine motif on one side and the image of a wolf suckling Romulus and Remus on the reverse, but is nevertheless not Roman. Rather than creating their own designs, the Saxons commonly imitated coins which traders would recognise and accept. Also unearthed were a bronze pin and possible strap-end, a bone pin and fragments of comb, two bits of curved iron from wok-shaped frying pans, and pieces of whetstones, including an unworked one. These discoveries are now on display in the Museum of London.

Subsequent digs on Covent Garden building sites unearthed further Saxon remains in Short's Gardens and the Peabody site in Bedfordbury, and it now seems likely that the area between Trafalgar Square and the Aldwych was the site of Lundenwic. Traces of a wooden waterfront retaining wall were discovered near York Buildings. The port lay where the ground begins to rise in a steep slope from the line of the medieval waterfront to today's Victoria Embankment Gardens. The earlier embankment had been built by piling brushwood on the sandy foreshore, weighed down by a thin scatter of stone rubble and discarded Roman tiles. This revetment was supported by stakes and planks hewn from alder and oaks felled between 670 and 690.

The old Roman road along the Strand, then as now, was the main street of the town. The mouth of the River Fleet was probably then deep enough for navigation; indeed, the Anglo-Saxon word from which it is derived means a tidal creek where vessels can float. Lundenwic would certainly have been an active port, and perhaps the only one through which the Saxon kings gained access to European markets in the eighth century. The settlement was probably founded by the East Saxons, clients of Kentish kings who acquired both wealth and prestige by strictly controlling the trade that passed through it. These were later displaced by the rulers of the kingdom of Mercia (the Midlands). The roads built by the Romans were still trodden by the middle Saxons, among them Watling Street, which connected landlocked Mercia to the vicinity of today's Oxford Street, just above the vital seaport along the Thames.

The quernstones found on the Jubilee Hall site could well be the lava millstones mentioned by Charlemagne in his letter to Offa, King of Mercia, and traded in exchange for cloaks: "As for the black stones which your Reverence begged to be sent to you, let a messenger come and consider what kind you have in mind and we will willingly order them to be given, and we will help with their transport, but as you have intimated your wishes concerning the length of the stones, so our people make a demand about the size of cloaks, that you may order them to be such as used to come to us in former times."

Saxon loomweights found on the site of the Jubilee Hall.
Museum of London.

The sceatta, an early eighth-century silver coin, discovered on the Jubilee Hall site.
Department of Greater London Archaeology, Museum of London.

Lundenwic probably covered 60 to 90 hectares, extending north–south from Short's Gardens down to the Thames, and from west to east between Trafalgar Square and at least up to the Aldwych, perhaps as far as the banks of the River Fleet, now submerged under Farringdon Street. It would have been one of the largest settlements in Britain at that time, surpassed only by the *emporium* at Ipswich. Like present-day city dwellings, the Anglo-Saxon urban living quarters were small and crowded, and used space with great efficiency. The town was densely packed with houses constructed of woven branches or wattle and smeared with orange daub made from brick-earth as an infill for timber frames. Some were whited with limewash. Food was cooked on open hearths inside or near these ramshackle buildings, and fire would have been a great hazard. Early writings record that the London settlement was destroyed by fire in 764, 798, and 801.

An impression of the interior of a Saxon home in the settlement near the Strand.

By John Pearson,
© Museum of London.

The people lived among their refuse, in yards containing numerous rubbish pits. The buried discards speak over the centuries: the occupants lived on cereal grains, meat and possibly dairy products, as well as shellfish and fish from rivers – roach, pike, and eels – and others brought upstream from the sea – herring, plaice, haddock, and whiting. They were craftsmen, producing woven textiles and other goods made of leather, wool, and animal bone, mostly from cattle but also sheep and pigs. Red-deer antler was used to make combs, needles, and knife handles, and the Jubilee Hall site contributes evidence of metal-working.

These humble artefacts, along with English slaves and hunting dogs, were exported in exchange for luxury items: spices, oriental silks, glass vessels, fine pottery, and wine from the Kingdom of Charlemagne, and millstones and glass vessels from the Rhineland. The rich port was an attractive target for Danish Vikings, who attacked in 842 and again in 851 and occupied the town from 872, when the Great Army wintered there. In 886 King Alfred the Great recaptured Lundenwic, and after this period, pottery and other artefacts disappear from the excavation sites. The settlement was probably abandoned as the population withdrew for protection within the walls of the old Roman city.

One of London's earliest chroniclers, Alderman Robert Fabian, had written in 1490 of a Dark Ages settlement along the Strand between Ludgate and Westminster, claiming that it was larger and better ordered than that in the City of London; but later scholars had disbelieved him. Like early historians in all cultures, his assertions were frequently drawn from fragments of mythology, and so heavily discounted by his descendants. In this case the source he cited was a 'Domesday Book'. Because none exists for London, his allegation was discredited. However, it may well be that Fabian was right when he went on to say that no one could read the 'Domesday Book' of London because it was written in the Saxon tongue, and so it was thrown away.

There is no evidence for social habitation of this area before the seventh century. Probably it was open countryside, although some flint remnants found at Maiden Lane suggest prehistoric connections. The Romans buried their dead by the wayside, and cremation urns which have been found around Trafalgar Square confirm that the Strand was once a Roman road connecting the City of London to Silchester, and passing by what was then an island in the Thames called Thorney, now the site of Westminster Cathedral. It was here that the ancient Abbey of St Peter at the West Mynster was erected (as the monks who occupied it were to claim as evidence of tenure) by the King of the East Saxons, Seberht, upon his conversion to Christianity around 600 AD. All of the land outside the City walls, as far westward as Chelsea, Kensington, and Bayswater, was part of the monks' vast holdings.

FOUR HUNDRED YEARS were to pass before the area the Saxons had inhabited appeared in recorded history, in a document attributed to the reign of King John (1199–1256), as Convent Garden. This was the name given to a forty-acre patch in the county of Middlesex, bordered west and east by what is now St Martin's Lane and Drury Lane, and north and south by Floral Street and a line drawn from Chandos Place along Maiden Lane and Exeter Street to the Aldwych. An ancient footpath called Aldewichstrate ('Old farmsteads way') issued from the western gate of the City of London a mile down-river at Fleet Street, and Drewerie Lane branched off here to the north. (Romantics point out that 'drewerie' or 'drowerie' meant 'a litel luste', hence a convenient rural 'Lovers' Lane', but a better-attested eponym was Sir William Drury, who fought for Queen Elizabeth I in the Irish wars). St Martin's Lane, too, was an old country byway.

In this quadrangle bordered by a thatch-covered mud wall, the Abbey or Convent of St Peter, Westminster, maintained a large kitchen garden throughout the middle ages to provide its daily food. Directly to the north the monks also owned seven acres known as Long Acre, and to the south, roughly where the Strand Palace Hotel now stands, two smaller pieces of land, known as Friars Pyes (a translation of *Freres Pyes*, or Pied Friars, a French order of mendicant monks who wore black scapularies over white mantles, and which had established itself in a house on this land in 1267). The monks of St Peter's Abbey cultivated orchards here, grew grain, and pastured livestock, selling the surplus to the citizens of London. Their records for 1327 report that the entire harvest of apples, pears, cherries, nuts, grains, and hay fetched £12. Over the next three centuries the monks' old convent garden became a major source of fruit and vegetables in London, and was managed by a succession of leaseholders by grant from the Abbot of Westminster.

The last of these leases was granted in 1530 to Sir Richard Weston, Undertreasurer of England. He transferred the title to Henry Dingley. His venture, one of the earliest recorded land speculations in Covent Garden, was exceptionally ill-starred. Dingley subleased the property to a Richard Browne, but in the same year the monks ceded their farm and orchard to King Henry VIII in exchange for some land in Berkshire. When Richard Browne prudently surrendered his interest to the King, Dingley took proceedings against him. The sovereign solved this and numerous other property disputes throughout his

John Russell, first Earl of Bedford.

kingdom by the stroke of a pen, when he dissolved the monasteries and appropriated their land in 1540. It was now royal sheep which grazed the open fields.

The next year, in exchange for some land in Devon, King Henry VIII granted both of the Friars Pyes (as a small part of a package of manors and lands which had belonged to the monasteries in several counties) to John, Baron Russell, Great Admiral of England, and later the first Earl of Bedford. In fulfilment of the King's dying wish, his son, Edward VI, bestowed the remainder of the convent garden in 1547 to his maternal uncle, Edward Seymour, the Duke of Somerset, who began to build Somerset House on the south side of the Strand the next year. When this politically powerful noble was beheaded for treason in 1552, the land came once again into royal gift, and was awarded four months later to one of those who had contributed to Seymour's downfall. Forty acres, that long fruitful rectangle known as 'le Covent Garden' plus 'the long acre', were granted by royal patent in perpetuity to John Russell, first Earl of Bedford, at a yearly rent of £6 6s 8d.

Though it had slipped from the control of the Church, the bucolic enterprise on the western outskirts of London continued to provide fresh fruit and vegetables to the local people who lived in the scattering of houses in the surrounding patchwork of meadows. The Strand was still just a rough track meandering along the course of the Thames as far as the Eleanor Cross at Charing (now Charing Cross). Following the completion of Somerset House in 1550, other magnificent aristocratic mansions began to rise up along the bank of the Thames – Drury Place, Arundel House, the Savoy Palace, Durham House, York House, and Suffolk House.

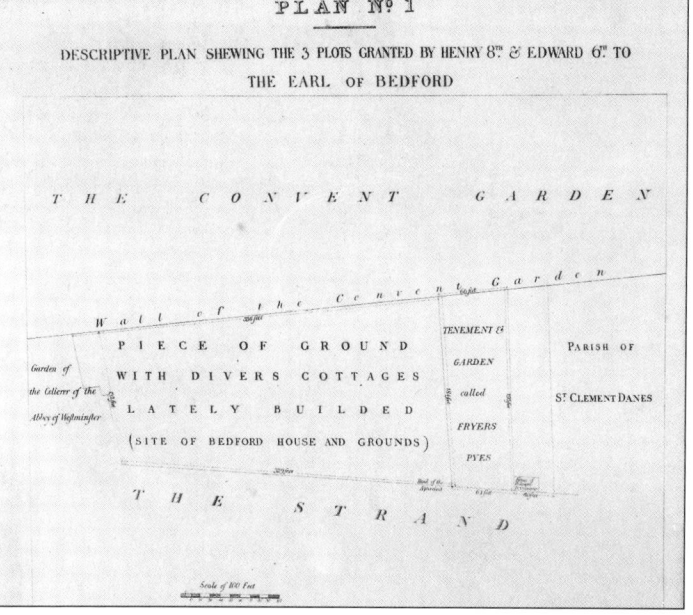

Map showing the Friar Pyes and other plots just under the boundary wall of the Convent Garden granted to the first Earl of Bedford.

By kind permission of the Marquess of Tavistock and the Trustees of the Bedford Estate.

In today's parlance, Covent Garden was ripe for development. At first the Russell family did little about it. But it was the start of a long landowning dynasty in what was to become the heart of London. Within a hundred years, the meadows where cattle grazed behind the straggle of small houses on the Strand had disappeared beneath a warren of streets lined with blocks of terraced buildings and houses four storeys high. Instead of cowpats, the 40 acres of Covent Garden were producing enormous annual rents. As Russell Street and Bedford Street remind us, the Russell family continued to own this property for nearly 400 years, and only severed its connection with Covent Garden after the Second World War.

Francis Russell, second Earl of Bedford.

The first Earl of Bedford died in 1556 and was succeeded by his son, Francis, known chiefly for his adoption of the family motto, *Che sarà sarà* ('What will be will be'). Francis, the second Earl, died in 1585. His eldest surviving son, also Francis, had died the day before, from wounds received in an affray, and so his

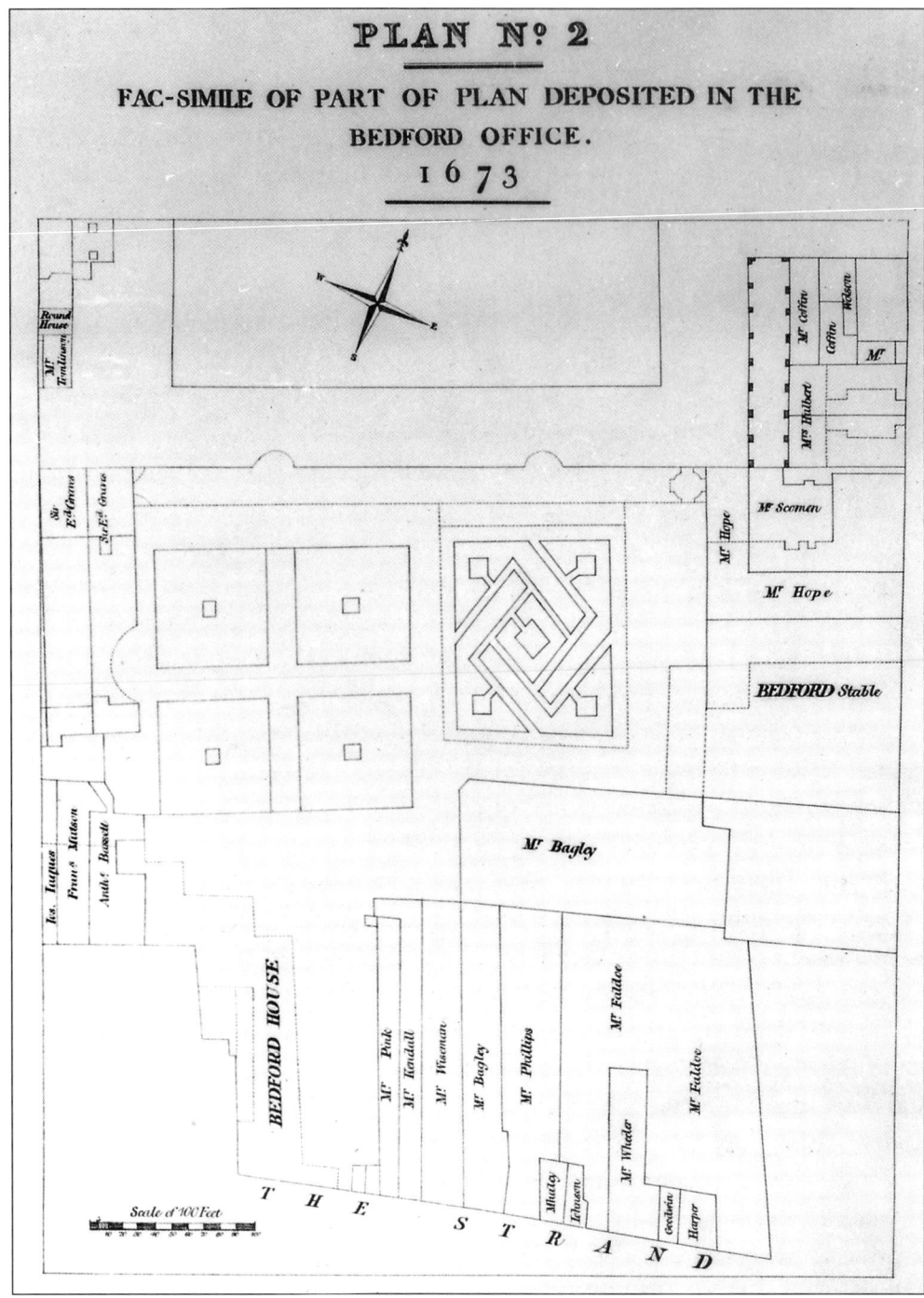

PLAN Nº 2

FAC-SIMILE OF PART OF PLAN DEPOSITED IN THE
BEDFORD OFFICE.

1673

*Plan of Bedford Ground,
1673, by John Lacy.*

By kind permission of the Marquess
of Tavistock and the Trustees of the
Bedford Estate.

grandson, Edward, still a minor, became the third Earl of Bedford. Sir William
Cecil had meanwhile built two grand mansions, Exeter House and Cecil House,
for himself and his son, Sir Robert Cecil, on land leased from the Bedfords. These
dwarfed the small houses and shops now lining the Strand, and upon coming into
his inheritance, Edward Russell elected to match this splendour. He chose Friars
Pyes on the north side of the Strand as the place to build his mansion, Bedford
House, in 1586. The Jubilee Hall today stands in what was a portion of its
extensive garden.

We know little about the appearance of Bedford House, but that glimpse is tantalising. There is an inventory dating from 1643, when the house and its contents were sequestered by the Long Parliament, some vouchers of 1657–94, and some map views and plans. These show a large irregular building, two storeys high, surmounted by a tower and a fringe of seven gables intersecting with a steep roof. The walled gardens behind it run up to the Piazza.

The house was framed in timber, and had a frontage of about 100 feet on the Strand, running eastward from what is now the corner of Southampton Street towards the Aldwych. Including large closets, there were 45 rooms, 23 of which appear to have been equipped with fireplaces (although there exists a 1673 tax bill for 60 hearths). In the second storey, three evenly spaced oriel windows gave light to a long gallery, hung with green cloth, overlooking the Strand. There was a dining parlour, a "waiteing roome", and a turret room in the tower. Tapestries adorned the family apartments, and there were many "turkey" carpets. Chairs of gilt and leather or crimson velvet provided seating in the principal rooms.

At the eastern end of the building a pair of great gates blocked an arched opening guarded by a porter's lodge. Within, there was a deep rectangular forecourt. From the western border of this courtyard a central passage led into a great hall hung with nine tapestries. In its north-east corner another gateway opened to a walled carriage-way leading eastwards into the Bedford stables.

From about 1600, lanes became streets as smaller thatched houses and stables began to fill in the meadows around Bedford House. Often this was done without official sanction. Both Queen Elizabeth and King James tried unsuccessfully to limit growth outside of the City of London. In 1619, Edward, the third Earl, was on the point of selling the elegant mansion he had built to pay off his debts (including a £10,000 royal fine for his complicity in a rebellion led by the Earl of Essex) when the heir apparent, his uncle Sir William Russell, intervened to prevent the loss of his inheritance. It therefore transpired that it was Sir William's son and the third Earl's cousin, Francis Russell, who took over the estate in 1619, becoming the fourth Earl in 1627. By that time the property had been reduced to some 20 acres. A brick wall had been built along Hart (now Floral) Street as its northern boundary, and the land within parcelled out in garden plots.

Francis Russell, fourth Earl of Bedford.

A shrewd property owner, the fourth Earl of Bedford (1593–1641) recognised the opportunity for developing his land, and prospered as one of London's first great speculators and property developers. He was quick to clear his Covent Garden holdings of the clutter of outbuildings and poor hovels which had accumulated there, and to clean out the open sewer which bisected it. In 1630 he petitioned the Privy Council and paid King Charles I the enormous sum of £2,000 for a licence, an early form of planning permission, to develop part of Covent Garden adjacent to his great house. To overcome royal reluctance to condone development outside the City of London, he used a classic example of 'planning-gain' argument: London would acquire a fine square with a grand open space, and the income from his rents would enable the earl to maintain the important thoroughfare of Long Acre, connecting Westminster with the City of London.

Probably at the insistence of the King, who wished to embellish his capital city, England's best-known architect, Inigo Jones, was employed to lay out the Italianate central square, measuring some 420 ft. by 316 ft., and the surrounding residential streets. It was town planning on a magnificent scale, so greatly admired that it has been copied ever since, though the original vision was never completed. The prospect to the west drew the eye across the Piazza to the dramatic entrance of St Paul's Church. The north and east sides were let to speculative builders for the construction of grand colonnaded terraced homes. These four-storey buildings were strictly uniform and generously proportioned, with ceilings ten feet high. On the south, the Piazza directly abutted the wall at the back of the fourth Earl's garden.

Construction began on the church in 1631, and by 1639 almost all the houses around the Piazza were occupied. The ancient fruit trees and vegetable plots disappeared beneath a neat grid of roads enclosing the Piazza; Russell Street, and four roads with obvious royal derivation – James, Charles, Henrietta, and King Streets – led directly into the new urban space. For some years the open square remained little more than a gravelled enclosure; at its centre was a tall sundial column topped with a gilt ball, with four 'gnomons', the pins of the dial which create shadows to mark the hour.

The City of London was overcrowded, and gentry were attracted westward to the open space of the Piazza. The handsome houses around the open square were leased mainly to titled ratepayers, while random, unplanned building to accommodate the servants and casual labourers who supported the life-style of the Piazza gentry spread along insanitary alleys and courtyards westwards past St Giles, and to the east beyond Lincoln's Inn.

It was the Civil War that started the long, slow slide into raffish decline. Most

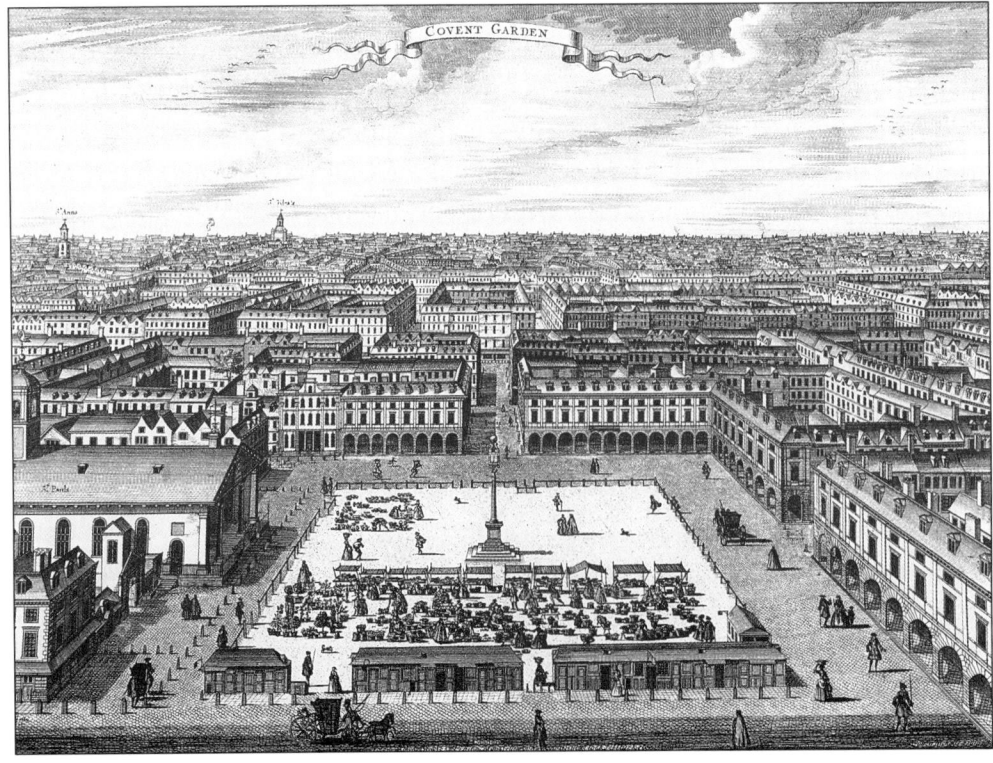

The Piazza, looking north, c. 1717–28.

From Sutton Nicholls's engraving, reproduced by kind permission of the Trustees of the British Museum.

of the residents were Royalist sympathisers and fled during the Commonwealth, when the Lord Protector, Oliver Cromwell, came to live nearby in the Long Acre. In 1647 more than a dozen Parliamentarians lived in or near the Piazza, including three regicides. After the Restoration some families with Royalist sympathies drifted back, but the convulsions of state and society did not encourage the lengthy aristocratic tenancies that would later determine the character of St James's and Mayfair. Artists such as Sir Peter Lely (1619–80) and Sir Godfrey Kneller (1646–1723) took up residence during the second half of the seventeenth century. But many of the fine houses surrounding the Piazza were left empty and vulnerable to vandalism and deterioration.

In 1641 Francis died, and the new fifth Earl (and later first Duke) of Bedford, William, made a dangerous return to Bedford House for his father's funeral. Parliament, angered by his support for the King, fined him £800 and sent in the bailiffs to seize his valuables. They found no gold or silver, and so in 1645 Parliament ordered that Bedford House and its contents be sold to cover the fine. This threat persuaded the fifth Earl to change his political allegiance, and in December he surrendered to the Earl of Essex. Thereafter, the rents continued to accumulate in the large Dutch chest which the fifth Earl kept in Bedford House as a family bank, and he devoted the rest of his life to his estates.

William Russell, fifth Earl and first Duke of Bedford.

In 1644 the residential covenants were breached as the first little shop opened under the portico of the Piazza. As early as 1656, when records noted that 30 shillings were paid to paint benches, market stalls had begun to nestle under a line of trees up against the garden wall of Bedford House for protection against the elements. They sold fruit, vegetables, herbs, and flowers, and also ironware. The impromptu market received a huge boost in 1665, as residents of the City of London fled the Great Plague for the open spaces outside its walls. Flower-sellers did a great trade in nosegays to combat the dreadful stenches. The very next year the Great Fire of London stopped just short of Covent Garden, and that, too, had a stimulating effect, as the merchants whose premises had been destroyed set up around the Piazza. They flourished under deregulation as the Russells freed the shopkeepers from the ancient restrictions of the City Guilds and Livery Companies of the City of London.

The fifth Earl knew a good business opportunity when he saw one. King Charles II had been restored to the throne in 1660, and in 1670 William Russell successfully petitioned him to formalise the market. The King granted to him and his heirs a royal charter – the continuing right to conduct a market and charge rents to traders: "for the buying and selling of all manner of fruit, flowers, roots and herbs whatsoever…for ever" throughout all seasons of the year "except Sundays and the Feast of the Nativity."

Two enterprising local craftsmen, Adam Pigott, a cutler, and Thomas Day, a tallow-chandler, had already been busy erecting small shops outside the garden wall of Bedford House and leasing them to market gardeners. In 1678 the fifth Earl effectively recognised them as market-operators, granting them an 11-year lease to build and sublease shops for £80 per annum. His planning regulations were

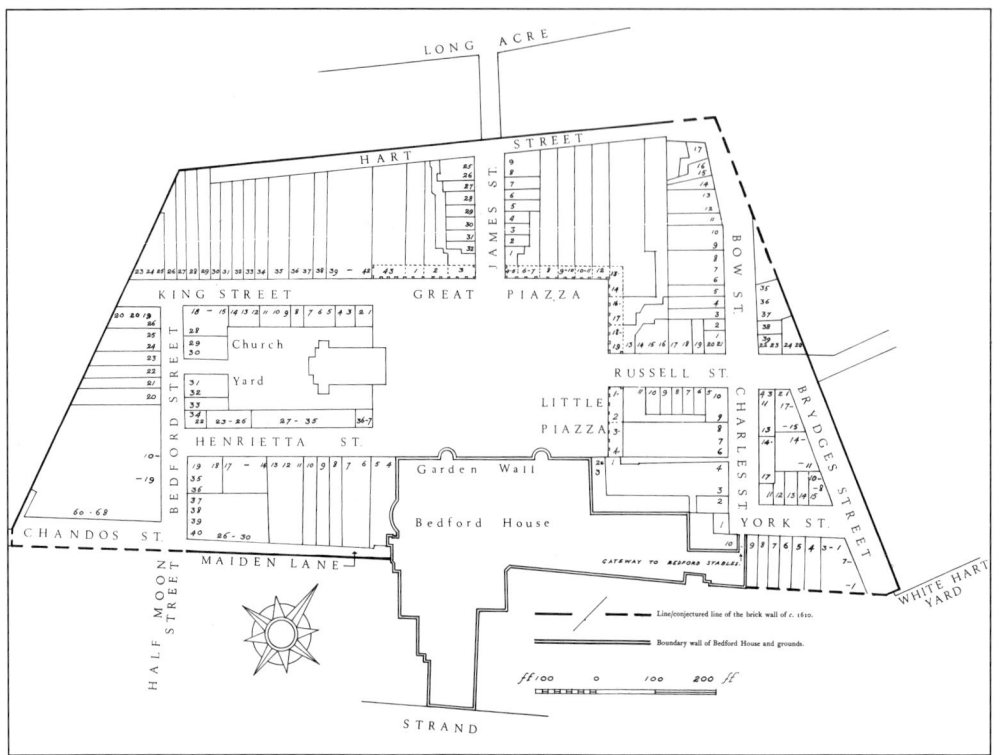

Extent of the Bedford Estate within the brick wall in Covent Garden, c. 1610, with the boundary wall of Bedford House and grounds at the bottom centre.

Reproduced from *Survey of London* vol. xxxvi, by permission of English Heritage and the Royal Commission on the Historical Monuments of England.

environmentally enlightened: the shops had to have a uniform frontage and their roofs were to be a foot lower than his garden wall, with no chimneys. Free passage for horses, carts, and coaches had to be maintained, and the buildings were to be kept clean and in good repair.

With the Restoration, life and gaiety returned to the centre of London. Thomas Killigrew persuaded his friend King Charles to grant him a royal patent for the first Theatre Royal and opened its doors in Drury Lane, not far from the site of the earlier, illegal, and notorious Cockpit Theatre, in 1663. Covent Garden became a centre of entertainment. There were taverns, coffee-houses, cockfight pits, and, in 1732 the first Royal Opera House opened its doors.

Up until 1692, continued alterations and improvements were made to Bedford House, mostly on the northern side, where its spacious garden extended across a raised terrace overlooking the Piazza. It remained the London home of the Earls of Bedford until William, the fifth Earl and first Duke, died there in 1700. It then passed with the rest of the Covent Garden estate to his grandson, Wriothesley. He preferred to live in his mother's house in Bloomsbury and thus the historic names Tavistock Street and Russell Square reappeared in that area.

In 1705–6, the 120-year-old Bedford House was demolished. The entire site, including the garden and courtyard, was laid out for redevelopment as the Bedford Ground. On its western border Southampton Street was built 50 feet wide, to permit the first access to the Piazza from the Strand. The new street was purposely narrowed at its southern end to create a bottleneck, and gated against the passage of market carts. A 35-foot wide corridor named Tavistock Street was driven east and west through the centre of the former garden, debouching into Charles Street at its eastern end. From its north side, a narrow 12-foot alley called

Tavistock Court led into the Piazza. This survives today as the passage between the Jubilee Hall and the Transport Museum. The opening to Maiden Lane was built only 18 feet wide and was named Southampton Court. In all, 80 building leases were issued for the whole of the Bedford Ground.

This reconstruction had a devastating effect on the market traders. The wall of the terraced garden of Bedford House against which they had pitched their stalls for half a century was demolished, and in 1706 they were pushed out into a railed enclosure in the open square. In their place, a row of houses known as Tavistock Row was thrown up on the south side of the Piazza, west of the narrow Tavistock Court passage, on what is now the site of the Jubilee Hall, between 1706 and 1714. This terrace adjoined three houses in two buildings east of Tavistock Court, Nos. 1–3, the only fragment of the original Piazza development to have

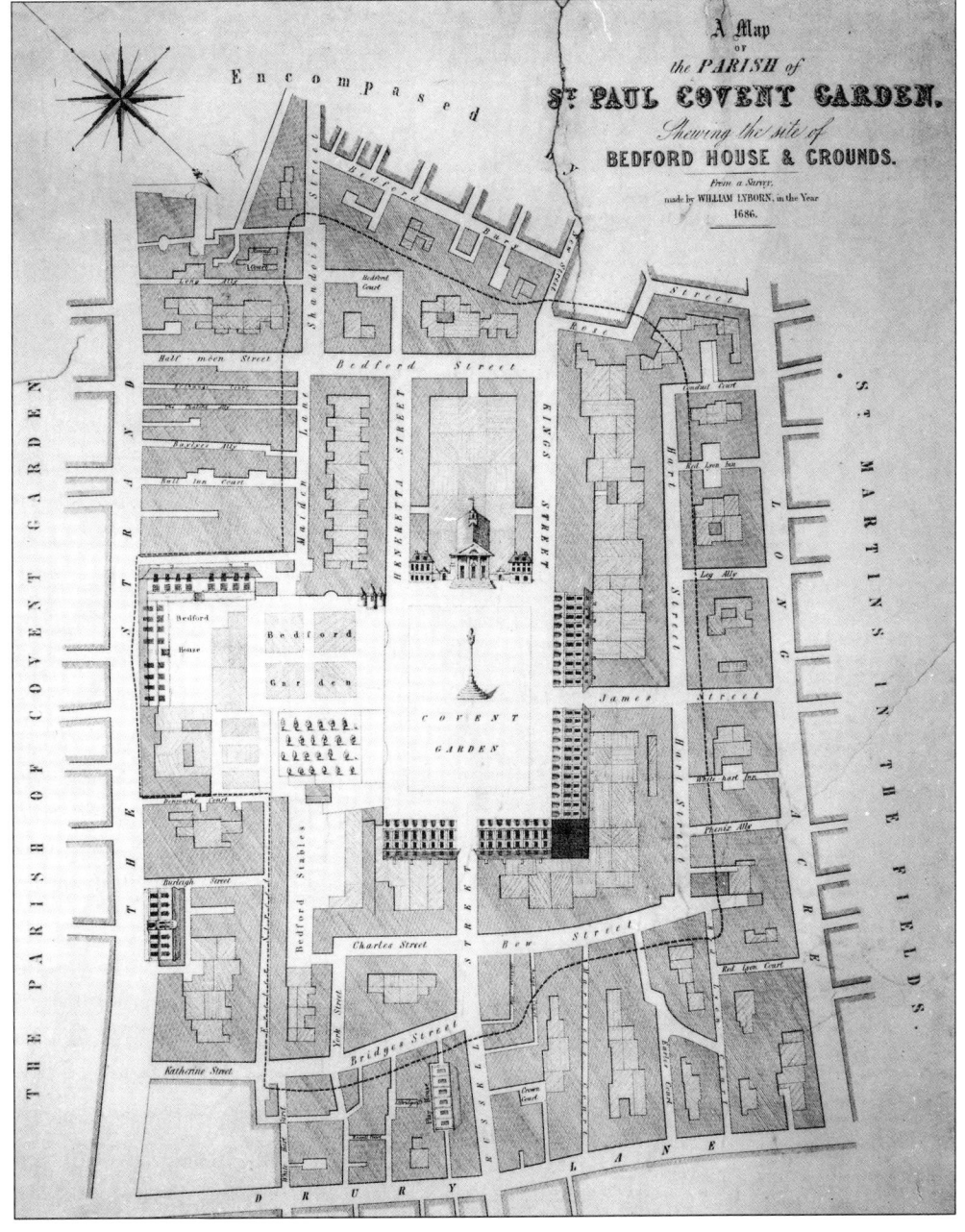

Map of Bedford House and grounds, reproduced from the survey of William Lyborn, 1686.

By kind permission of the Marquess of Tavistock and the Trustees of the Bedford Estate.

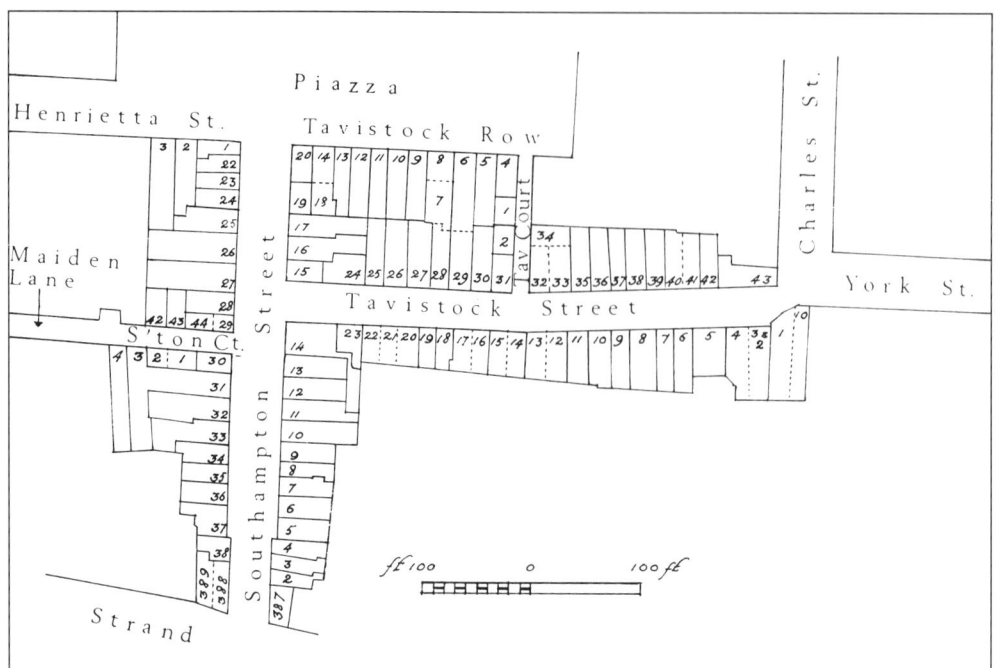

A plan of the Bedford Ground in 1706–14, showing individual plots and house numbers. Based on original leases and a plan of 1795 in the possession of the Trustees of the Bedford Settled Estates and now deposited in Greater London Record Office.

Reproduced from *Survey of London* vol. xxxvi, by permission of English Heritage and the Royal Commission on the Historical Monuments of England.

been realised on the south side. Though of good character, the new houses which were built at Nos. 4–14 were not required to match the classic Inigo Jones design of the old porticoed buildings on the north and east sides of the Piazza. They were not even uniform to each other, because the later houses in the group had to comply with new regulations contained in the two London Building Acts of 1701 and 1708, which were passed during the granting of the leases. So, although all were four storeys high, this row of 11 new houses comprised two basically different types. The earlier buildings had flat arched windows and wooden-eave cornices, sometimes surmounted by a later brick parapet, and in one case by a Chinese fret railing of wood. The later constructions had windows with segmental arches and prominent triple keystones, and their fronts were carried up to form plain stone-coped parapets. These houses were not sufficiently grand to attract the aristocracy, but residents included successful actors and artists. The marine painter Samuel Scott lived in the row during the 1730s, and the portraitist Nathaniel Dance was at No. 13 in the 1770s. No. 4 became the scene of one of the great eighteenth century scandals of London society. The milliner who lived there attracted the attention of Lord Sandwich while he was strolling through Covent Garden, and became his mistress. She presented him with nine children before being murdered by a jealous suitor in 1779.

Miss Martha Raye, mistress of Lord Sandwich, who was murdered on 7 April 1779, painted by Nathaniel Dance RA in 1777.

FROM BEFORE THE TURN of the eighteenth century market forces began to prevail, and the area gradually subsided into debauched decline. In 1681 Robert Lazenby had opened the first *bagnio* in a basement in the Little Piazza, as the eastern end of the square was called. Soon other houses in the Little Piazza were converted into these Turkish baths, which became known generically as 'Hummums'. *Haddock's* and *Lovejoy's* joined *Lazenby's Hummums* in the Russell Chambers corner, now occupied by *Tutton's* and the entrance to the present day

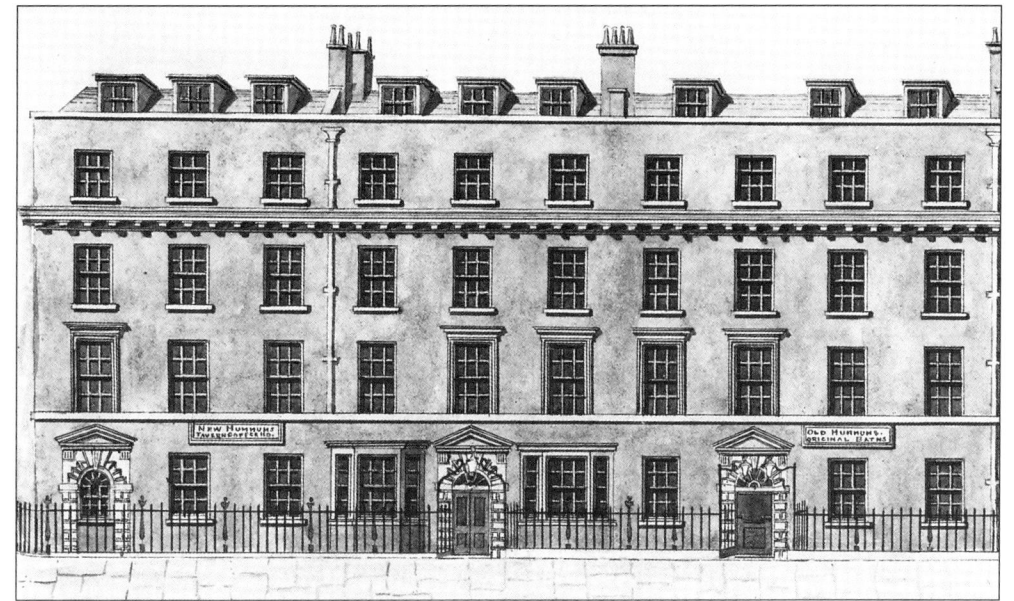

The Little Piazza on the east side of the square, showing the NEW and OLD HUMMUMS, Nos. 1–3 (consec.), in 1769–70.

From a watercolour in the Westminster City Archives.

View of the Piazza in 1751, looking north from where the Jubilee Hall stands today.

From an engraving by T. Bowles, reproduced by kind permission of the Trustees of the British Museum.

Transport Museum. These soon degenerated into places of assignation and then straightforward brothels, imposing a new meaning on the word *bagnio,* formerly simply the Italian for a solitary and innocent hot bath. The original *Lazenby's Hummums* was the most notorious, and in the closing years of the seventeenth century it was shut down. It reopened in 1701 under new management, admitting men only, with the advertising boast that "no smoak or any noisome or stinking savors" were allowed.

By 1748 a collection of 229 stands and 106 shops, low but substantial buildings, sprawled in the centre of the Piazza. The market became a noisy, messy neighbour. The gentrified tenants of the arcaded buildings around the Piazza packed their bags and resumed their westward drift to the wards of Mayfair, Bloomsbury (also owned by the Russell family), and St James's, where other grand squares had arisen. The last of the titled gentry were gone by 1757.

Rents fell in the wake of their departure and Covent Garden entered a raffish, Bohemian phase, attracting men of letters, politics, arts, the theatre, and, of course, market traders. The fine houses around the Piazza were turned into taverns, hotels, and coffee-houses, and "resorts for drink, talk or assignation." Hogarth prowled the nearby gin palaces of Drury Lane and Earlham Street for life

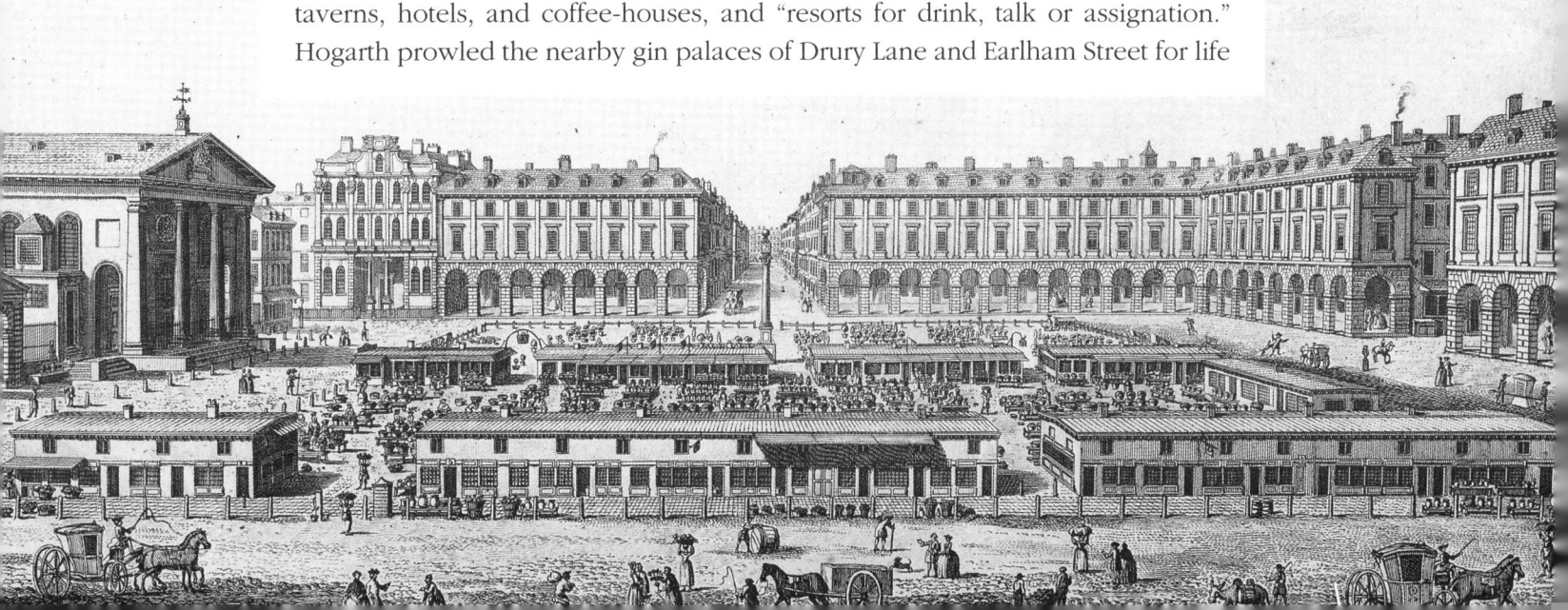

Facing page:
'Morning', by William Hogarth, shows a lady, her face adorned with beauty patches (originally used to disguise smallpox scars), hesitating outside TOM KING'S coffee-house, installed under the portico of St Paul's church. Lord Archer's impressive mansion at 43 King Street, which still stands today, is included on the right.

Looking south past the sundial in the centre of the Piazza to Tavistock Row in 1750.

From a drawing in the Westminster City Archives.

studies for his comic and compassionate series of etchings, *The Rake's Progress.* Covent Garden was to make its mark in history as London's principal pleasure garden, awake and active from before dawn when the market opened until the small hours of the night. It was almost always thus. As early as 1632, before its brief elevation as a residence for "Gentlemen and men of abillity", the turbulent tavern life of the secluded lanes of Covent Garden had been described in a contemporary stage comedy as peopled with "the lewdest blades and naughty-packs."

Manufacturing came too. Busy workshops sprang up in the alleys and byways all around: barrow-makers, coach-builders, tailors, goldsmiths, mercers, sedan chair-makers, and fan-mounters all practised their crafts here. Booksellers and auctioneers also particularly favoured the area. Gradually, the noble houses in Tavistock Row were converted into shops and pubs. By 1720, No. 10 had already become a tavern called *The Queen's Head,* and in 1730 No. 1 was converted into another, *The Bedford Arms.* In 1800 it was transformed again, into a hotel called *The Imperial.* The building survived until 1859 when, together with its companions Nos. 2 and 3, which had continued to be leased as separate residences, it was demolished to create more room for market activities.

In 1813 the Covent Garden Market came under government regulation. It was, however, still owned by the Dukes of Bedford, who throughout the centuries managed their estate with great care, if not social compassion. Throughout the nineteenth century, the Bedford Estate carried out a regular programme of clearing out and renewing decaying areas, including the construction of new, wider roads to replace narrow streets which disgorged traffic into the broad

The south-east corner of the Piazza in 1837, showing the OLD HUMMUMS at No. 4 Little Piazza and the IMPERIAL hotel and private residences at Nos. 1–5 (consec.) Tavistock Row, where the Jubilee Hall now stands.

From a watercolour by C.J. Smith in the Guildhall Library, City of London.

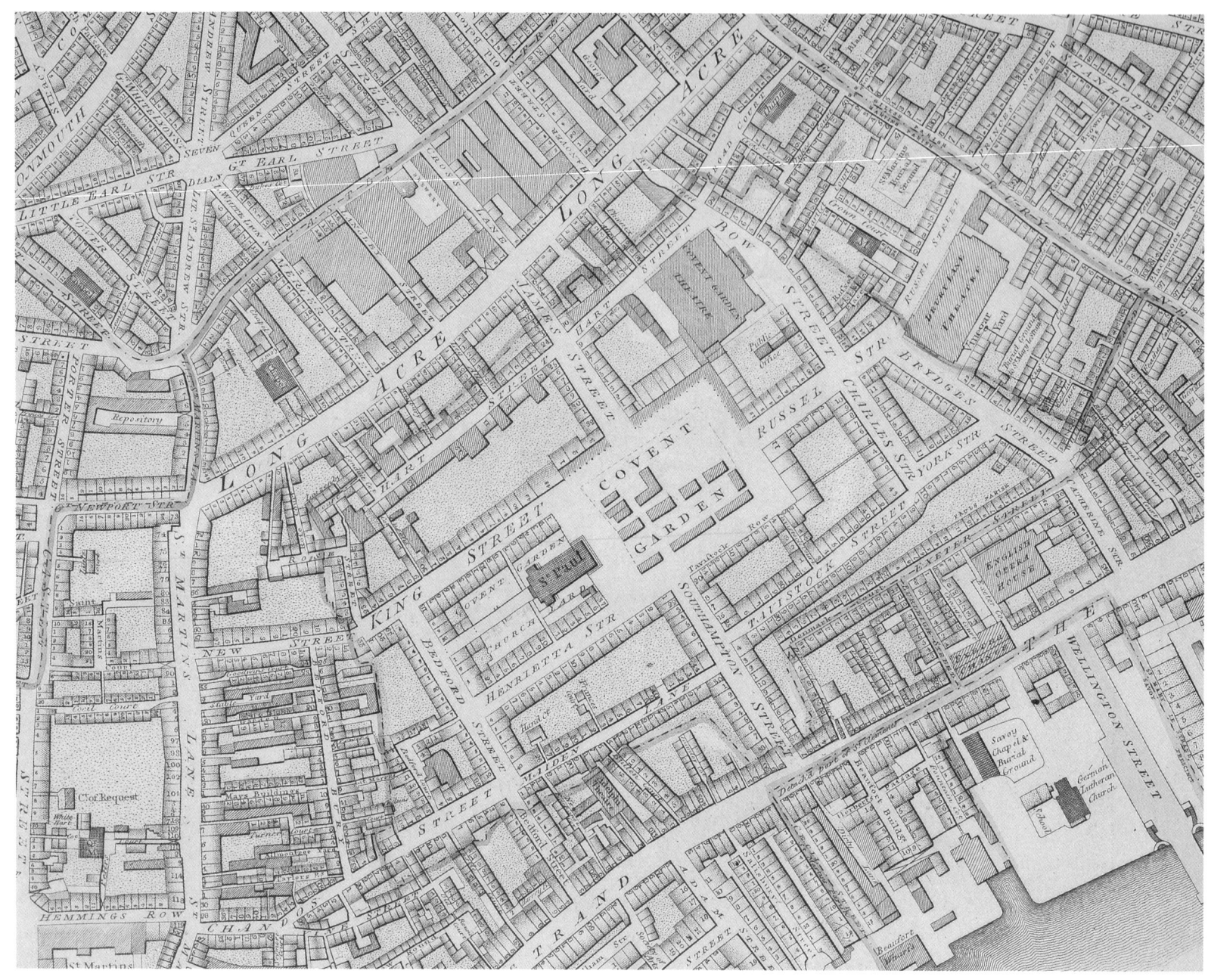

Covent Garden in 1819, a decade before the Central Market Building was constructed.

Extract from Horwood's map, reproduced by kind permission of the Trustees of the British Museum.

approaches to the Piazza.

In the process, whole neighbourhoods were obliterated, of the type described by Dickens in *Sketches by Boz*, in 1836. In Drury Lane he saw "wretched houses with broken windows patched with rags and paper; every room let out to a different family, and sometimes two, or even three – fruit and 'sweetstuff' manufacturing in the cellars, barbers and red-herring vendors in the front parlours, cobblers in the back; a bird fancier in the first floor, three families on the second, starvation in the attics, Irishmen in the passage, a 'musician' in the front kitchen, and a charwoman and five hungry children in the back one – filth everywhere – a gutter before the houses and a drain behind – clothes drying, and slops emptying from windows…". In 1844 the Duke of Bedford remarked to his surveyor, C. Haedy, "I cannot conceive what becomes of all the poor people who are compelled to leave their homes and lodgings for the improvement of Covent Garden." It was a comment which was to be echoed more than a century later, and with considerably more heart, by a Greater London Council planner.

The cholera epidemic of 1850 spread rapidly through the insanitary tenements of Covent Garden and stung the Bedford Estate into action. To prevent further decay it introduced strict controls against underlets and change of use. Only with the Duke's specific consent could leases be sold to a butcher, publican, cow-keeper, chimney sweep, pawnbroker, gold-beater, bone-burner, undertaker, coffin-maker, bookbinder, or dealer in rags, birds, or caricatures. And the land agents of the Duke maintained an absolute ban against the frivolities of music halls, ballrooms, billiard rooms, auction salerooms, shooting galleries, madhouses, and school seminaries.

It was a losing battle. By 1886 a survey by the Bedford Estate Office tallied 120 lodging-houses in Covent Garden. Most of the tenants were of the poorest classes – porters, shoe-menders, labourers, laundresses, and charwomen. The Bedford Estate reported: "there are few of the absolute destitute class, though the pinch of poverty must be felt, and thieves and prostitutes will shortly appear unless sharp measures are adopted…".

The commercialisation of the area had long been completed with the erection of the covered market in the middle of the Piazza. Work started on the new market building designed by Charles Fowler, with perimeter colonnade and lodges, in 1828. When it was finished in 1830, it looked very much as it does today, except that the two main aisles were uncovered. The glass roofs were added separately, in 1875 and 1889. The central avenue was lined with fruiterers, and two conservatories on the first floor of the west terrace fulfilled the constant demand of the Victorian household for plants and cut flowers.

In 1860, following the construction of the new Royal Opera House, the fine line of the arcaded buildings was cleaved to insert the Floral Hall, the glass and

Construction of the Floral Hall in the Piazza, June 1858.

After G. Sargent. Guildhall Library, City of London.

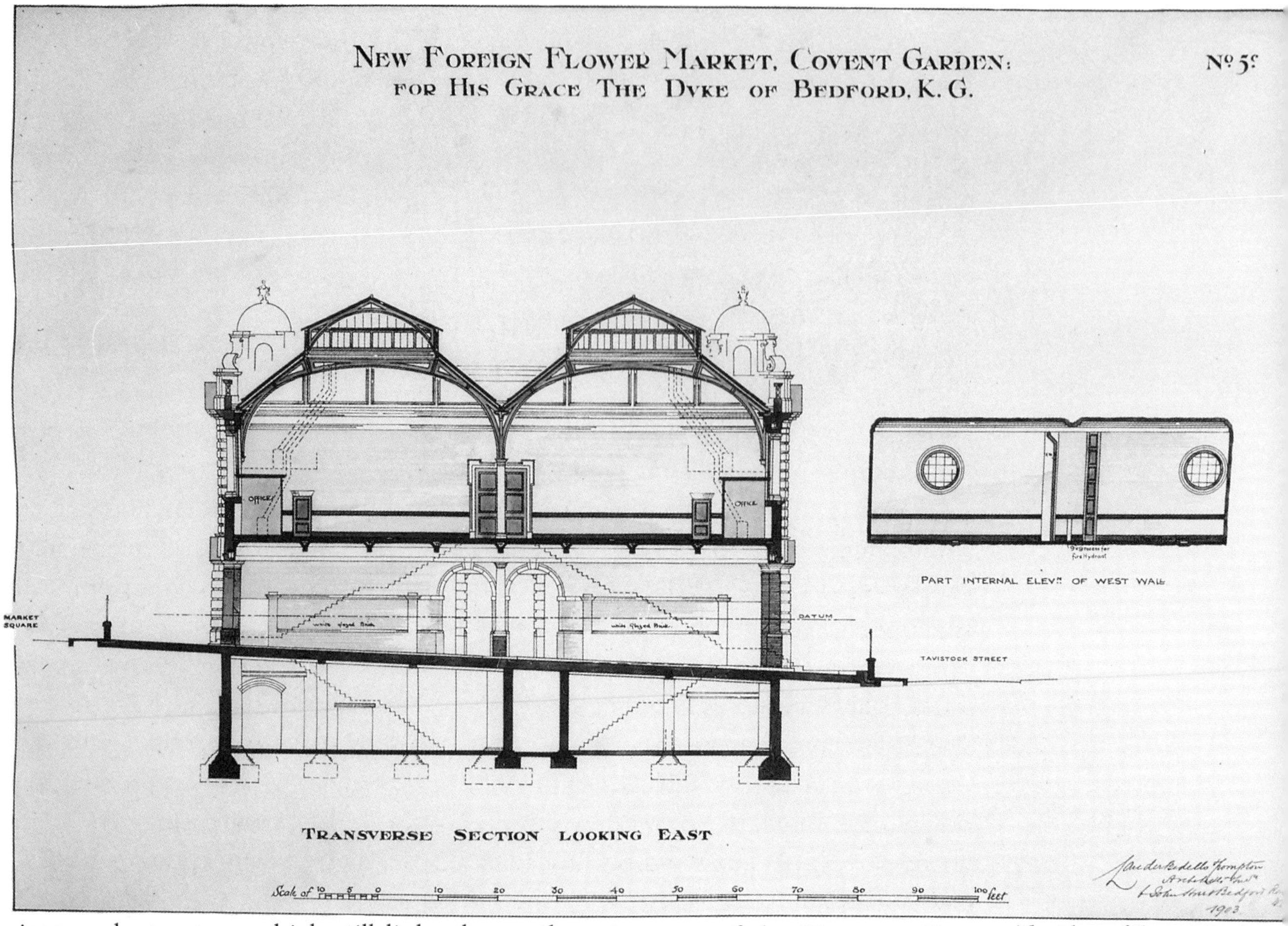

NEW FOREIGN FLOWER MARKET, COVENT GARDEN:
FOR HIS GRACE THE DVKE OF BEDFORD, K.G.

Nº 5ᶜ

PART INTERNAL ELEVⁿ OF WEST WALL

TRANSVERSE SECTION LOOKING EAST

Scale of ¹⁰ feet

The plan of the original Jubilee Market Hall, east elevation, by Lander, Bedells and Compton, 1903.

By kind permission of the Marquess of Tavistock and the Trustees of the Bedford Estate.

ironwork structure which still links the north-east corner of the Piazza to Bow Street. It was, of course, intended to house the flower market. However, the flower dealers perversely preferred to operate under canvas in the south-east corner, and so the Floral Hall was actually used as the foreign-fruit section. The flower-sellers were eventually persuaded to move indoors when the building now used to house the Transport and Theatre Museums was completed in 1872. The iron flower-stands it once contained are still in service as the permanent stalls which stand in the small 'Apple Market' in the north hall of the new Central Market Building.

In 1884, to satisfy the market's voracious appetite for space, the demolition crews began to level the remainder of Tavistock Row and other early eighteenth-century houses, 26 in all, which had been erected on the old Bedford Ground in the block bounded by Tavistock Row, Tavistock Court, Tavistock Street and Southampton Street. Demolition was completed in 1891 at a cost of £15,709, and the open space remained as a temporary 'lay bye' for market vehicles for another six years, when the

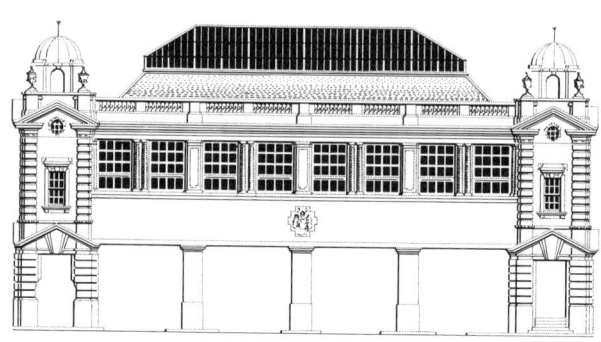

Drawing of Jubilee Market Hall, Covent Garden, before restoration.

By Alan Fagan,
© The Heritage of London Trust.

Interior of the foreign-flower market on the first floor of Jubilee Hall, looking west, 1904.

Duke of Bedford commissioned a new home for the section of the market which sold imported cut flowers. An increasing volume of trade was coming from the Channel Islands, the Isles of Scilly, and the French ports.

Built by James Cubitt, the new foreign-flower market was designed by Lander, Bedells, and Compton as a substantial, free-standing, oblong building of two lofty storeys, both divided lengthwise by a row of widely spaced columns. Unusually, the market was located upstairs. The magnificent vaulted first floor, lit by clerestory windows and supporting a splendid long peaked glass roof on iron girders, was conceived as a trading floor. The north and south walls were fringed with 16 small salesmen's offices, each with its own display area, and there were another 34 stands and counters in the centre. The floor was served by two electric lifts in the south-west angle of the pavilion. The ground storey was left largely open to the street, with wide spaces and few points of support, to provide a maximum wheel area for wagons and other vehicles. The pavilions were deliberately angled to avoid the appearance of a block standing on stilts. Below was a high-ceilinged basement to be used for storage. Each of these three floors was around 1,000 sq.m. in area and more than five metres in height.

The symmetrical facades of the Jubilee Hall were dressed in red sand-faced bricks and Portland stone and, in the baroque style fashionable in Edwardian times, there was lavish detail, customary in a civic building, but unusual in a functional market hall – a generous scatter of keystones, cupolas, cartouches, and broken pediments. Venetian windows graced the east elevation and each corner flourished a pavilion ornament of two pedimented stages surmounted by a small dome. The architectural style was described in *The Builder*, in its October 1904 issue, as the 'later English Renaissance manner.' This fashion was dubbed 'Wrenaissance' by Sir E.L. Lutyens, who used it for the offices he built for *Country Life* magazine, just opposite in Tavistock Street. The renaissance reflected Wren's improvements at Hampton Court, and, owing much also to the Free Arts and Crafts movement of the era, the design was considered quite advanced at the time.

The building covered about half the site; the rest was left empty. Though completed in 1904, it was named the Jubilee Hall in honour of Queen Victoria's Diamond Jubilee, commemorating the sixtieth anniversary of her reign, which had been celebrated in 1897, the year that construction first began. Until 1974 it served a useful role in the market as a warehouse

Detail, the Jubilee Market Hall, 1974.
Greater London Photograph Library.

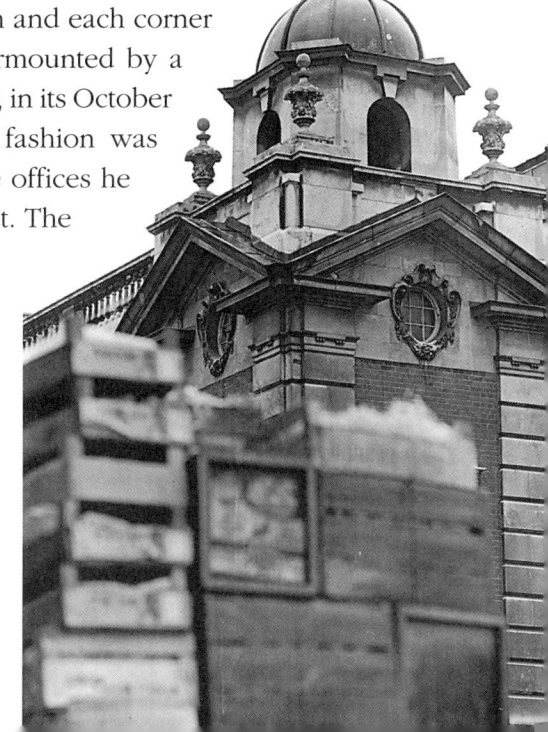

and trading floor, latterly specialising in potatoes.

Long before these expansions were undertaken, it had become obvious that the colourful wholesale fruit and vegetable market, congesting the narrow streets with heavy traffic in one of the choicest parts of central London, would sooner or later have to be relocated. *Punch* magazine fulminated against the general mess of what it called the Covent Garden "mud salad" market. In the new political climate which emerged towards the end of the nineteenth century, many of the landed gentry were disposing of their great estates, and aristocratic control of public facilities such as markets was an anachronism. The Bedford family was unnerved. By 1910 the eleventh Duke of Bedford would have been content to hand over control of the operation, but both the Metropolitan Board of Works and the City of London Corporation declined to take it over.

'Early Morning in Covent Garden Market'.

The Central Market Building in 1902.
Greater London Photograph Library.

In 1913, a £2 million private option for sale of the Central Market area comprising 19 acres of the family's holdings was agreed; but it was not until five years later that the offer was officially taken up by a syndicate led by Sir Joseph Beecham, pill-manufacturer and father of Sir Thomas, the famed conductor. (The Bedfords retained the freehold for the Theatre Royal, Drury Lane, and Bow Street Magistrates Court). The syndicate's holdings were managed by a company called Covent Garden Estate, and in 1920 it, too, tried unsuccessfully to sell off the market to the London County Council. A year later, a government committee decided the buildings were obsolete and the location quite unsuited to modern motor transport. For the next four years the future of the market was debated. A plan to move it to St Pancras was killed in Parliament in 1927. The Utopian Abercrombie plan for London, prepared in 1943, suggested the fruit and vegetable market be moved to the outskirts, on the edge of the 'green belt' surrounding London. Still nothing was done, while in 1945, 300 years of exploitation of Covent Garden by the Russells quietly ended when the twelfth Duke sold the family's last remaining property, No. 26 James Street.

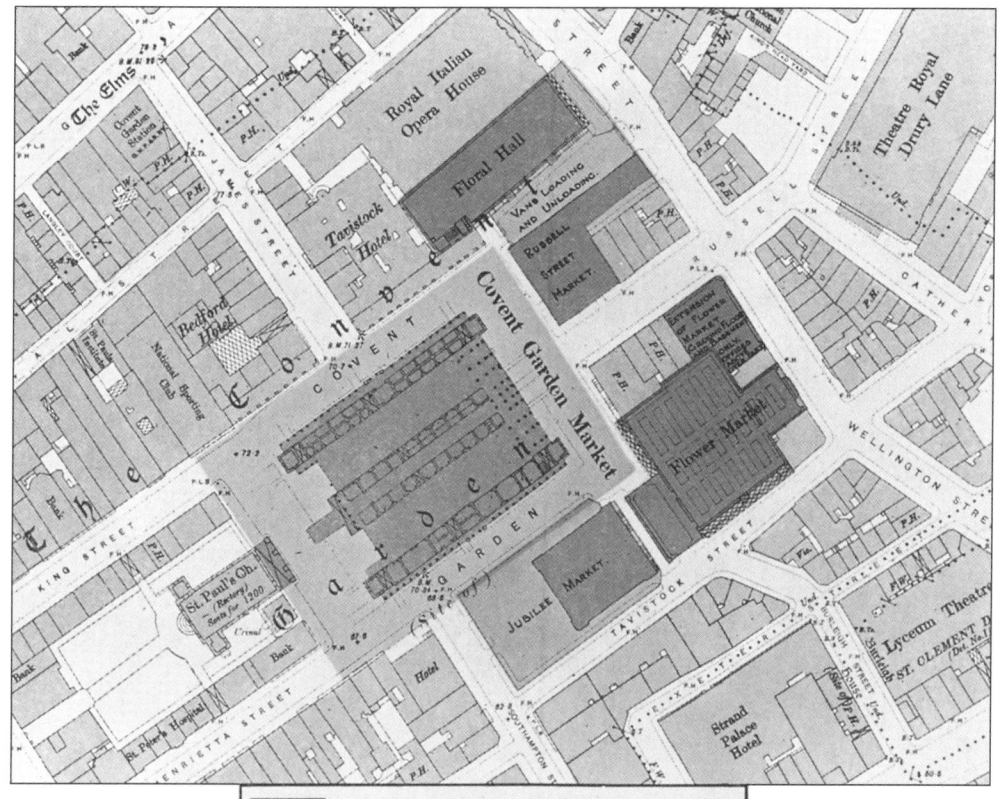

Plan of the Covent Garden Market in 1926, showing chartered and unchartered areas.

From the report on Covent Garden Market by the Town Clerk of the City of Westminster, reproduced from the 1910 Ordnance Survey map and *Survey of London* vol. xxxvi, by permission of English Heritage and the Royal Commission on the Historical Monuments of England.

The Covent Garden Market had long since become an institution, part of the folklore of London. It never slept. The new work-day started at midnight as the last trains and buses brought in the porters. Throughout the small hours of the morning lorries arrived from market gardens all over Britain, laden with crates of lettuces, mushrooms, and roses, potatoes from Norfolk, apples from Kent, oranges and lemons from the western ports. Some produce started the trip by air – daffodils from the Channel Isles or anemones from France – and trains brought tulips from Lincolnshire and primroses and violets from the woods of the West Country to the main-line London stations. But everything ended its journey stacked on a lorry crammed into one of the congested streets around the Piazza.

The porters, wearing aprons over their waistcoats, and long coats, cloth caps, and scarves against the cold, unloaded the sacks and crates and boxes by hand, bearing them by head, by barrow, and trolley to the stalls where the 'night men' set up their displays. Everywhere throughout the market there was a cheerful burble of Cockney camaraderie over cups of tea boiled up and cigarettes shared, and the tuneful whistling of men enjoying their work. Each 'night man' had 400 boxes or more to open, check, and display by 4.30 a.m. He could take a break

Covent Garden Market at the beginning of the twentieth century.

*Covent Garden Market,
under the portico of
St Paul's.*

From Reid's *Views of Westminster*,
London vol. iii,
© Museum of London.

then, when the salesman arrived to start his shift, and push off to warm his hands
at *Albert's Café*, or *Frank's*, over another mug of tea and a bacon roll, or a saveloy
wrapped in a thick slice of white bread, as the buyers began to trickle in at 5 a.m.

At daybreak more lorries would turn up, loaded with the ordinary
vegetables from the farms near London – cabbages, leeks, carrots and more
potatoes. Farmers' stalls went up on the cobblestones of the Piazza, and by 7 a.m.
the market was in full, bustling swing. Female porters worked in the flower
market, and by shop opening time at 9 a.m. they had dispatched boys bearing
colourful basketfuls on their heads or by barrow throughout central London.

Later, when the prices had fallen, the old ladies who sold flowers in the
London streets would come along to stock up. By 11 a.m. there was nothing left
except the squashed fruit, leaves, and vegetable litter discarded on the pavement.
The square would still be packed with lorries, some loading up for out-of-town
deliveries, others beginning to bring in tomorrow's supplies. The market would
just tick over now, until a new working day began at midnight.

Finally, in 1961, the Covent Garden Market Act was passed. The following
year most of the properties owned by the market landlord, notably excluding the
Royal Opera House but including Jubilee Hall and the empty adjacent site,
together with the other market buildings, were disposed of to a public body newly
created with the backing of the Government, the Covent Garden Market Authority
(CGMA), for £3,925,000.

The new Authority controlled 4,000 workers and 340 companies which
processed £70 million worth of fruit and vegetables and £10 million worth of
flowers each year, predominantly as wholesalers. In 1964 it decided to move the

Covent Garden Market, the Little Piazza, showing the Floral Hall.
© Museum of London.

market, wavered over alternative sites (one was the nearby Seven Dials, which had most of the same drawbacks), and eventually chose Nine Elms in Battersea, where surplus railway land was available by the side of the Thames near the Vauxhall Bridge. Parliament gave its blessing in 1966.

With the market destined to resettle south of the river some time in the next decade, an era which had lasted more than three centuries was about to come to an end, leaving a gaping hole in the centre of Covent Garden. The choice chunk of central London acreage that was left behind would require new owners, and the square mile of surrounding area now called Covent Garden, which the market had so long dominated, would require new thought and a new city-centre role. Abroad, the closing of *Les Halles* in Paris and Amsterdam's *Nieumarket* was prompting similar thinking about urban regeneration.

In 1965 a joint planning group was established by the two local authorities which controlled the area, Camden and Westminster, with the Greater London Council (GLC) overseeing strategy. In 1968, the properties owned by the CGMA were purchased by the GLC for £6,050,000, and its planners published exciting new proposals for radical change in a Comprehensive Development Area – not just the 14 acres of land to be vacated by the market, but the entire 96-acre district of Covent Garden.

The Covent Garden Market by St Paul's, 1930.
Greater London Photograph Library.

Covent Garden porters.

From *Street Life in London*,
© Museum of London.

CHAPTER THREE

Life under the portico of St Paul's Church in the 1970s.
© Clive Boursnell.

The New Jerusalem

1968–1972

WHEN JIM MONAHAN became a student at the Architectural Association in Bedford Square, he lived in digs in Covent Garden. His connection with the area was marginal, yet it was he, rather than any of its native sons, who became the most effective and durable leader of protest against the threat of wanton destruction which hung for decades over the colourful neighbourhood at the heart of London. Covent Garden exists today, in the way it is, only because people like Jim Monahan, who lived and worked there, decided it was worth fighting for, and brought a mighty, faceless, planning bureaucracy to heel. It is owing to them that here, in the middle of a huge, busy city, nestled between the modern-arts complex of the South Bank, the gallery treasure-houses of Trafalgar Square, the vulgarity of Leicester Square, and the edge of the financial powerhouse of the City of London, there survives the remnant of a small-scale urban village.

In the late 1960s, Covent Garden had industry, too. It was a chaotic commercial jumble of 1,700 firms employing 34,000 workers. The boisterous wholesale fruit and vegetable market was its pulsing heart, but also within its borders were the headquarters of two national newspapers, the *Daily Herald* and the *Sun*, 27 publishing houses, and half of London's 36 theatres, including the oldest, the biggest, and the grandest.

Clustered around in the narrow streets, hundreds of small businesses serviced these key industries, some through a craft tradition extending back to the eighteenth century. James Keeley invented the wheeled costermonger stall and founded his business in the same year Covent Garden's Central Market Building was erected. His descendants were still making barrows in his Neal Street workshop. At *W. T. Morrell & Co.*, a firm first founded in 1861, books had been bound by hand in an upstairs workshop in Nottingham Court for 60 years. George Russell established a business in 1770 to supply every kind of material needed by horse-drawn traffic, from loincloths for horses to waterproof covers for the bowler hats that cabbies wore. Now evolved into *Russell & Chapple*, the Monmouth Street firm specialised in canvas goods, from tarpaulins to theatrical backdrops and artists' canvases. There were two frame-makers, one, *Noah Mann & Sons*, the fifth generation in a family business founded in 1849. *George Parker & Sons*, a saddlery in Upper St Martin's Lane, had been established two years later.

There were a myriad theatrical suppliers, including costumiers, makers of masks and ballet slippers, a French horn manufacturer, and in Neal's Yard a three-man enterprise called *Robert White & Sons, Armourers,* where skilled metal-workers had been cladding stage knights for 200 years. There were five hospitals, 26 stamp dealers, and 126 publishers or printers, including *Odhams*, the company behind many leading national magazines. In warehouse workrooms everywhere, sprinkled like yeast in dough, was a more recent admixture of, in the word of the age, 'trendy' jewellery designers, glass blowers, potters, and silversmiths, and a growing Bohemian culture of artists, writers, photographers, and film studios. Many of these were on short leases. Speculators had bought the property in anticipation of redevelopment. The days of the heterogeneous business

In 1968 the open space next to the Jubilee Market Hall was used to park cars and barrows.
Greater London Photograph Library.

community, flourishing in echoing former warehouses and dilapidated nineteenth-century buildings, were coming to end. In a nation without rent controls, the same was happening all over Britain.

In most inner-London areas the population had been dropping for more than 100 years, as family size diminished and, with increasing general prosperity, the enticements of suburban life beckoned. In the late 1960s, about 3,300 people actually lived in Covent Garden. However, many were elderly, widowed, and living by themselves or without children. The average occupancy was just 2.1 people in the 1,660 homes, almost all of them flats. Half of these shared both bathroom and lavatory, and almost one-quarter shared a kitchen. The bulk of housing was private, unfurnished, rented accommodation; more than a quarter was council-owned, and almost another 10 per cent belonged to the Peabody Trust, a body of Victorian philanthropic origins. Some of the buildings had no water supply to the flats. Communal sinks and toilets on the open stairs were often unwillingly shared with local dossers and tramps who hung around the market. Over the past 80 years the number of cheap lodging-houses had reduced from 120 to two. It was time for a change.

"They're luverly!" chirped the headline of the *London Evening Standard* on 6 November 1968, describing the £140 million plan for the redevelopment of Covent Garden called "Covent Garden's Moving". A model was on display in an exhibition in Wellington Street sponsored by the Greater London Council. In the brave new world of city planning, the news was greeted as a welcome sign that at last Britain was catching up with the rest of postwar Europe. We could think big, too – or, as the newspaper article described it, could dream up "a compulsive vision which blends the best of the old historic area with innovation on a grand scale."

Time had finally been called on the Covent Garden wholesale fruit and vegetable market. With a clang! It would leave a huge void in land use, in employment, in community life. The GLC proposed to fill it by building a New Jerusalem in the heart of the metropolis. It would replace two-thirds of the 96 acres now known as Covent Garden, the entire area bounded by Kingsway to the east, the Strand to the south, Charing Cross Road to the west, and Shaftesbury Avenue and High Holborn to the north. Monumental constructions the size of whole street blocks would virtually demolish the existing street pattern, imposing a multi-level roadway system and a modern complex of offices, conference centres, hotels and new theatres, shops, and restaurants. In the correctspeak of the go-ahead 1960s, "a multiflexible interdisciplinary entertainment/sports hall" would be dropped into the Cambridge Circus "node", planspeak for a knotty place. There would be new housing, too, schools, and a park. In the process, however, many familiar landmarks came under threat. Five of London's historic theatres would be bulldozed, eleven others disrupted. And eight out of ten of the places where people lived were to be demolished to make way for three tidy bands of specialised uses.

The plan envisioned two great slices of new development, on the south a "bright lights" entertainment area running from the Piazza to Leicester Square, and a northern range of residential high-rises. A character route of conservation was

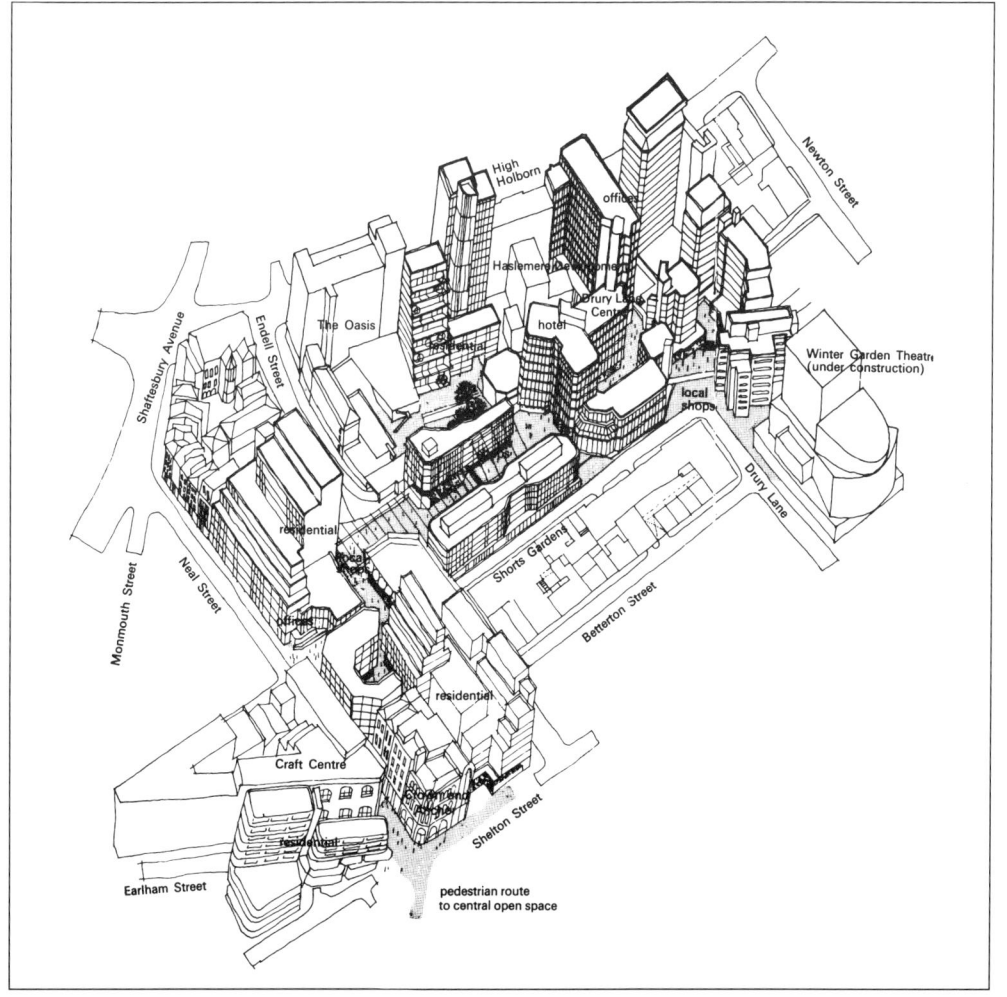

Phase one renewal, north spine, from 'The Next Step', published by the GLC Covent Garden Committee in 1971.

Reproduced by permission of English Heritage and the Royal Commission on the Historical Monuments of England.

left in the middle to lard the white-bread sandwich of technology with the savoury spread of history. The motor car was greatly favoured, with two new four-lane highways, one sunk into Maiden Lane and another low-level spine road in the north, both connected to a circulatory system; the widening of Charing Cross Road and Shaftesbury Avenue; and, of course, car parks. These would multiply the number of parking spaces in Covent Garden from 600 to 4,300. The plan allowed for a working population of 31,000–37,000, and 6,000 residents.

The principle then in vogue, and which was to be responsible for the desolation of many city centres in Britain today, was the separation of pedestrians and vehicles via 'traffic architecture'. Foot passengers would be elevated to a new system of aerial public transport linked by bridges and walkways which could then be extended to other parts of the central metropolitan area. In architectural musings, the lofty buildings would "heighten dramatic situations and episodes, create landmarks, and provide contrast." The new Covent Garden was expected to become a major tourist attraction and exert a seminal influence on ideas for urban form.

This proud plan emanated from a task force of professionals called the Covent Garden Team. It had been brought into being in September 1965 by an

Market traders in the Central Market Building.
© Clive Boursnell.

intricately balanced consortium of the two local authorities, Westminster and Camden (the very different boroughs between which the area is uncomfortably split in an approximate 2 to 1 ratio) and the GLC, the transcending regional authority. This was called the Covent Garden Joint Planning Committee (CGJPC). Its purpose was to save Covent Garden from haphazard, piecemeal redevelopment by imposing an overall plan under public control. Landownership in Covent Garden was fragmented. The councils would encourage the assembly of large parcels to ease the implementation of their plan by private developers.

THE GLC WAS CREATED by the London Government Act of 1963 under the government of Harold Macmillan as a means of securing Tory hegemony of the capital. However, it often came under Labour control, and was eventually abolished in 1986 by Margaret Thatcher. An extra tier of government, it was a flawed structure without ultimate power, and throughout its life came under persistent attack from both above and below. Under both Tory and Labour rule, GLC plans for investment in infrastructure to keep London services running were overturned by central government. And its strategic planning jurisdiction straddled the elected governments of 32 local boroughs, each of which was responsible for planning within its own boundaries. This overlap often provoked conflict, too. While the local authorities dealt with specific land use and planning applications, the GLC had a statutory mandate to approve or reject proposals for strategic projects, and its Historic Buildings Board had powers of control over listed and historic buildings. Covent Garden qualified for GLC involvement on both counts. (At the time, although there was a national Historic Monuments Committee, the GLC department was entrusted with a specific remit for London. Both reported separately to the Department of the Environment (DoE). Today they are conjoined as English Heritage, and the London region is no longer autonomous).

Local councils tackle complex issues through an elaborate structure of standing committees, each dedicated to a particular issue. These planning committees mirror the party division of the full council, and are chaired by a member of the majority party. As amateurs, they depend heavily on the professional advice they receive from local government officers such as the Covent Garden Team, who consequently can wield a great deal of influence; but it is in the hands of the elected representatives who have been appointed to the standing committee that the decision-making power rests. Their recommendations are usually accepted by the full council without demur.

These committees did not, by and large, consult the man on the No. 9 Covent Garden omnibus about the planning issues which would affect his life. There were no citizen 'planning commissions' advising councils in the American pattern, and information was closely controlled by the local bureaucracies. The only remedy available to objectors was to wait until a major planning decision had been published, and then appeal to the Secretary of State for the Environment, hoping to reverse it.

The national government retained an overriding interest in the area, as it had from the decision to grant a royal market charter to the Earl of Bedford in 1670 through to the decision to uproot the market nearly 300 years later. The Secretary of State for the Environment had to approve all major redevelopment projects, and judgments by the GLC or local authorities on planning applications could be referred to him for review. He might then call a public inquiry on contentious issues. These inquiries are presided over by an inspector from his department, who makes a recommendation upwards for a final decision.

Conservative Alan Greengross, leader of Camden Council, was also in the planning chair of the CGJPC, and the new scheme was expected to go through, as was customary, more or less on the nod. The routine process of consultation began, and the three councils gave it general blessing. Major property companies circled around, speculatively assembling sites in anticipation of the building boom which would follow the market's eventual departure some time in the early 1970s. Land prices soared.

This grandiose scheme was destined to arouse loud and sustained opposition. The citizens and workers of Covent Garden were to take up their pikestaffs and poster paints, and throughout the next decade the area would exist as a community under siege. The proposed redevelopment became one of the major political issues of the day, and fortunes shifted as each of the two political parties twice replaced each other in control of County Hall, home of the GLC, during the period.

At first, however, there was little hostile reaction. Franz Schumacher's opinion-shaping book *Small is Beautiful* would not be published for another five years. In go-go Britain of the late 1960s, weary of the privations of austerity, people were keen to share in the higher standards of living that progress would bring. Old buildings were thought inefficient and uncomfortable. Modern architecture could create the better society, and planners were folk heroes. They had their teeth clamped on the bit and their eyes fastened on the wild blue yonder. All over Britain, worn inner-city communities were collapsing under the wrecker's ball as progressive councils built bypasses, underpasses, overpasses, and inner ring roads to ease the passage of the new icon of success, the motor-car.

Planners' drawing boards sprouted multi-level pavements-in-the-sky. From these, pedestrians who took to the aerial walkways of Covent Garden would also be able to amble over to gawk down on Piccadilly Circus, where Eros was to be elevated to an upper-level concourse, in the shadow of a 435-ft. skyscraper rising over the Criterion Theatre. Regent Street was to become a grand multi-level galleria worthy of Inigo Jones, under a weatherproof glass canopy. The bomb site near St Paul's in the City would boast another sunken highway with an overhead pedestrian walkway. Other lofty schemes were in the offing, too – a Mies van der Rohe tower at Mansion House, and a new Home Office building to replace New Scotland Yard. Of all of these dreamy confections, only the monumental Barbican Arts Centre would actually rise up from the drawing board into the airy world of the pedestrian deck.

In spite of this euphoria, informed opinion was beginning to turn in favour of conservation, local participation in development projects, and small-scale infill and renewal. Questions began to surface about the Covent Garden scheme. Ironically, one of the earliest authoritative protests came from across the Atlantic. The architectural historian Ada Louise Huxtable had come to view the GLC exhibition in Wellington Street. In the article she wrote for the *New York Times*, she criticised the planners' cavalier disregard for so many historic buildings and streetscapes, of the sort which, she said, "Americans are beginning to wrap in cotton wool." Of course, cynics replied, the Americans had far fewer of these souvenirs, and they already had their thruways.

The original brief for the plan had been quite sensitive to public needs, and it did contain social amenities. It was in advance of contemporary practice on conservation and the need for open spaces, it included a sports centre and traffic control, and it would provide a great deal of housing. But it would demand vast amounts of private, as well as public, finance, which could only be attracted by adding a vast acreage of large office blocks, hotels, and other commercial facilities. The plan virtually wrote off the housing stock which already existed, and, fatally, it ignored the human-sized problems and inevitable social upheaval

Scavenging for beans outside the Floral Hall.
© Clive Boursnell.

it would create for those who already lived and worked in Covent Garden.

It was the sheer audacity of the scheme which was to topple it, like a modern tower of Babel. Little more than four years after it was proudly proclaimed, the Covent Garden redevelopment plan had crashed under the weight of aroused and angry popular protest.

Ironically, the traditional charm of Covent Garden, which the planners aimed to exploit, would be erased by the demolition required to put their plan in place. The families who lived in Covent Garden were generally low-income and had lived there for generations. The community roots were deep. One-third of residents had relatives in the area. Of those who worked, one-third were employed locally in small businesses and craft shops. Neither they nor their employers could afford to buy into the new Utopia. By any definition, Covent Garden was a neighbourhood. Yet, apart from consulting the powerful landowners, the professionals made no attempt to approach individuals who had a local interest, and thus gained little understanding of the dynamics of the area they were attempting to preserve and improve.

After the brief public exhibition which had alarmed Ada Huxtable, but to which the public response was generally apathetic, the GLC and the Councils of Westminster and Camden approved the Draft Plan in principle. However, in January 1970, under pressure from the private sector to simplify dealings, the Conservative-dominated GLC, now led by Alan Greengross, decreed that Covent Garden was of strategic importance, and that a single authority would lubricate the planning process for developers. The two local councils saw it as a straightforward grab for political power. Against the opposition of the minority party, the GLC disbanded the original tripartite planning group and in June 1970 created a new body, renamed the Covent Garden Joint Development Committee (CGJDC), on which the two boroughs could sit, but over which the GLC had full control. Conservative Richard Brew took over the chair from his colleague, Cllr Greengross. Both local authorities complained, though Westminster, which had other fish to fry with the GLC in Piccadilly Circus, soon fell into line. Camden councillors were infuriated and refused to play any further part until 1974. Meanwhile, the GLC continued to back an increasingly unpopular plan.

I T B O D E D I L L for the scheme that one of the first strong individual voices raised against it was that of one its creators. Brian Anson, a deputy principal planner on the Covent Garden Team, gradually became aware that aspects of the scheme were grossly in conflict with his personal strongly held left-wing principles. He tried to persuade the Team to involve, indeed to help organise, local community interests, but failed, and in January 1971 was transferred off the project. According to his boss, Geoffrey R. Holland, Acting Deputy Team Leader, Anson's viewpoint had "switched from an architecturally radical solution to a socially radical solution [and he] was shipped out of here because it was impossible to run the team with him on it." Anson gave journalists his side of the story, and the issue of public participation boiled to the surface in the national and

London press. The future of Covent Garden quickly became a political football.

As the 1970s began, the several developers who had been lined up by the GLC jumped the starting whistle and kicked the football into play. In 1918 the Bedford Estate had sold almost all of its 19-acre Covent Garden holding for £2 million. Now land was fetching £2 million an acre. Foreseeing a slick passage for the Draft Plan through the various legislative procedures, the developers began to apply for planning permissions to develop various sections of the area. The planners co-operated; they saw these applications as a wedge to insert features such as the development of the new road network. Soon GLC tenants were, in the GLC planspeak, being "decanted" from their flats. By the end of 1971 more than 10 per cent of the people living in Covent Garden had already left. They were not legally obliged to go, and a 1969 survey had shown that 84 per cent of Covent Garden residents preferred to remain in the area, despite the primitive living accommodation. But the GLC owned public housing in the area, and when this powerful landlord pressed residents to leave and clear the way for redevelopment, they usually went. It was *de facto* eviction by persuasion; no statutory body had yet approved the plan.

Long before the expression 'not in my back yard' took on its political colour, most people in Britain were generally opposed to the idea of physical change and redevelopment as a matter of principle. These days, articulate special interest groups have learned how to manipulate the media with skill. However, the revolt which began to gather momentum in the narrow streets of Covent Garden in the early 1970s was truly popular. It was impromptu, ingenuous, and embraced all sections of the community. The issues it brought to the surface struck resonances amongst a much wider audience. People all over Britain and abroad sat up and took notice. The legends of Covent Garden are engraved deep in the romantic view of English history, and peopled by figures such as Nell Gwynne, Hogarth, Dickens, Boswell, and the cast of *My Fair Lady*. Inevitably, the protest campaign enjoyed frequent and sustained media coverage.

A disparate but forceful body of protest began to form: fourth-generation residents, long-term proprietors of traditional small shops and businesses, craftsmen and professionals who had moved to the area more recently. For various reasons they all resented the conversion of their back yard into a concrete testbed for planners' airy notions. As early as July 1970, Alfred Calder-Brown, an architect, former Westminster County Council planning officer, and a resident of Drury Lane, threatened to create a Drury Lane Association to protect the area against the extension of the Waldorf Hotel, which was to demolish two GLC-owned tenement blocks, the Siddons and Stirling Buildings. Local rents were expected to increase by 400 per cent. Young people without his experience, but articulate and angered by the planners' presumptions, began to spring up as leaders of popular protest.

THE LAMB AND FLAG, reached through a tiny covered passageway off Floral Street, is one of four pubs which can reasonably claim to be the oldest in Covent

Russell Street traffic in the 1970s.
© Clive Boursnell.

Garden. Certainly, intrigue and protest have simmered in its smoky alcoves for centuries, possibly including the plot to offer GBH to the poet Dryden in the adjacent Rose Alley in 1679.

In the autumn of 1970 the historic pub was the venue for the first public confrontation with the planners. It was arranged by a Bohemian element which had been attracted to the fray. This group included local potter Kenneth Clark, Robert Dunbar, Director of the London Film School, which was housed in a disused market warehouse, and photographer Gordon McCleish, who worked from a studio in the area. Representing the establishment viewpoint of the GLC was a pair with divided loyalties. Ron Reynolds was a valuer from the GLC's Organisation and Methods Team who had been appointed to lead the planning Team into the active phase of financing and building the scheme. As his design spokesman he brought along senior planner Art Muscovitch, a young Canadian architect. Muscovitch was a close friend and collaborator of Brian Anson, and already shared his grave doubts about the plan which he had helped design. Eventually this would lead to his dismissal, too, some years in Anson's wake.

Students who had been working on projects based on the area were invited to attend. Jim Monahan was persuaded to come along by his flatmate, Ben Crow, who was studying traffic engineering at Central London Polytechnic. Monahan had just set up an architectural practice with four young colleagues in a converted cellar underneath the arches of Charing Cross station, and he was interested primarily because he was hoping to find premises in Covent Garden. He was appalled by what he heard, and began to stir up resistance to the plan throughout the area. He would stay in the front lines of the struggle throughout that decade, and the next.

The Public Enemy was ignorance; the local people simply did not know what was in store for them, and were in any case habituated to obeying officialdom with little question. The establishment was solidly behind the GLC proposals, the professional bodies held their tongues, and the media was at first indifferent or actively hostile to public protest.

One of the local people who opened the door to Jim Monahan was Revd Austen Williams, vicar of St Martin-in-the-Fields, in Trafalgar Square. Ever since the First World War, when the previous vicar gave shelter to troops in transit to and from the battlefront via Charing Cross Station, this church had been in the forefront of enlightened community service. The first complete broadcast of a religious service took place here, in 1924. (Not without opposition: supposing a wireless were on in a public house – men might listen to the service with their hats on!). Since 1964 Mr Williams himself had encouraged the Chinese residents of Soho to use the church as a community centre. When Jim Monahan warned him that something was about to destroy much of his parish, he needed little prompting to descend from his pulpit into the role of Churchman Militant. A Royal Chaplain, he was to engage in rancorous public meetings, take the witness box at an extraordinary public inquiry, and become the elected chairman of two new community associations. He would write a letter to *The Times* warning of a mood of civil "desperation and violence", and he was also to be manœuvred into the uncomfortable position of condoning a forceful and unlawful occupation of a GLC Information Centre at 1–4 King Street, a commando raid plotted by Brian Anson, which was thwarted only at the eleventh hour. One of his earliest engagements was with Ron Reynolds and his GLC Team at Ronson House in the Strand. An informal committee including Revd Williams, McCleish, and Monahan registered a protest which fell on deaf ears, and served only to fuel the fires of indignation.

Another colourful figure now entered the scene. In a smooth public relations manœuvre, in March 1971 the GLC moved Cllr Richard Brew on, replacing him as Chairman of the CGJDC with the Lady Raine, Countess of Dartmouth, who was the daughter of the romantic novelist Barbara Cartland. Lady Raine was to marry Earl Spencer five years later, acquiring a young stepdaughter who would become the Princess of Wales and presumably, some day, Queen of England. An accomplished establishment politician, she had earned her conservationist credentials by chairing the GLC's Historic Buildings Board. Her appointment was designed to quell the opposition and reassert the intellectual authority of the planners, but faced with a community behaving as though it were under enemy occupation, the PR veneer was soon to show signs of distress.

Inevitably, Jim Monahan and Brian Anson met, and on 24 March 1971 in the architect's studio underneath the arches, they hatched the idea of a public meeting – to be held in a week's time. Jim was rapidly discovering a talent for publicity. At short notice he had thousands of leaflets printed and distributed, and aroused national press notice of the event. Lord Soper, a socialist clergyman, lent Kingsway Hall, headquarters of the Methodist Church on the eastern fringe of Covent Garden, on April Fool's Day, and opened the meeting before handing over the platform to Revd Austen Williams. Other speakers were George McRobie, an associate of Franz Schumacher and Director of the Intermediate Technology Development Group, which was located in Covent Garden; Irene Chaplin, a Labour member of the CGJDC, who spoke of the need for urgency; and John Toomey, a local resident who worked as a printer, one of the traditional Covent Garden trades. He was one of the organisers, and he expected to speak to a couple of dozen people. Six hundred turned up – housewives, market porters, students, artists, pensioners, and businessmen – and John Toomey rose to the occasion with a rousing oration, ending with the rallying cry "Covent Garden is for the people." A resolution was passed calling on the GLC to guarantee the preservation of the community, and an *ad hoc* Steering Committee was formed. Austen Williams was elected Chairman and John Toomey Vice-President of an embryonic group which was to evolve into the primary local community-action organisation.

On 22 April, with spirited help from Jim Monahan and his flatmate Ben Crow, they convened a large outdoor meeting in the Piazza in front of St Paul's. The people who united against the brutal development scheme were a mixed lot. While Brian Anson mobilised support from whole generations of old Covent Garden families, such as the Toomeys and Driscolls, many of the featured players in the drama that began to emerge hardly conformed to his working-class stereotype. The speakers who were attracted to the Piazza that day included socialist Paul Foot, who wrote for *Private Eye*, disc jockey David Jacobs, and actress Amanda Barry. Christina Smith, who had worked as an assistant to Terence (now Sir Terence) Conran, and had started her own importing company, *Goods and Chattels*, in Neal Street, brought her enthusiasm and business know-how to the campaign. In her premises and elsewhere, a nomadic group of young people, with students from the London University Bartlett School of Architecture at its core, published the weekly *Independent Covent Garden Workshop News*, price one penny, a modern version of a penny broadsheet. Robert Harris, who owned *Charles H. Fox* in Tavistock Street, suppliers of make-up to the theatrical profession since 1878, played a role in the community drama, too. Simon Pembroke was a lecturer in Ancient Greek at London University. David Bieda ran *Street Aid*, a community action group devoted to providing facilities for local children. Its premises in Southampton Street were scheduled to disappear. So would the oldest restaurant in London, *Rules*, and its owner, John Wood, became deeply involved, representing business interests. Not all of these potential allies were welcomed by the instigators of the movement, whose views were fixated on the working-class community. Although it supported local shopkeepers enthusiastically, the people's organisation had little time for trendy new craft shops and media businesses now busily buying up leases and renovating old properties.

C O V E N T   G A R D E N became a hot issue in the 1971 borough council elections, particularly in Camden, as Labour candidates campaigned on the failure to consult the public on the plan. In May, Lady Raine, Countess of Dartmouth attempted damage limitation by staging a press conference at which she launched a glossy brochure presenting a slightly revised 1971 version of the plan. Jim Monahan, wearing a badge that read 'Stuff the GLC Covent Garden Plan', ruined the party by making an uninvited riposte at the end, claiming the scheme would devastate the neighbourhood of Covent Garden.

Jim Monahan confronts Lady Raine, Countess of Dartmouth beneath the portico of St Paul's, 6 May 1971.

Greater London Photograph Library.

The protest movement gained coincidental support from an unlikely quarter when *Coutts*, the top people's bank, was drawn into the fray in April 1971. A public inquiry was held into its application to renovate its head office, the familiar triangular listed landmark with pepperpot corners located on the outer limit of the area, on the Strand, across from Charing Cross station. The bank wanted to rebuild, preserving the popular pepperpots, while inserting a new glass-fronted banking hall. The GLC insisted that the proposal should allow for part of its Draft Plan, a road link directly under the bank to siphon traffic from Trafalgar Square, and *Coutts* objected.

While the verdict of the Secretary of State for the Environment was awaited on the *Coutts* case, the main bout got under way. To implement its plan the GLC required his special approval to designate all of Covent Garden as a Comprehensive Development Area. This would authorise special powers, including government funding and compulsory purchase, to impose drastic urban renewal. The authority itself would be enabled to assemble sites currently under fragmented private ownership to permit large-scale rebuilding by private developers. The Secretary of State was obliged to instigate a public inquiry under the direction of inspectors from the DoE. Their job would be to listen, record, and recommend.

Like a wartime resistance movement, the protesters prepared ground they knew well for the battlefield. In June, Brian Anson resigned from his post with the GLC. He was given a job with the Architectural Association, and spent the next few weeks helping to prepare the case for the opposition. With his inside information, he was the key figure amongst a regiment of witnesses lined up for the hearing on the Covent Garden Draft Plan on 7 July 1971. The night before there was a mass public meeting in Kingsway Hall. Afterwards, the audience filed through the streets bearing candles, in a silent procession to Cavell House on Charing Cross Road, on the other side of Covent Garden, the venue for the hearing. It was a moving testimony to the strength of the local movement.

Programmed by the GLC to last no more than a month, the public inquiry was to extend to three. The list of objectors grew and grew. One hundred and fifteen people and organisations, from the Peabody Estates to Moss Bros, the Borough of Camden, two major clearing banks, and the Duke of Bedford, submitted written complaints; 53 of them repeated their written arguments in the witness box. It stretched into one of the longest planning inquiries ever held in Britain, consuming 42 days of court hearings. The media found endless newsprint fodder as the local people, passionate but untutored in the legalistic procedures, tangled with the smooth professional manners of the GLC planners and politicians and their solicitors and barristers (who had already routinely booked their next cases on the assumption that the inquiry would be short, if not particularly sweet). These met their match in witnesses of the calibre of Cambridge graduate David Bieda and his *Street Aid* colleagues, who testified passionately and wittily for two weeks. The locals were fascinated by the quasi-judicial proceedings conducted in the sombre Victorian council chambers, with its marble halls and mahogany panelling, and spear-carriers turned up in platoons. The community group's case, advanced by Revd Austen Williams, took six days, and included the presentation of a petition signed by 1,896 residents.

John Taylor, the barrister employed by the GLC, directed his counter-attack more at the body of community protesters than at the issue, implying it was an unrepresentative group manipulated by outsiders. The legitimate defender of the people against the depredations of over-zealous development, he maintained, was the GLC, with its Draft Plan.

Brian Anson was fully primed for the role of star witness. He asserted that the planners had never sought any meaningful public debate. He cited a devastating note from Richard Brew, chairman of the CGJDC, which described pressure groups as "troublesome" and instructed his planners to "backpedal" on public participation.

The Poet laureate, Sir John Betjeman, insisted on appearing on behalf of *Rules*. As always, he appraised architecture in human terms, advancing the metaphysical argument that a restaurant used by actors and other celebrities somehow acquired an aura, in the same way that churches absorbed the pious thoughts of the faithful. He concluded, "The village of Covent Garden needs a champion against the developer, and that champion should be the GLC." At the time that seemed highly unlikely, but eventually that is precisely what came about.

Whilst emotionally rousing, the headline-making polemic of such witnesses was, as the GLC legal advisers knew, largely irrelevant. The inspectors conducting the public inquiry could ignore issues of sincerity, fair play, and cultural climate. Their exploration of justice would be confined to cold examination of facts and figures within the terms they had themselves set. More to the point was the analysis offered by historian Graham Shane, a building by building evaluation of Covent Garden's architectural heritage, which made a strong case for large-scale preservation.

By the end of the public inquiry on 16 September 1971, it appeared to most people, not least the press, that the deficiencies of the GLC's grand scheme had been clearly exposed, and its perpetrators ostracised by the community they purported to serve. The issue had escalated to heights which could now only be resolved at the highest levels of political decision-making. The community celebrated with a party for 1,500 people in the courtyard of the tenements in the Wild Street Estate, but would have to wait sixteen months for the decision of the Secretary of State for the Environment which would follow the publication of his inspectors' report.

With the aid of a grant from the Rowntree Society Service Trust, the impromptu community-action steering committee formally reorganised itself in October 1971 as the Covent Garden Community Association (CGCA), under the same leadership. Jim Monahan was one of the founders, and a Vice-Chairman. Its charter was: "To suggest alternative proposals for a gradual renewal in keeping with the area's character and based on public participation, and to protect the rights of people living working, studying or with businesses." Its early meetings were held, in the style of a revolutionary cell, in local kitchens and parlours, and in a windowless cellar beneath a shop in Neal Street, reached through a trapdoor by a wooden ladder. At street level, the CGCA kept up the political pressure by setting up an efficient network of 50 neighbourhood representatives, distributing leaflets, issuing press releases, and organising fund-raising events and

Porters at the Covent Garden Central Market.

© Clive Boursnell.

demonstrations. Buildings scheduled for the bulldozers were fly-posted. One hard-hitting poster showed Hitler, with the headline, "He could not destroy Covent Garden. Don't let the GLC."

The community received heartening news in January 1972, when Peter Walker, the Conservative Secretary of State for the Environment, ruled against the GLC in the *Coutts* case. That would effectively scupper the Maiden Lane sunken roadway scheme. The tide seemed to be on the turn. Meanwhile speculators continued to gamble by gobbling up Covent Garden property at handsome prices. Sixty per cent of businesses in the area were on short leases of five years or less; other buildings were allowed to decay. By April 1972, when the CGCA held its first Annual General Meeting, it was reported that one-sixth of all the buildings in the area were boarded up or had already disappeared.

The titled lady who now occupied the GLC Covent Garden planning chair, the Countess of Dartmouth, responded to public disquiet with carefully arranged 'meet the people' televised walkabouts. The CGCA spy network inevitably rumbled these performances, and disrupted them with heckling. In January 1972, angry demonstrators laid siege to her fashionable Mayfair home. In a conciliatory gesture a few months later, she invited a number of the protesters to a gracious lunch at County Hall, complete with the formal municipal silver service and cut-glass goblets. If she thought that the grand surroundings and the presence of a Royal Chaplain, Austen Williams, as leader of the CGCA would encourage docility, she seriously misjudged the quality of her opposition. The occasion was a fiasco. The locals went away angry and hungry for satisfaction, if not sustenance. Austen Williams complained to Brian Anson that it was "all a waste of time. She's just brought us here to soften us up with prawn cocktails and salmon sandwiches." The press statement issued by Lady Raine's office the next day gave her side of the story: "Negotiations have broken down; the community had only destructive criticism and would not face facts."

Friday 7 July 1972 brought bad news. Over the signature of DoE Inspector Hilton, a defensive report on the public inquiry was published, which not only completely upheld the position of the GLC but rebuked the objectors for not proposing a viable alternative. It was now referred to the Secretary of State for the Environment for his final decision.

Three weeks later the Countess of Dartmouth created further headlines by reconsidering her position on the issue and resigning her office. In her letter to the GLC's Tory leader, now Sir Desmond Plummer, she explained, "No individuals or bodies who represent the general public have supported us and I have felt increasingly that our proposals are out-of-date and out-of-tune with public opinion, which fears that the area will become a faceless concrete jungle. I am unable to work for a project in which I no longer believe and which could do unnecessary and irreparable damage to an historic part of London." Considering the quality of the establishment figures now ranged against the Draft Plan it was a pragmatic political conversion, and two other Tory members of the Committee resigned in her wake.

Lady Raine was replaced by another well-known but more demotic personality, former Olympic swimmer Robert Mitchell. When he took over her chair, construction had already started on a link of the massive roadway scheme where the new Drury Lane Hotel was rising in the north-east corner of Covent Garden, and planning permission had been granted to widen Charing Cross Road. CGCA member Simon Pembroke kept up the attack by analysing the GLC's own daily transcripts of the inquiry and producing a 105-page detailed assessment of the evidence, which he dispatched to the DoE in the autumn of 1972.

Community warfare continued, triggering secondary explosions. Ed Berman, the American director of the *Almost Free Theatre* in Soho, staged a confrontational public meeting of community action groups with GLC and Westminster politicians; and late in 1972 theatre managers and unions combined to launch a "Save the Theatre" campaign, with the objective of preserving the threatened playhouses. Meanwhile the job took its toll of the new Chairman. Robert Mitchell was temporarily forced out of action by a heart attack just before the New Year, when the long-awaited final judgment on the inquiry was due.

Geoffrey (later Lord Geoffrey) Rippon had taken over from Peter Walker as Minister for the Environment, and there were some encouraging portents. In September, Dan Cruickshank, of the *Architect's Journal*, was asked by the GLC Historic Buildings Board to prepare a roster of important Covent Garden buildings. Jim Monahan interpeted this as a belated response to a lecture the CGCA had given to that department's staff association a year previously, which had provoked considerable discussion. Meanwhile, at street level whispers circulated. In November 1972, a few weeks before the day of decision, a portentous group was observed going around the area looking at individual buildings. They were, rumour deduced, the Secretary of State for the Environment and his Permanent Secretary, on a personal tour of the battlefield with members of the Historic Monuments Committee of the Department of the Environment.

CHAPTER FOUR

Ironmonger Fred Collins holds the floor at a CGCA meeting in the basement community centre.

© Clive Boursnell.

The Renaissance of Covent Garden

1973–1980

WHEN GEOFFREY RIPPON'S decision was produced, on 15 January 1973, it was singularly astute. While the Department of the Environment gave the Greater London Council the comprehensive development powers it sought, the new large-scale road plan and the increased shopping and hotel space were rejected. The proposed increased in housing was approved; however, any such development was to be of the same scale and character as the existing fabric, and should be accompanied by appropriate provision for schools and open space. And the master stroke was that the Secretary of State for the Environment extended the boundaries of the conservation area and added 265 buildings to the official list of sites of outstanding historic and architectural merit. These included *Rules*, pubs with literary associations, and structures with plain frontages but of interest inside, such as the premises of a former coachmaker. Because these buildings were scattered all over the area, affecting 42 different streets in the 96 acres, the manœuvre effectively pulled the rug out from under the blockbuster developers. Geoffrey Rippon was not modest about his role. "Almost the best thing I ever did – saving Covent Garden," he said afterwards.

Buildings have been listed in Britain since 1947. The policy extends to most structures built before 1840, as well as selected later ones. While listing is not an ultimate deterrent to development, a building on the statutory list cannot be modified or demolished without special permission from the local planning authority. In Covent Garden that would involve Westminster or Camden Council as well as the GLC, and the Secretary of State for the Environment could also decide to intervene. As such, it was extremely offputting to potential developers.

They would shortly have lost interest in Covent Garden in any case. The property market had been inflated under the Barber budget during the Heath administration. The *Yom Kippur* War, the oil crisis of 1973, and the three-day-week triggered a property crash which effectively drained the available pool of investment. Nevertheless, Rippon's judgment was a landmark decision. In the era of soaring land values in the late 1960s, development plans had usually gone through relatively unscathed. Now developers had been served warning that they could not rely on the government to rubber-stamp appeals for permission to demolish old property to make way for modern blocks, particularly as the decision had emanated from a Conservative administration. Lady Dartmouth congratulated Geoffrey Rippon on rejecting major points of the plan she had defended so bravely before her resignation, and the Labour Party chortled about the power of the people. *The Sunday Times* called it a muddled political decision dictated by the need of the Conservatives to steer a cautious course to the forthcoming April elections, while saving face for the Conservative leader of the GLC, Sir Desmond Plummer.

Jim Monahan saw only "a partial victory [because] the developers have moved in now and own 75 per cent of the land...I want to see a living area of a city, rather than something which is just dead and to be preserved." Official listing of buildings could save only the physical exterior fabric of the area; the social fabric could yet be shredded by gutting those buildings and converting them into luxury offices. Covent Garden was still officially recognised as a Comprehensive Development Area, and the GLC had been granted all the powers it wanted for dealing with it. But, significantly, the Secretary of State now required the GLC to consult the public in drawing up new plans for the area. Whom it was to consult, and how, was left open. And the key question remained unanswered: in the face of rising land costs and competitive economic pressures, exactly how were parts of inner London to be preserved for small-scale neighbourhood development?

The bureaucracy of the planning procedures was awesome. Development had first to be approved by the Covent Garden Joint Planning Committee, which the GLC had set up with special responsibility for the area, and afterwards referred to its Central Area Planning Committee, its Finance and Scrutiny Committee, then probably the Policy and Resources Committee, and the Historic Buildings Board, where required. Because the area is split between two local councils, consultation was also necessary with their respective similar committees. Finally, particularly if housing were involved, the permission of the DoE was required. It was hardly surprising if through this elaborate system of baffles the *vox pop* could rarely be heard.

By this time, those voices were cacophonous. The display of unity which the community had mustered under threat was already beginning to fall apart. The protest movement was riven by disputes, and some of the veterans of the battle to save Covent Garden will take unhealed psychic wounds to their graves. Brian Anson was deeply disillusioned that no strong leaders emerged from the mean streets of Covent Garden. He declared that his revolution had been hijacked by the energetic middle-class radicals who were fighting for the architectural integrity of the area and their own upmarket way of life, and gave only lip-service to the concerns of the indigenous working class. He felt they might save the fabric of Covent Garden at the cost of destroying the simple quality of the life which was lived within it. He expressed these views at a chaotic meeting of the Covent Garden Community Association on 7 February 1973. Two days later he resigned from its Executive Committee, and gradually drifted away from the conflict.

Relations improved when Labour wrested control of the GLC from the Conservatives in May 1973. A fair deal for Covent Garden was a major plank of its political platform, and a number of candidates backed by 'Homes Before Roads' pressure groups captured the spirit of the moment, demonstrating that the public was no longer apathetic about callous urban planning. The Tories had been forced on to the defensive, and Labour changed its policy on motorway development. The GLC professionals and their political bosses knew that now they would have to learn how to work with the community. Labour Councillor Tom Ponsonby, former secretary of the Fabian Society and later to become a London Tourist Board chairman, a member of the House of Lords, and Opposition Chief Whip, now took over the Covent Garden planning chair and the challenge of producing a new plan and a peaceful atmosphere of public participation.

A public meeting on 13 June 1973 ushered in a new era of participation. This time it was called by the GLC. Although held outside Covent Garden, in Conway Hall, Red Lion Square, it attracted an audience of 500. Saddled with an obligation to consult on development, but finding no group with which the GLC felt able to deal, Cllr Ponsonby insisted that he would not impose decisions about types of consultation; that it was up to the local people, not him or the GLC, to decide on the way they wanted to work with the planning bodies. A temporary Working Party of 12 was elected from the body of the audience to create a structure to work alongside the GLC planners, developing its own ideas and reviewing and commenting on all other proposals. John Wood, of *Rules*, was named Chairman. Other members included Jim Monahan, Christina Smith, and George Clark, a professional activist who had been attracted to join the CGCA and its struggle. Only two of the leaders, John Toomey and Sam Driscoll, were drawn from the old Covent Garden families.

A series of public meetings of the new Working Party followed. At first they overflowed with dissidents and the atmosphere was hostile. Only slowly did the number attending decrease, and with it the vituperation. It was a long and frustrating process. The CGCA and its supporters were determined that Covent Garden should be preserved for the people, and in their view the only politically correct solution was council housing. More pragmatic business and commercial interests argued that, without funding, this was unsustainable. They were concerned about restoring economic vitality to the area.

Because Chairman John Wood appeared to be genuinely concerned about the needs of the local people, particularly housing, and not just for the future of his restaurant, he won respect on all sides and helped to resolve strongly held differences of opinion amongst the various sections of the community. "The main problem with these protest meetings is packing," he observed. "You don't get a truly representative result." His aim was to air all the very different points of view and somehow achieve a balance. Eventually, he opened a register on which any legitimately concerned individual could record his or her position. "It went on night after night, about three nights a week. I declined to take votes."

From this debate gradually emerged the most ambitious exercise in public participation that had ever been attempted anywhere in the United Kingdom. Wood's registration programme evolved into a new constituency with specific representation from all sections of the community including the different types of tenants, home and business property owners, local employers and employees, plus theatre and public organisations. Residents automatically qualified for the vote to elect this council, and people who worked in Covent Garden or declared a special interest in the area could vote as well, if they bothered to register.

Elections were held in May 1974. Despite the enthusiasm of local activists, the response was apathetic. Of a total adult residential population of about 3,700, fewer than 1,000 actually troubled to take part in the process. People who worked in the area and other 'interested parties' far outweighed them, bringing the total voting electorate to 4,374.

This specialised democratic body was ratified on 6 June 1974 as the Covent

A meeting of the Covent Garden Forum in the Africa Centre.
© Clive Boursnell.

Garden Forum of Representatives. Its role was to be the official negotiating body representing local interests to the GLC, which also financed it. Its constitution provided for 30 elected members serving two-year terms, consisting of nine representatives from each of the main interest groups – residents, businessmen, and services such as theatres and welfare, plus three local property owners. The Executive Committee of the CGCA joined the Forum almost *in toto*. Jim Monahan, John Toomey, Sam Driscoll, and Fred Collins, whose family had been ironmongers in Earlham Street since 1835, moved onto the Forum. Less likely bedfellows were Alan Spence, a member of the local Communist Party, and Basil and Alex Moss, the inheritors of those renowned outfitters to capitalism, Moss Bros. The CGCA Chairman, Revd Austen Williams, also became Chairman of the new organisation. The Forum met regularly in the vestry of his church and generated a number of committees covering different aspects of community life, including one which reviewed planning applications. Later, it operated out of a small office in Bedford Chambers. It was a pro-active style of democracy. Under its idealistic slogan "For All", it set out to enforce discussion between potentially antagonistic economic and social interests, with the aim of eventually reconciling them by compromise.

The GLC responded to the new situation with apparent goodwill in the only way it knew – by reshuffling bureaucratic labels. The Covent Garden Joint Development Committee re-emerged as the Covent Garden Planning Committee (CGPC), an executive arm of the Central Planning Committee at County Hall, with the specific brief to look after this highly sensitive area.

Reporting to it was the Covent Garden Team, a multi-disciplinary task force of GLC officers – architects, planners, and surveyors. Responsibility for developing and administering a new plan for the future and for the refurbishment of the GLC-owned properties fell upon Brian Anson's former boss, Geoffrey Holland, who was appointed Team Leader in April 1974. His planners put a new, blank pad of paper on their drawing boards. By and large, however, these were the same people who had devised the original Draft Plan for the 96-acre Covent Garden Comprehensive Development Area, elevated to a new role, and the community continued to view the GLC with deep distrust and hostility. This began to ease during the summer of 1974, when the Team published the results of a survey and a number of discussion papers on community issues which were objective and conciliatory in tone.

Based on site, in the heart of Covent Garden, at 1–4 King Street, the Team provided technical advice on the formulation, appraisal, and project management of all schemes approved by the council. Information and argument were provided in papers which the Team prepared for the agenda of every meeting of the CGPC. It was responsible for the active management of all the commercial properties owned by the GLC, making recommendations about refurbishing or rebuilding, and rentals, and undertaking disposals. The Team also had powers to recommend planning permission for GLC-owned freeholds, which amounted to about 10 per cent of the Covent Garden area. All of its work was filtered through meetings of the local representative groups, the CGCA and the Forum, for their comment before presentation to the CGPC. The two local Councils, Westminster and Camden, were consulted, but exerted much less influence on the affairs of those who lived and worked in the area.

Over the next decade, before it was itself to be dissolved, the GLC, now planning with and for the local people, managed to achieve massive changes in Covent Garden which the more compromise-minded members of the local community were able to find largely acceptable.

ON 11 NOVEMBER 1974, the fruit and vegetable market left Covent Garden for good. There was no fanfare, no wake. More than three centuries of history just quietly slipped away. By then the Team was well launched into a lengthy process of consultation, and soliciting a degree of local involvement unprecedented in London. A new Draft Plan was gradually taking shape.

Meanwhile the CGCA got stuck into a vigorous grass-roots programme. Its manifesto was parochial and practical: "We want homes now, making the best of what we have, not grand plans that will never be realised. We don't need planners; we want builders, plumbers, and carpenters."

It started a food co-op shop and sponsored a flourishing community centre in an Earlham Street warehouse. While the builders were ripping out the heart of Covent Garden throughout the 1970s, the CGCA created several charming temporary community gardens on building sites. The most popular was a sunken Japanese Water Garden, designed by Keith Chang and created through a £1,000 grant from the GLC and a labour of love by volunteers. A green oasis in a desert of concrete and rubble, it blossomed on a site next to *Odhams* printing works in the centre of Covent Garden, which had lain derelict since it was devastated by a V-2 rocket 30 years previously. When the builders moved in to put up housing here, the garden was shifted to the adjacent *Odhams* half-acre, bulldozed and awaiting redevelopment. Always open, the garden attracted a happy mix of sunbathers, mums and toddlers, and kids playing football. It also became a useful outdoor venue for community protest meetings.

But the main concern of the CGCA was housing provision. It undertook planning studies, organised tenants' associations in council and trust housing estates, maintained an information network through its own weekly newsheet, and kept up the political pressure through press relations and direct lobbying of the GLC Central Planning Committee and its dedicated CGPC.

The Forum, meanwhile, was having its successes too. The GLC generally accepted its ideas on planning matters. But was this because the Forum was effective, or because its proposals were sufficiently anodyne? The CGCA came to realise that the creation of the Forum presented it with a quandary. On the one hand it was an official recognition of the validity of community interests; on the other, it diluted the effectiveness of CGCA's own high-pressure lobbying tactics. Precisely because the Forum was so broadly based, representing every conceivable interest in the area, elements within the CGCA felt that it had degenerated into a bureaucratic talking-shop, impotent to inject any significant new ideas into the GLC's programme. Jim Monahan resigned from the Forum and at the 1975 AGM of the CGCA he secured the passage of a resolution that none of its leaders could also be represented on the governing body of the Forum. As a result, a number of community stalwarts declined to resubmit their names for re-election to the Executive Committee of the CGCA, including its Chairman, Austen Williams.

During the latter half of 1975 the Covent Garden Team prepared a series of 13 policy reports, stimulating yet more public discussion, and at this time Jean Merriton of Westminster took over Labour's chair of the Covent Garden Panel from Tom Ponsonby. In May 1976, the GLC produced a policy options report which took on board a number of modifications which had been suggested to it. From this document a new Draft Plan emerged, which was fleshed out with detailed feasibility studies for individual sites. Throughout the entire process, there was continual participation by the Forum and the CGCA, and local public meetings were sponsored which were open to anyone who took an interest.

The objections of the Forum to the new Draft Plan were minor, and largely accepted by the planners. The CGCA, however, had a different axe to grind. It had drawn up its own plan for the area called 'Keep the Elephants [i.e. large-scale development] out of the Garden.' Its vigorous opposition to the entertainment route and demand for controls on tourist facilities fell on closed ears. However, the GLC Team had also advanced various options for the demolition and redevelopment of nine specific listed sites, and the community had its own ideas about these. Impatient with the GLC's planning bureaucracy, the CGCA had already launched its own housing programme, working with the local housing associations. The first Sainsbury shop had been in Drury Lane, and a grant was obtained from the Monument Trust, sponsored by the Sainsbury family, to explore alternative infill solutions for the redevelopment of Covent Garden.

Martin Dyke-Coomes had been a couple of years ahead of Jim Monahan at the Architectural Association, and later they found themselves sharing an office while working for adjacent architectural practices. Both men were pretty bored with their jobs. When the Monument Trust grant came through, Jim persuaded Martin that there were more exciting things to do in Covent Garden. He was right. The two architects chucked up their jobs and went to work full-time for the CGCA. Martin met and soon married Maggie Pinhorn, the energetic founder of *Alternative Arts*, sponsored by the Arts Committee of the GLC to create festivals and street theatre to enliven the deserted pavements. He was to spend the next ten years working closely with Monahan on community-based projects.

The pair of youthful architects quickly established their credentials by refurbishing a group of derelict buildings in Short's Gardens to provide housing for local residents, while installing a shopfront office for the CGCA underneath. They housed sixteen people through a Department of Environment grant of £9,000, the same amount the GLC had estimated just for repairing the roof. Protecting its planning options, the GLC would grant only five-year leases, but it was a start. It was the first family housing to be built in Covent Garden since the Second World War.

As the professionals on the GLC Team made the rounds of the nine key sites scheduled for potential redevelopment, the two CGCA architects chased around at their heels, drawing up imaginative and economic alternative proposals for every one of them, so the local people would have the means to argue with the local authorities at a professional level, demonstrating what they wanted to happen and that it was technically possible.

The planners rejected most of these challenges as unworkable, but the final word lay with their political masters. In October 1976, when the Team's recommendations came up before the Labour-controlled CGPC under Chairwoman Jean Merriton and her deputy Alex Kazantsis, the community won hands down. On eight of the nine feasibility sites, the committee approved the alternative schemes drawn up by the two CGCA architects in preference to the proposals of their own planning officers. The bureaucrats were livid because they had lost control of their committee, and bemused by the two young architects, who seemed to be pulling rabbits out of hats.

A second local public inquiry was convened on the new Draft Plan in March 1977. Significantly, the venue was the homely community centre in Earlham Street, a far cry from the stately legal atmosphere of the first hearing; and despite widely divergent views, a new atmosphere of co-operation and conciliation prevailed. The hearing lasted six days. In a comradely sleight-of-hand manoeuvre in clever contrast to the bludgeoning tactics of the original inquiry, the GLC enlisted both the Forum and the CGCA as 'counter-objectors', a new wheeze in the planning process. It was a tactic to avoid a subsequent appeal to the DoE, because in this role they could pre-empt any other objectors who might surface. John Taylor, the barrister who had sought to destroy the credibility of the CGCA in the first inquiry six years previously, now found himself standing shoulder to shoulder with its leading activist, Jim Monahan. The inspector's report at the end of May accepted the new Draft Plan with few amendments, and referred it to the GLC for final approval.

In the mean time, there had been another sea-change in the political waters. On 5 May 1977, Labour suffered a devastating defeat in the GLC election. So when the new Covent Garden Action Area Plan was finally published in January 1978, ironically it bore the signature of Alan Greengross, the former chairman of the old Covent Garden Joint Development Committee responsible for the original plan, He had been reappointed to the planning chair, replacing Labour's Jean Merriton. However, party politics had apparently yielded to the genuine interests of the community, and Greengross now gave Conservative backing to the social objectives, especially the housing element.

A decade had been lost, but there had been significant gains for the community. Reflecting its mixed authorship, the plan tried to serve a balance of local interests. Like the original scheme, the new version aimed to increase the resident population to between 5,000 and 6,000. However the emphasis had switched from large-scale redevelopment to conservation, combined with a sensitive mix of small-scale uses. Against prevailing social and financial trends, the plan plumped for traditional high-density city housing. Half of the homes were to be big enough for families. Council residents who had already been forced to move out, even their children who had grown up in the mean time, could now move back if they wanted to return. Others who would lose their homes were given rehousing guarantees.

Office provision was to relate to central London needs, but with an emphasis on small suites. Light industry was to be encouraged, and this was interpreted to include dance rehearsal space and sound-proofed recording studios. Shops were favoured, too, but showrooms had to provide a proper window display to enliven and lighten the street. New cafés and restaurants were also allowed, but there were strict controls over nightclubs, discotheques and restaurants with music and dance licences. The authors of the plan were wary of infiltration by the infamous massage parlours, saunas, strip clubs, casinos, gaming clubs and street arcades of nearby Soho, and none of these are to be found in Covent Garden today. Museums and art galleries were deemed acceptable only if the premises or site were not suitable for housing, industry, shops, or offices.

The planning process was now highly practical, the GLC acting, as John Betjeman had pleaded at the original inquiry, as a good lord of the manor. As a property owner it looked to long-term profitability from sensible estate development and management. As trustee for the people of London it was also responsible for achieving new economic, social, and physical vitality for 96 acres in the heart of city, and ensuring tangible improvements for the people for whom Covent Garden was quite simply their home.

A central need was an important new source of employment. Covent Garden had lost 6,000 jobs in the printing industry, and another 3,000 connected with the market. Entertainment and tourism were identified as crucial areas for potential investment and jobs to spark the area's economic regeneration. Inevitably, the centrepiece of the plan was the Piazza.

The GLC now had deeds of ownership to a motley collection of buildings in and around the Piazza, including the Central Market Building, the Flower Market, Bedford Chambers, the west side of James Street up to the corner of Floral Street, and the Jubilee Hall. As in the original plan, the Central Market Building was vaguely intended to become some sort of shopping galleria. The model was Ghirardelli Square in San Francisco, an international success. Another example was the renovation of the old Faneuil Market Hall in Boston, already under way, though concentrated more on snack eating and drinking. Nearer to home, the success of the Brent Cross Shopping Centre in north London was also encouraging. But the idea of festival shopping in some formerly derelict commercial building had not yet been recognised as a formula for inner-city regeneration. "We found it incredibly difficult at the time to describe what we wanted to do," admitted Geoffrey Holland, the GLC Team leader. As late as 1977 the GLC was receiving suggestions that the site should be used as a gigantic ice-rink on the lines of Manhattan's Rockefeller Plaza, or a dual-purpose helicopter landing-pad and atomic shelter.

Although details of its reincarnation were still unclear, preliminary work began on the Central Market Building in 1975. The Flower Market was scheduled to be converted into two museums, for the theatre and London Transport. Other properties would be let short-term, at least, to begin to attract people back in to fill the void. The GLC encouraged temporary use of some of its old buildings and sites, sometimes secure in the knowledge gained from the continuing process of participation and consultation that the temporary would stand an excellent chance of surviving into permanence.

And so, in the late 1970s, architects, small computing businesses, and photographic and design studios servicing the creative industries of publishing and advertising found themselves able to set up in older property. Street life gradually revived as some restaurants were lured by cheap rents. Brian Stein was one of the first of the new wave of entrepreneurs to rediscover Covent Garden when he opened the *Brahms & Liszt* wine bar in Russell Street to overnight success. Directly across the road, the bookshop where Dr Johnson first met Boswell became a modern coffee-house. Other early arrivals included the *Rock Garden* and *Tutton's* restaurants in the Piazza, and *Rumours* in Wellington Street. These brought the rest of the catering industry in their wake. Purveyors of speciality goods such as *Penhaligon's*, the perfumier, were attracted, too, but there was a dearth of local services for residents. The proverbial candlemaker came, but, to the chagrin of the CGCA, the butcher and baker simply were not interested in the sparsely populated inner-city area.

Covent Garden began to flourish once again. In Neal Street, Christina Smith was refurbishing the Earlham Street warehouse to extend her Covent Garden manor, which now includes most enterprises in the area with the word Smith in the title, as well as her Neal Street East flagship emporium. She was Chairwoman

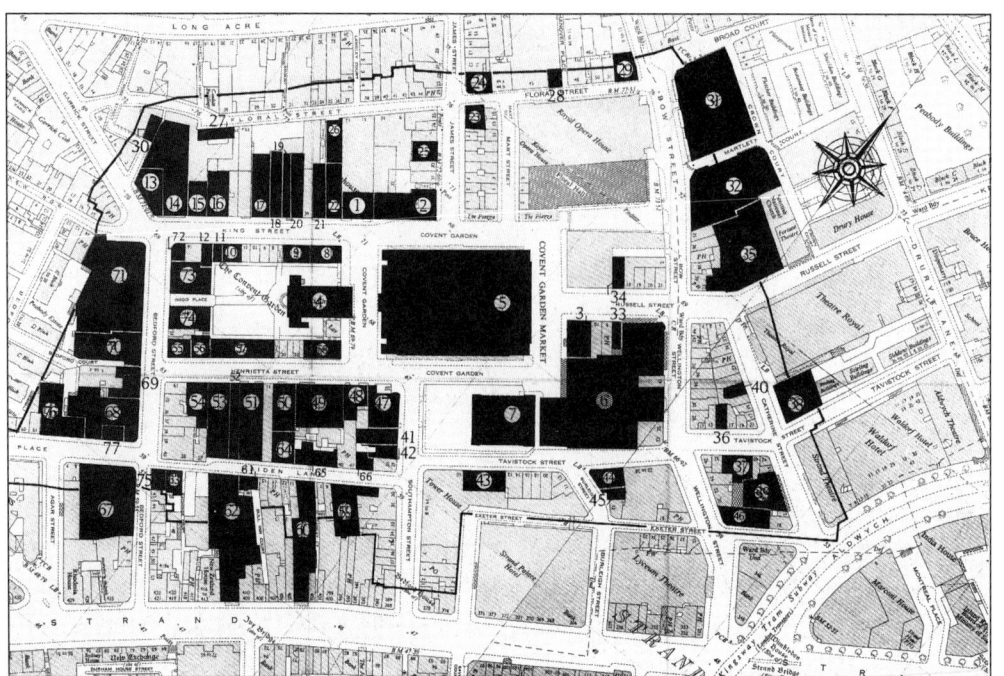

Map of the Parish of St Paul, Covent Garden, 1970, indicating buildings of historical interest and architectural merit.

Reproduced from *Survey of London* vol. xxxvi, by permission of English Heritage and the Royal Commission on the Historical Monuments of England, and the Ordnance Survey map with the permission of the Controller of Her Majesty's Stationery Office, © Crown copyright.

of the Piazza Committee of the Covent Garden Forum. Her former employer, Terence Conran, had his design headquarters nearby; entrepreneur Nicholas Saunders established a remarkable wholefood co-operative in Neal's Yard; the Dance Centre opened in Floral Street, followed by the Pineapple Dance Studios in Langley Street, forerunners of today's health and fitness centres. *Alternative Arts*, under artistic director Maggie Pinhorn, brought street theatre back under the portico of St Paul's. Small businesses sprang up in former warehouses everywhere, and people surged into the area. Covent Garden once again became, as Mary Ann Lamb, sister of the poet Charles, described it in the late eighteenth century, "a place all alive with noise and bustle."

The GLC invested a total of around £4.6 million in the Central Market Building, including an exceptionally high figure of £2.8 million for building costs, owing to the difficulties posed by restoring the historic structure; and the Tory GLC leader, Sir Horace Cutler, opened the new building on 18 June 1980.

In any shopping centre the precise mix of occupants is crucial. The GLC was aiming to recreate the kind of zest and life that imbued the Pompidou Centre in Paris, which had also been built on the site of a former market, Les Halles. There were 3,900 sq.m. of selling space on offer, and the policy was to exercise a high degree of selection to achieve a balanced mix of speciality shops, even if this might result in somewhat lower rents. The pitch to retailers pointed out that about 150,000 people worked within a 15-minute walk of the Piazza. Additionally, the potential tourist draw was immense, though at this juncture highly speculative. More than 1,000 applications flooded in. The GLC was able to choose as it pleased, eliminating start-up enterprises, and making incognito vetting visits to existing shop premises before accepting candidates.

The development was an outstanding commercial success. By the time the GLC was disbanded in 1986, this operation was producing an annual income of

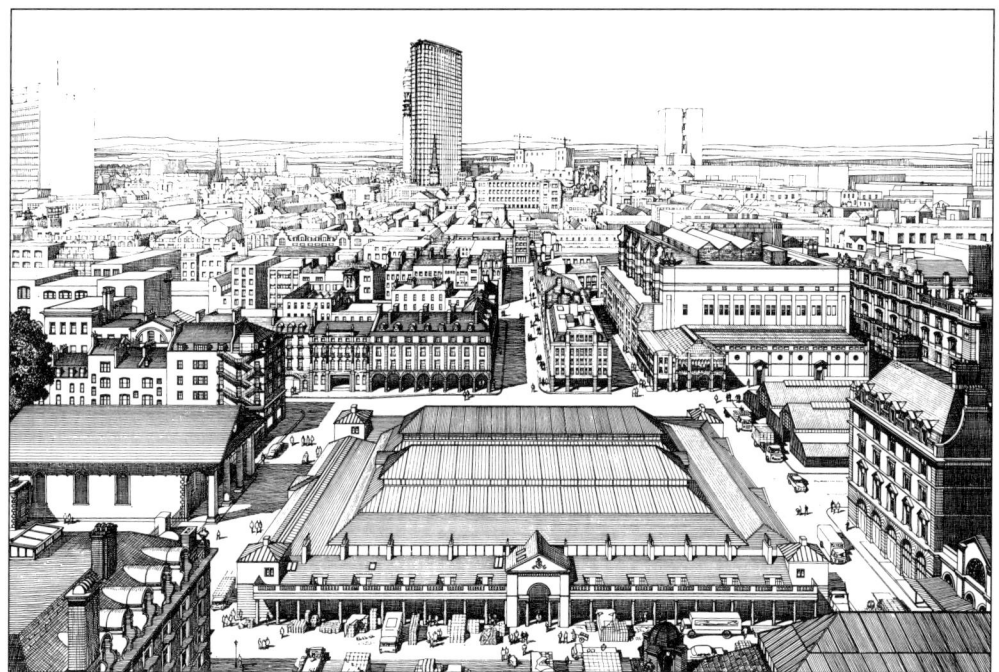

Bird's-eye view of the Covent Garden Market area, looking north, c. 1970.

Drawn by F.A. Evans and T.P. O'Connor and reproduced from *Survey of London* vol. xxxvi, by permission of English Heritage and the Royal Commission on the Historical Monuments of England.

£1 million and its capital value had multiplied almost threefold, to an estimated £17 million.

In spite of the laborious process of consultation, to misquote Abraham Lincoln, "You can't please all of the people all of the time," and by no means everyone was satisfied with the way the Covent Garden plan had eventually turned out. But by the time the Central Market Building opened, it appeared to many that the financially practicable objectives of the community had by and large been fulfilled. People who had lived in substandard housing had been rehoused in new flats built by housing associations and the two local councils, and in these neighbourhoods at least the village atmosphere lingered. When Labour regained control of the GLC in 1981, most Londoners thought the battle of Covent Garden had been won.

Brian Anson disagreed. He published a book that year called *I'll Fight You For It!*, explaining why he had left the struggle by the end of 1974, "when the protest movement had a choice of directions and in my opinion took the wrong one: to work for reform within the system instead of developing a revolutionary struggle against it." He viewed the conflict not as a fashionable community action to reform the British planning system but as a stark class-political battle for property. As a Liverpudlian of humble background, Anson identified with London's Cockneys in the universal class struggle, and was contemptuous about former comrades whom he describes as pseudo-radicals: "It was a freedom struggle about people's rights to their land. I don't think it's about environment at all."

Jim Monahan and others in the CGCA at least agreed with Anson that there was much left to be achieved: the struggle was never-ending. Soon they were to take to the streets again.

CHAPTER FIVE

The Sports Hall

1974–1978

*Roller-skating in the
Jubilee Hall, 1975.*

© CGHP.

SOON THE BANNERS of protest were flying again in Covent Garden. With the Central Market Building completed, the planners were at last able to turn their attention to the demolition and redevelopment of the nearby Jubilee Hall, the former potato warehouse erected in honour of Queen Victoria, and the unsightly adjacent farm shed which had been slapped up against it in the declining years of the Covent Garden wholesale market. The Jubilee Hall was unprotected: it was the only one of the 11 major buildings which the Greater London Council had acquired as part of the package of freehold land and buildings from the former Covent Garden Market Authority in 1974 which Geoffrey Rippon had not deemed worthy of listing. There had been considerable government pressure for the GLC to acquire the CGMA property to offset the cost of moving the market to Nine Elms. The government also made it clear that no further preservation orders were contemplated, and the council was thus encouraged to pay the full potential redevelopment value for the building under the compensation rules. This was apportioned at £1,350,000 out of the £6,050,000 paid for the entire CGMA portfolio.

Ian McNicol, Alan Tattersall, Jim Monahan, and other members of the Covent Garden Community Association had been campaigning to get hold of the site ever since the market moved out – through the letterbox, the media, and on the streets – in a typical highly visible and audible Covent Garden community protest. They felt the building itself was worth keeping, and they wanted to use it as a community sports hall. There were few designated open spaces in Covent Garden, so indoor recreational facilities were essential. At first they simply squatted. Maggie Pinhorn was one of a gang organised by CGCA Co-ordinator Penny Saunders to clear the first-floor space of mounds of potato sacks and other debris to make room for the first indoor five-a-side football tournament between local teams.

Because it was unlisted, the Jubilee Hall was not one of the nine sites for which the GLC Covent Garden Team (and the CGCA) had prepared specific feasibility studies. The squatting locals eventually extracted a temporary permission from the GLC to use it on an *ad hoc* basis, and a typically Covent Garden co-operative venture emerged, with the CGCA and a number of other organisations from as far afield as Soho keeping the still unconverted building in

A view of the Flower Market, showing the entrance to the first floor of the Jubilee Hall on the right, in the closing days of the fruit and vegetable market, 1974.

Greater London Photograph Library.

regular use. The enthusiasm of David Bieda of *Street Aid* convinced the local organisations, the Covent Garden Community Centre and the CGCA, that, having got a foot in the door, they wanted to stay there. Although the CGCA was not entirely convinced that *Street Aid's* ambitious schemes were practical, an organisation was established to begin negotiations with the GLC about the future of the site. The CGCA continued to supply most of the physical energy, while David Bieda took on the administration.

The Jubilee Hall site was still in a planners' limbo. The Action Area Plan called for its demolition and replacement by a mixture of offices and (presumably expensive) housing. The argument was that the GLC, having bought the site at a development price of £1,350,000, had to redevelop it in order to get the ratepayers' money back. During the second public inquiry in March 1977, many local organisations objected to its redevelopment, among them the CGCA and the Covent Garden Forum, but the most vociferous was *Street Aid*. It wanted to create a permanent sports facility for the local community by retaining the Jubilee Hall and putting up a construction on the adjacent empty site. On this matter, the CGCA's protest was uncharacteristically muted; its tactic was to concentrate on getting a lease from the GLC, a situation which could strengthen its hand for preserving the building at a later date. The Forum sat on the fence, taking the view that it was too early to decide the future of the site.

The first floor of the Jubilee Hall, before restoration.
© CGHP.

The inspector supported the GLC's Draft Plan, remarking: "the existing building has no special attributes which would warrant its retention." However, as there was no early prospect of financing its redevelopment, a formal proposal was incorporated into the Draft Action Area Plan to delay demolition of the Jubilee Hall until 1982. It was also noted that, in line with the GLC policy to promote temporary usage of sites scheduled for redevelopment, the building could be made available as a sports hall in the mean time; with some flexibility, a permanent sports facility might later be accommodated within the plans.

Unfortunately, internal ructions hit the *Street Aid* organisation almost immediately, and it suddenly fell apart. David Bieda left to set up a similar organisation, the Central London Youth Project, elsewhere in Covent Garden. The CGCA took over the administration of the sports hall, but the credibility of the project was in tatters. It was apparent that a new organisation would have to be set up very rapidly in order to convince the GLC of the practicality of the scheme.

Through its contacts with the GLC's Covent Garden Planning Committee, the CGCA found a useful sponsor in Councillor David Guy, representing Bloomsbury district on Camden Council and a Labour member of the GLC. Working with him, the CGCA set up the Jubilee Hall Recreation Centre Ltd (JHRC), with a charter to provide low-cost, community-based recreation facilities for people living and working in central London. David Guy joined its board, and lobbied the majority Labour Party to grant the company a licence on the Jubilee Hall. With Cllr Guy supplying the energy and ideas, and Alec Kazantsis, Deputy

Chairman of the CGPC, providing the political clout, the venture drew a sympathetic response. The GLC swiftly approved a licence for the use of the first floor as a temporary sports and recreation centre, subject to planning permission, at a rent of £1 per year. The licence could be renewed annually, provided the operation continued to be financially sound, until April 1982. Ian McNicol, who had worked at the defunct Street Aid, became the JHRC's first Co-ordinator.

THE DECISION WAS TIMELY. A week later the Conservatives swept into overall control of the GLC under Horace Cutler in the May 1977 local elections. The elections were a disaster for Labour, but Dick Collins, who had replaced Alec Kazantsis as Labour's candidate in Camden, squeaked through by 122 votes. The Tories had plans to do away entirely with the GLC, and the outlook was poor for the diverse local groups which the Labour-controlled council had encouraged and financially supported. One of these was the plan for the recreation centre in the Jubilee Hall. Nevertheless, when Cllr Collins died in office less than two years later, it was while he was attending an official ceremony at the community sports hall.

Many of those who had worked to achieve it feared that the Conservative-led GLC would work behind the scenes to dismantle the guidelines of the Labour-approved Action Area Plan. The community's sports hall project became a race against time over hurdles placed in the way by the GLC. The licence could be revoked if building works were not started within six months, and there was no money in the kitty. The fund-raising task fell to Jim Monahan, now working full-time for the CGCA, and Ian McNicol.

The sports hall under renovation, looking north-east, 1977.

Greater London Photograph Library.

The Monument Trust offered a sizeable loan of £30,000 and a grant of £5,000, but in order to qualify for it, the limited company had to restructure as a registered charity. Amazingly, David Guy managed to achieve this in two weeks flat, and 12 unpaid directors were appointed, drawn from the GLC, Camden and Westminster Councils, the Covent Garden Community Centre, and other community and user groups. Jim Monahan was also project manager. He had to draw up the renovation brief, put it out to tender, and then raise the money to make it possible. As architect he engaged David Pritchard of the practice of McCormac Jameson. Having signed a contract for £75,000 and counting only £30,000 in the bank, his movements around Covent Garden became ever more frenzied. In the end, he and McNicol were able to raise all of the funds to make the 70-year-old former potato warehouse safe and suitable from charitable trusts, industry, and commerce, and grants contributed by the GLC and the Westminster City Council (WCC). As well as undertaking remedial work on the fabric of the building, a new floor was laid, and showers, toilets, changing rooms, and storage facilities installed.

London's first community-inspired and community-run sports and recreation centre was officially opened on 30 January 1978, but without its royal guest of honour. HRH the Duke of Edinburgh caught flu and had to cry off. However, he agreed to come to an Open Day on Friday, 1 December 1978. Spectators wondered why the Duke's motorcade was delayed. As he was finally escorted up the front stairs, the body of the GLC Labour councillor from Camden was being discreetly evacuated through another exit. Dick Collins, seized by a heart attack, had fallen dead at the feet of his stunned political colleagues, an event which triggered a chain of repercussions which was to have a profound influence on the fate of the Jubilee Hall.

To the dismay and fury of some members of the GLC, the Jubilee Sports Hall was an immediate popular success. Its policy was to provide a small, intensively used public facility at the lowest possible cost to the community. Open seven days a week, the large first-floor hall was used for indoor team sports – football, badminton, basketball, netball, and volleyball – as well as table tennis and rollerskating. It offered a range of keep-fit activities, too, with classes and equipment for weight training, trampolining, judo, and yoga.

The sports hall was well-fitted and its organisation was efficient, but it had no revenue funding. Fortunately, its opening happened to coincide with a fad for roller-skating. On Saturdays and Sundays the hall was packed with so many people whizzing about on wheels that, even at the nominal rates charged, the JHRC was able to generate a lot of income to help pay operating costs. The infant charity continued to live hand-to-mouth, begging, borrowing, and scraping, until eventually both Westminster and Camden Councils chipped in with grants. It was, of course, also indirectly subsidised by the GLC through the peppercorn rent for the premises. Residents, children from schools and nurseries, students, and commuting workers flocked to the new recreation centre, not just from Covent Garden, but from Soho, Holborn, and Fitzrovia, too. Within six months it was being used by 1,000 people a week, and by 1982, when its licence was due to expire, the weekly traffic had reached 2,500. By then, it was earning 75 per cent of its operating costs from membership fees and charges for services. But from the day of its conception, the Jubilee Sports Hall was living on borrowed time.

Badminton and volley-ball at the sports hall in the late 1970s.
© CGHP.

The new GLC administration had announced its intention to develop the Jubilee Hall site in partnership with the private sector almost as soon as it installed itself at County Hall. The Covent Garden Action Area Plan was formally adopted by the CGPC under Chairman Alan Greengross on 24 January 1978. Compared to the original plan published ten years previously, it allowed for about the same working population (32,000–33,000), and a slightly diminished number of residents (5,150–5,850). With regard to the Jubilee Hall it stipulated: "This is a most important site, enclosing the south side of the Covent Garden Piazza. Redevelopment is proposed for public or semi-public uses at ground floor level, commercial and office space on the lower floors with housing above. The building would be in scale with the Piazza surroundings, particularly Bedford Chambers and the Flower Market, and will use a sympathetic range of materials. A new pedestrian arcade will be created for the south side of the Square."

Detailed proposals for the Jubilee Hall site were published on 30 March 1978. The redevelopment offered an exciting final opportunity to complete the original classical design of the Piazza by incorporating a section of covered galleries on the south side for the first time. The site represented the largest remaining potential housing gain in the Covent Garden renewal programme, a net increase of 200 persons, with non-residential space limited to about 6,500 sq.m. Later, at the request of the WCC, new public lavatories and underground car parking for 250 vehicles were added to the brief. But it did not include a sports hall.

Henry T. ("Jim") Cadbury-Brown, OBE was yet another architect with an interest in Covent Garden. He lived at 32 Neal Street, where he also maintained a practice with John Metcalfe. While Jim Monahan and Martin Dyke-Coomes were at the beginning of their careers, he was a well-established architect who had made his reputation as one of the chief architects of the Festival of Britain in the 1950s. Cadbury-Brown had also been involved with the Royal College of Arts building facing Hyde Park, the World's End development, and sections of the new University of East Anglia. He was also Chairman of the Covent Garden Conservation Area Committee (CGCAC), and naturally interested in the ideas of the CGCA. He and Martin Dyke-Coomes decided to design their own proposal for the Jubilee Hall site, which they hoped would derail the one-track planners and jolt them into considering a more imaginative solution. They felt the GLC could achieve quite a lot of what it wished to do by creating a mixed-use scheme on the adjacent site, while preserving the Jubilee Hall.

Their plan for the preservation and restoration of the Jubilee Hall building, which comprised 2,627 sq.m. of space overall, was to retain the sports hall in 935 sq.m. of space on the first floor, while providing for a flexible mix of commercial lets, perhaps including a theatre and arts centre and workshops, on the 1,098 sq.m. ground floor and in the 1,132 sq.m. basement. Commercial viability would be achieved by erecting a new building on the adjacent 614 sq.m. site where the temporary 1970s shed stood, which would contain both residential accommodation and a substantial commercial element.

They called their proposal to save the old potato warehouse "From Spuds to Sports". It departed from the GLC planning brief in three major respects. There was less housing than had been called for, but the authors argued that the shortfall could be compensated for by the redevelopment of the GLC-owned property in James Street, above the Piazza, which was perhaps a more amenable place to live. There was only a token provision for car-parking: the architects claimed that a massive car park was inconsistent with other provisions of the Action Area Plan, which called for parking controls in heavily congested areas such as Tavistock Street. They used the extra space to house the sports and recreation facilities instead, which were not called for in the plan. Aesthetically, the two architects pleaded that the buildings now surrounding the Piazza represented two main styles. Bedford Chambers, Russell Chambers, Lloyds Bank Chambers, and the end blocks to St Paul's retained the spirit of the original Inigo Jones conception. The other major buildings, clustered about the Central Market Building, were market halls – the Floral Hall, the Flower Market, and the Jubilee Hall – and these had their own late-Victorian style. Therefore the retention of the Jubilee Hall was not inconsistent with the architectural enclosure of the Piazza. Their design sketches offered several variations of a four-storey post-modernist building, lower than Lloyds Bank Chambers across Southampton Street, and linked to the Jubilee Hall at street level by a graceful series of repeated arcades reminiscent of the Inigo Jones Piazza.

On 23 October 1978, Martin Dyke-Coomes and "Jim" Cadbury-Brown presented "Spuds to Sports" as the local community's solution to the future of the Jubilee Hall site, making application to the Secretary of State for the Environment, Peter Shore, to preserve the building, repairing the omission of 1973 by including it in the list of buildings of architectural and historic interest situated in an Outstanding Conservation Area. They had no financial backing for the scheme; their objective was simply to demonstrate to the GLC, and any potential developer, that there was a socially useful and commercially viable alternative to the demolition of the building.

The next night they participated in a meeting at 13 New Row aimed at drumming up popular support for their proposal. "Jim" Cadbury-Brown came in his capacity as Chairman of the CGCAC, Martin Dyke-Coomes and Jim Monahan represented the CGCA, Austen Williams was there from the Forum, Alan Tattersall came from the sports hall, and Dan Cruickshank of the *Architect's Journal* also attended. Key players attracted from interested amenities groups were Marcus Binney, chairman of SAVE Britain's Heritage, Peter Robshaw of the Civic Trust, and Hugh de Quetteville and Tim Revere of the Monument Trust. It was agreed to start a campaign to Save the Jubilee Hall, which the Monument Trust offered to fund. A committee of seven was elected, representing the various groups, and began an intensive effort to lobby support from politicians and establishment figures. They swiftly recruited the affable Peter Brooke, then Conservative MP for Westminster South, who later rose greatly in stature to become Secretary of State for Northern Ireland, Chairman of the Tory Party, and then National Heritage Secretary. The Victorian Society, though unconvinced of the building's architectural quality, lent support because "to demolish it seems a waste of an asset to the community." Other local activists who rallied to the cause included Alec Kazantsis, Joe and Pearl Dennis, Ian McNicol, and Mary Searles.

The GLC failed to take any action whatsoever on the "Spuds to Sports" application for outline planning position. It could have been easily dismissed: the site was, after all, in a Conservation Area and the plan clearly contained insufficient detail. Instead it was suspended.

The Local Government Act 1972 requires local authorities to obtain "the best consideration available" whenever they dispose of land or property. So, in March 1979, in line with the projection of the Action Area Plan for redevelopment by 1982, the Covent Garden Team invited tenders for the Jubilee Hall site from development agencies. While not specifically demanding the demolition of the Jubilee Hall, the brief clearly envisaged its removal. And it contained no provision for a permanent sports hall. In the heady economic climate of the late 1970s, this was pure oxygen to property developers, and dozens of different groups began to put together first-stage "schemes and bids", the initial hurdle intended to eliminate cranks and time-wasters.

There were 200 applicants, and by the closing date 23 of these had made submissions. As the developers' schemes began to come to light, Jim Monahan and Martin Dyke-Coomes found them ugly and insensitive. Only expensive flats could offer the developers a proper return, and local people could never afford them. The local community leaders reasoned that their best chance of thwarting the demolition plans was to drum up public support to get the Jubilee Hall officially listed. To gain publicity they took to the streets with a "Save The Jubilee Hall" campaign, supported by reports, demonstrations, marches, and sponsored walks and runs.

The stalwarts of the CGCA were now politically astute enough to know that though the propaganda battles could be fought on the streets, the political victories were won in council chambers. A by-election for Dick Collins's seat on the GLC was held in March 1979, in the waning days of an unpopular national Labour government under Jim Callaghan. At the suggestion of Camden Cllr David Guy, who had done so much to make the sports hall a reality, Jim Monahan was one of those who was put forward for nomination. His community activities had gained recognition in left-wing circles, and his chances of securing backing were good.

However, Jim Monahan's political adventure was short-lived. Belatedly discovering that only members of recognised unions could become candidates, he enrolled in a union and was endorsed in three voting districts. Unfortunately the union he chose accepted new members only at its annual meeting, and he was ruled out on this technicality. The Labour party's nomination went instead to another political amateur, Charlie Rossi, an unfancied Camden Council rat-catcher and street-level activist for the National Union of Public Employees (NUPE).

Today the Jubilee Hall still stands, and a greatly enhanced community recreation centre occupies the first floor. It is managed by the JHRC as a registered charity, with a large representation of the great and the good – professionals and politicians – on its board, and the operation is now well funded. But to make that come about, the community activists of the 1970s had to find new allies in a new decade.

CHAPTER SIX

The Short Happy Life of the Jubilee Market

1975–1980

Illtyd Harrington, deputy leader of the GLC, with Pearly King George Major and family at the opening of the Jubilee Market, 18 August 1975.

Photograph by Paul Armiger, the Daily Telegraph.

WHEN THE WHOLESALE fruit and vegetable market moved out on 11 November 1974, the heart of Covent Garden stopped beating. Warehouses were shuttered, and the busy streets all around were suddenly quiet and deserted.

Under the Greater London Council plan to revitalise the area, priority was given to the renovation of the Central Market Building with the help of grants from the national government. Later, the Jubilee Hall would be demolished and replaced by a new building, but that work on the redevelopment of the whole south side of the Piazza was not scheduled to begin until 1982. To Tony Sherman and Cyril Waterman, who ran a busy outdoor market at the Brentford roundabout in Chiswick, the ground-floor arcade of the deserted building, together with the adjacent shed, now a refuge for carts, wooden boxes, and displaced market cats, seemed a natural for a temporary market site. Where else could a street trader rent a barrow for a couple of quid a day, less than half a mile from Piccadilly Circus?

Street markets in Britain are in the main run by local authorities, sometimes, as in Covent Garden, under royal charters stretching back centuries. Despite the barrow-boy image, they are financially an important sector of the retail industry. Today markets are a growth area, as the unemployed and those who have been made redundant from regular jobs take up the more haphazard career of the street trader. There are around 1,500 markets in Great Britain, crowded each week with 120,000 stalls operated by half a million robust and fiercely independent proponents of free enterprise. The local authorities often just provide the space, and put the management of the sometimes unruly markets out to tender. In London a market lease can fetch as much as £700,000 a year.

Today some 25 big private market-operators dominate the sector nationally. Sherman & Waterman Associates (S&W), which manages 14 markets up and down the country from an office in Covent Garden's Henrietta Street, is now one of the three or four largest. Tony Sherman's desk faces his partner's, Continental fashion. On the wall behind are several photographs of Cyril Waterman, grey-haired and distinguished, and the younger Tony Sherman, bearded and bulky, in company with Her Majesty the Queen. Nearby is another photograph of Sherman side by side with former prime minister, Margaret Thatcher. The one of Margaret Thatcher is a realistic cardboard cut-out, but Her Majesty is real enough. Her photographs were taken just a few yards down the road on the site of the Jubilee Market Hall.

In his time Cyril Waterman was known amongst market traders as one of the best pitchers in the business, though most of them knew him as 'Peanuts', rather than Cyril. He got his start by buying monkey nuts in bulk from the *Percy Dalton* importing company in the Covent Garden fruit and vegetable market, decanting them into small bags, and peddling them at the dog tracks in Haringey and White City. Later he branched out into other lines, including furs, earning a national reputation in the trade the hard way, by travelling to markets all over the country selling from the back of a lorry. When he met property consultant Tony Sherman, the two saw an opportunity to join their skills, and formed S&W to manage private markets in temporary locations.

When they got wind of the site at Jubilee Hall in 1975, they went to the GLC Team headquarters at 1–4 King Street and suggested the idea of opening a covered street market to Team Leader Geoffrey Holland and one of his valuers, Norman Shifron. The GLC jumped at the opportunity to make a few bob from the doomed property while construction work went on hammer and tongs all around it, but the partners in S&W were less pleased when they realised their proposal would have to go out to tender. When the GLC advertised the covered 1,850 sq.m. site on an annually renewable lease, with a preference for a traditional street market, it received 70 applications.

The S&W team had the nous to recognise the traffic nuisance that a market would create in the congested alleys of Covent Garden, and prudently allocated space for on-site parking of traders' vans in its site plan. Although it limited the market-operator's potential income by reducing the maximum number of stalls to about 100, this foresight particularly impressed the Westminster City Council, which had to cope with parking problems, and the S&W bid to pay a base rate plus a percentage of the gross revenue won the street market licence from the GLC. S&W took on an annually renewable lease, and in turn rented stall space to traders, and on 18 August 1975 the Jubilee Market opened with a flourish. A band of the Grenadier Guards marched up the Strand, the Pearly Kings and Queens of London turned out, and with a fanfare of trumpets Illtyd Harrington, Deputy Leader of the GLC, officially opened the Jubilee Market. There were around 50 stalls at first, and the market had a life expectancy of perhaps two to four years.

I N I T I A L L Y, the traders were justly dubious about their prospects. Although the site was dead in the centre of London, it was literally dead, too. The once bustling square was empty, surrounded by shuttered warehouses, at its heart the forlorn hulk of the Central Market Building, shrouded by hoarding to conceal the

Opening of the Jubilee Market, 18 August 1975.
Greater London Photograph Library.

The deserted Piazza, October 1975.
Greater London Photograph Library.

refurbishment works. These were slow to start, and for a year there was little activity of any kind in the centuries-old Piazza. Most of the traders agreed to give it a whirl only because 'Peanuts' Waterman said it was a good idea. Without his credibility the market would have been a non-starter.

Traders paid about £2 per day for a stall in an everyday general market selling food, clothing, and giftware. Effectively it was a one-hour market, sustained by local office workers who were delighted to be able to find a convenient place to have a snack and do their shopping during the lunch break. It was only open from Tuesday to Friday. Most of the traders worked long hours at well-established markets on Saturday and Sunday. Generally, they took Monday off to rest or re-stock, and on weekends, without the office workers, the Piazza was deserted.

Slowly, the market began to thrive; and as more traders were attracted to the site, permanent stalls came into keen demand. S&W maintained order by banning fly pitchers and controlling the mix of goods to avoid swamping the market with high-profit fashion lines. Jellied eels and cabbages were on offer alongside twinsets and coney coats. Butcher Len Bassett, incorporated as *Ideal Entertainments and Catering Ltd*, projected the spirit of the market, auctioning lamb chops or a side of beef from the back of a van. You could buy live mussels at *Ginger's* shellfish stall at 25p a quart, and oysters at 15p each, and whelks and cockles to eat at the stall for 10p a plate. Street trading tends to be a family business. Joe the Flowers and his wife, Nellie, had been flogging freesias for thirty years with lines like "Love, if I sold them any cheaper, I'd be done for begging." *Johnnie's*, owned by 'Peanuts' Waterman, sold sheets at £6 the pair, his daughter, Rosalyn, ran *Buddy's Baubles*, selling wooden bracelets and shell pendants, and later one of his sons, Vince, was a market 'toby', street market argot for a

*The first day of trading a
the Jubilee Market.*
Greater London Photograph Library.

hands-on supervisor, derived from *tobermory*, a Romany term meaning 'boss man'.

Cyril Waterman also ran a linen stall at the Wembley Market on Sundays. When a vacancy occurred for a fabric stall at the Jubilee Market, he thought of his neighbour at the Wembley Market. Ray Green, originally a tailor's cutter, had become a street trader in 1967 and had stalls in four locations – in Brixton, Lewisham, and on East Street off the Walworth Road, as well as Wembley Market.

Still in his thirties, Ray Green was a typical London street merchant – quick-witted, cheerful, and street-wise, a hard-working family man with three small daughters. Second-generation English, all of his grandparents were immigrant Jews from Poland or Russia. He was born in north London just in time to live through the Blitz, and left grammar school at 15 to work in the garment trade. In his twenties Ray Green had set up his own cutting service in a Southwark basement with a couple of ex-workmates, John Povey and Gordon Andrews. The business started well but fell off after a couple of years, and Ray began to work East Street market with fabrics to supplement the cutting service. In 1973 the three partners bought a fabric shop in Electric Avenue, Brixton, called *Bits of Cloth*, and opened a branch in Lewisham the following year. With his two partners managing the shops and Ray in the East Street market Tuesdays and Thursdays and Wembley on Sundays, the cutting business wound down to zero. So, when Cyril Waterman spoke to Ray about the Jubilee Market, he reckoned he could give it a whirl on Wednesdays and Fridays.

But compared to his other locations, which were crowded with customers, Covent Garden was a desolate place. In 1976 the Piazza had not yet been pedestrianised and road traffic surged one way all around it. Business had slowed down again in the Jubilee Market. By now the potential value of Covent Garden property had become too valuable to tolerate large-scale industrial activity. When the British Printing Corporation sold up *Odhams* printing works and moved south of the river, they took around 4,000 employees with them. These had become so attached to the market that for a while the firm hired buses to cart them back to the Jubilee Market at lunchtimes. But it was clear to most of the stall-holders that the future was dodgy for a street market on the traditional pattern in Covent Garden.

Their landlords, S&W, responded quickly and creatively to the challenge. They reckoned they could attract a different type of customer by opening an antiques and flea market on Mondays, when the general market was closed. It was a good day to choose, fitting in well between the traditional antique markets in Bermondsey on Fridays, the Portobello Road on Saturdays, and Camden Passage on Wednesdays. They opened with just 15 dealers, but as the word got round a whole new set of traders moved in, setting up their stalls by 6 a.m. every Monday to do business with each other and buy and sell with the general public later in the day.

Inspired by this success, S&W determined to make capital of the remaining dead days of the week, and on 25 November 1978 chanced their luck again by opening a weekend crafts market. Ron Vere-Field, a lecturer and teacher who ran the Rotherhithe Community Workshop and was a practical wood-carver, ceramic sculptor, and puppet-maker, came on board as their crafts consultant and 'toby'. The guiding principle was that the people serving behind the stalls had to have actually made the goods they were selling. To create additional interest, S&W offered stalls at half-price to those who were prepared to demonstrate their skills on the spot. And so, on a raw November day, Tony Sherman and Cyril Waterman

The first day of trading at the Jubilee Market.
Greater London Photograph Library.

The Jubilee Market, 1977.
Greater London Photograph Library.

stood in a cold wind watching a potter at his wheel, dipping his hands in freezing water while he showed a group of numbed children how to throw pots.

He was one of only 11 traders who turned up on opening day, but the idea took hold. Soon the Jubilee Market was bustling with handworkers and their wares on weekends – up to 200 weavers, jewellery designers, silversmiths, knitters, shoemakers, leather workers, potters, and makers of wooden toys and dolls houses and furniture, macramé hammocks and hanging baskets, hand-painted textiles, and ingenious novelties made of pressed flowers, beans, glass, pipe-cleaners, and almost anything else.

S&W livened up the market with showbiz: licensed buskers entertained the shoppers, and Percy Press, the uncrowned king of the Punch & Judy show, was hired to entertain on weekends and throughout the summer months. The market was jumbled and disorderly, but it was colourful, and breathed character and excitement into the area. By now 700 different traders converged on the site each week. As the stall layouts were different for each of the three markets, busy night shifts worked until midnight on Fridays, Sundays, and Mondays to set up for the next day. The moribund Piazza was humming again.

While the Jubilee Market blossomed, a dark shadow loomed just a few yards away. The building activity behind the hoardings shrouding the slumbering, humped shape in the centre of the Piazza was now palpable and highly audible. The renovated Central Market Building, designed by GLC architects, was rapidly taking new shape, and the future of the Jubilee Hall site was still murky.

The first section of the repaved granite-sett Piazza opened in April 1979 and quickly became a favourite venue for fashion and advertising photography. During the autumn of that year, at night and on weekends, veteran railway locomotives, coaches, tube-cars, and trams lumbered mysteriously through the streets of Covent Garden. These were the exhibits for the London Transport Museum being trundled to their new home in the elegantly restored iron and glass Flower Market just next door.

When lettings were announced for 26 retail and six catering units in the Central Market Building, 1,000 applicants queued up. Some Jubilee Market traders took the precaution of putting their names down but they were rejected. Evidently, they did not represent the kind of 'shopping experience' the GLC had in mind for its new Covent Garden complex. When it was announced that the Central Market Building would open in June 1980, thoughtful traders like Ray Green realised that time was running out. Action had to be taken to preserve their market. However, their landlords did not encourage any representations. S&W's advice to the traders was simply to keep their heads down. Otherwise, they said, the GLC might be provoked into terminating their lease forthwith.

The Jubilee Market, from Henrietta Street in 1978, with the Central Market Building under reconstruction in the foreground.
© CGHP.

CHAPTER SEVEN

Death by Development

1979–1980

Jim Monahan confronts Dr Mark Patterson, chairman of the GLC's Covent Garden Planning Committee, in the Piazza.

© Clive Boursnell.

*I*F THE POLICE hadn't thrown Charlie Rossi over a hedge into a cowpat, it is unlikely that the Jubilee Hall would exist today. It couldn't have been easy. Though only a scrap over five feet tall, he is a sturdily built, tough and independent-minded Glaswegian.

In the 1950s Charlie Rossi was working as a bricklayer on a building site and living in digs with workmates in Old Harrow. Though not a political animal, one night he put on his best suit, a sky-blue Frankie Laine cut, to attend a Labour Party meeting with some friends. He wasn't particularly impressed, and was walking back to the building camp when the patrol car pulled up.

"They took a look at my suit," he remembers, "and said I was a vagrant. They bundled me into the car, drove me up to Bishop's Stortford and gave me a right seeing to by the side of the road. Then they threw me over the hedge, where I landed in a lot of cow shit. I wasn't worried about my body and my face. I was worried about my sharp blue suit and what they had done to mess it." He found his way back to Old Harrow, and at half past two in the morning knocked up the local political agent, Paddy Coyle, "all cow shit and shouting for a form to sign to get in the Labour Party."

Years later Charlie Rossi was employed by the Camden Council Environmental Health Department and had become a dedicated trade unionist fighting hard for the National Union of Public Employees. He had been a tireless worker for Dick Collins's successful campaign, and in 1979 he was one of four candidates nominated by various political factions in Camden Council to serve out the unexpired term of the deceased GLC councillor. Surprisingly, when the General Management Committee of 32 members representing seven different wards and affiliated unions met to consider the nomination, they selected the politically unseasoned rat-catcher over three more plausible choices.

It was not until much later that Rossi realised he had probably been set up to take a fall by more moderate elements in his own party. The Borough of Camden was in the grip of a paralysing and hugely unpopular strike, and his own union, NUPE, was at the heart of it. Official support from the Party was lukewarm, and Rossi soon found he was doing most of the canvassing himself.

A physical affray on the steps of Camden Council with Labour Councillor Tony Craig tipped the balance of the election in candidate Rossi's favour. NUPE fell in solidly behind him, and suddenly the campaign received immense popular support. Not only Labour Party members but activists of all hues came out to canvass and leaflet for him. On 8 March 1979, just eight weeks before Maggie Thatcher's national government swept to power, the unlikely Labour candidate scored a stunning upset in a by-election which the professional politicians had written off as unwinnable. It took four counts before a mysteriously mislaid parcel of one hundred ballots dramatically bobbed to the surface to show that Charlie Rossi had won by 113 votes, only nine less than Dick Collins's previous result.

Within days, before he had even taken his seat at County Hall, Rossi was targeted by the politically sensitive defenders of the Jubilee Hall Recreation Centre. His first encounter with Jim Monahan was not altogether auspicious.

Having been invited to a meeting at the Covent Garden Community Centre, the brand-new GLC Labour councillor for Holborn and St Pancras afterwards found himself swept aboard a mystery coach tour of North London. Two busloads of demonstrators disembarked to surround a private house, loud-hailing through megaphones fixed in the trees, leafleting the neighbours, and generally making a nuisance of themselves. When a woman and her two children came to the door, Rossi discovered that this was the residence of Dr Mark Patterson, a haematologist with offices in Wimpole Street, and ex-MP for Chipping Norton, who had now replaced Alan Greengross as the Conservative Chairman of the GLC Covent Garden Planning Committee. The GLC was beginning to sell off its property holdings in Covent Garden, and the nub of the dispute was its plan for a change of use in the James Street buildings from housing to offices, which incidentally would impinge on the Covent Garden Community Association's strategy for the use of the Jubilee Hall site. Advised by Team Leader Geoffrey Holland, Patterson's committee had reversed the 1977 Action Area Plan which designated these buildings for housing. The CGCA had challenged the GLC decision in the courts, and, in the usual pattern, was seeking publicity on the issue by exporting civil disturbance to the calm residential suburbs of north London. However, as far as the new councillor was concerned, the tactic backfired. Charlie Rossi's sense of civil justice was deeply offended by the barracking hurled at his political opponent's family while Patterson was not at home to confront the protesters himself.

Just a few days later, at his maiden GLC meeting, Cllr Rossi was thrown off his stride by another Monahan manoeuvre. A petition to save the Jubilee Hall was listed in the agenda for 3 p.m., but failed to appear. It wasn't until nine that night that Jim Monahan and Alec Kazantsis arrived at County Hall to deliver it, rolled up like a great loose cylinder of wallpaper. An elaborate game of pass the parcel ensued. The Tories waved the petition over to the new boy. Cllr Rossi had no knowledge of procedure, but he smelled a rat, and returned the huge roll to the Tories. The messenger was sent back again, and again rejected by Rossi. Tory Cllr David Ashby (later an MP) taunted him to present it but, working on instinct, he refused to acknowledge the petition.

After the meeting, Rossi checked with GLC Labour Cllr Illtyd Harrington, who confirmed that it would have been politically naïve to present the petition six hours out of context. Rossi had narrowly avoided making an embarrassing blunder. Whether by design or default, he felt he had been let down by Monahan, and particularly by Alec Kazantsis, a man of great political experience. The latter, he reflected, had been deposed by his own vigorous campaign on behalf of Dick Collins for the very seat that he himself now occupied. Before long Charlie Rossi would learn a great deal more about the Jubilee Hall issue, which was to become a very hot potato in GLC Labour politics.

In 1979 the three-year grant of the Monument Trust expired and the CGCA housing initiative was dismantled. Martin Dyke-Coomes and Jim Monahan were both out of a job. They decided to join together to commercialise their altruism in a private architectural practice which they called Covent Garden Housing Project (CGHP), and continued to rehabilitate flats in the neighbourhood with funding attracted now from the private sector. Martin Dyke-Coomes shrewdly insisted on including an architectural solution for the Jubilee Hall site within their ambitions. Local agitation to save the neighbouring sports hall was gathering steam. But what it needed was a commercially practical architectural package to get the show on the road.

One day in September 1978, during the height of the "Save the Jubilee Hall" campaign, a flamboyant guardian angel had appeared on the threshold of the shopfront office of the CGCA in Short's Gardens. Martin Landau was a total stranger, but with a smooth and impressive personal presentation. He took a great deal of interest in the "Spuds to Sports" proposal and said he could supply the financial contacts to back a Jubilee Hall scheme. From the circumstances of its conception, the CGCA had a congenital suspicion of property developers. But Landau name-dropped appropriate *bona fides*, and he was willing to help.

Landau, who, it was said, had lost most of his relatives in the Holocaust, was a man of enigmatic complexity. An ex-theatrical impresario, he had also been curator of the Ben Uri Art Gallery, the jewel in the crown of the Jewish art establishment in London, housed in the West End Great Synagogue in Soho's Dean Street, where the works of Bomberg and Epstein are on permanent exhibition. As far as anyone who worked with him was ever able to discover, he was a front man employed as the Director of Arts of an organisation called the Jewish Cultural Foundation (JCF), which proposed to establish a Jewish cultural centre on the site of the Jubilee Hall. He worked out of a fifth-floor office at 241 Regent Street, owned by Eros Properties. Behind that was an entrepreneur called Norman Hyams, who, coincidentally, was an ex-pupil of architect "Jim" Cadbury-Brown. Hyams was associated with two well-known names in the London property market, Sydney Corob (Corob Group of Companies) and Peter Levy (D.E. & J. Levy).

Martin Landau invoked a long list of eminent Jewish public figures as reputed sponsors. They included the Chief Rabbi, Sir Immanuel Jakobovitz, two other highly placed Rabbis, Sir Isaiah Berlin, Greville Janner, QC, MP, who was President of the Board of Deputies of British Jews, Yehudi Menuhin, Daniel Barenboim, Isaac Bashevis-Singer, Sir John Clements, and a Professor Nathaniel Lichfield, and also the Archbishops of Southwark and York. Landau shrewdly reckoned that, with the political backing of the high-profile local group, he could put a credible package together. Over the past eight years the CGCA had become a neighbourhood force the planners had to reckon with. But to a savvy commercial developer, the grass-roots democracy must have appeared idealistic, amateurish, and ridden with dissension. Landau may thus have underestimated its commitment and staying power on the fundamental issue of including uncommercial local recreational and housing uses within the scheme.

It was an odd marriage, but the two interests began warily to work together. The Jubilee Hall Recreation Centre Ltd and the CGCA threw their support behind the JCF scheme. Martin Dyke-Coomes wrote to Norman Hyams on 22 September

1978 confirming the points of agreement between the two parties: the Jubilee Hall would be retained, the first floor to continue to be used as a community recreational centre, while the ground and basement floors would be refurbished as an arts centre. The whole would be financed by a "maximum return" new building to be erected on the adjacent site, featuring shops and offices but also including rented housing, possibly funded by a housing association. The plan was based loosely on the "Spuds to Sports" project conceived by Dyke-Coomes and Cadbury-Brown, and the two returned enthusiastically to the drawing board. Jim Monahan, however, was disquieted by Landau, and the two refused to meet each other.

Monahan remained active on the political front where there was plenty to keep him busy. In January 1979, the GLC initiated a meeting with the Design Council at which "unofficial" soundings were taken for a scheme for a "Palace of Design" on the Jubilee Hall site, to include an exhibition and conference centre plus offices, and allegedly backed by the Royal Society of Fine Arts. The CGCA sniffed a GLC diversionary plot to win wider support for the demolition of the building.

In April 1979 the GLC advertised an invitation for first-stage tender for the Jubilee Hall site. By the closing date of 15 June, 23 proposals had been submitted to the GLC Covent Garden Team. Seven of these were vague and contained no financial offer, and these were eliminated. The remaining 16 serious bidders were invited to make formal presentations. It was not simply a case of making the highest bid – all the schemes were rigorously examined in terms of design quality, the track record of the applicants, and their financial substance, as well as an evaluation of the components of their financial offer.

Only one of the applicants argued that it was not necessary to demolish the

The Jubilee Hall Market and the recreation centre, open for business as construction work continues on the Central Market Building – looking west from the Flower Market, 1979.

Greater London Photograph Library.

building in order for the GLC to recoup its financial outlay. The JCF/CGCA scheme proposed to leave the Jubilee Hall standing and retain the community sports facilities while erecting a new building next to it, where the old shed stood. It would contain a Jewish Cultural Centre on the ground floor, housing for 48 people, and, to provide the financial basis for the scheme, a block of shops and offices.

The CGCA could not count on the support of the planning bureaucracy employed by the GLC. The professional members of the Covent Garden Team, who had at first dismissed the community's ideas out of hand, had been deeply shocked by their rout on the proposals for the nine listed sites after the 1977 public inquiry. Jim Monahan and Martin Dyke-Coomes had risen from the streets of Covent Garden like dragons' teeth to overturn their professional judgment; the planners now overestimated the influence of the two maverick architects. This attitude made dialogue and compromise between the community architects and the GLC officers virtually impossible. If Monahan and Dyke-Coomes took one stance, the planners were disposed to take another.

The Director-General of the Conservative-controlled GLC, Sir James Swaffield, circulated a memorandum charging the CGCA plan with "sacrificing housing and car parking elements of the brief." He also attacked the sports hall, claiming "many local children no longer use the centre, having been alienated by its new image and other clientele." The Committee to Save the Jubilee Hall fought back. Marcus Binney, chairman of SAVE Britain's Heritage, spurred Labour MP Frank Dobson to repudiate the GLC criticisms in the House of Commons. Whilst accepting that the community scheme would provide housing for only 48 people, as opposed to 79 in the most feasible of the other schemes being considered by the GLC, car-parking, he pointed out, had already been subtracted from the brief. Further, he alleged, Sir James had "circulated a slur about a registered charity." He averred that the sports hall facilities, now attracting 1,600 people per week, were intensively used by a wide range of youth clubs, local nurseries and primary schools.

The CGCA appealed to the minority Labour contingent on the CGPC, but it could only hope to fight a delaying action. When the JCF plan came up on the CGPC's agenda, along with rival schemes, in the Chair was the Conservative Mark Patterson, the target of the CGCA's urban guerrilla tactics, and one of the Labour councillors on the committee was the man who had recently unwittingly participated in picketing his house, Charlie Rossi. He recalls that when the JCF representatives made their presentation, Chairman Mark Patterson went straight for their pockets. "Who are you?" he demanded. "Who's backing you? Show us your money. What have you got?" The gladiators championed by Labour could not reply. Martin Landau's backing had not yet materialised. When the JCF was challenged to put up its money or shut up, silence prevailed.

The surviving proposals were considered by the CGPC on 25 September 1979, in the confidential section of its meeting, and a shortlist of four developers was chosen to be invited to prepare more detailed schemes in a second stage

The three redevelopment schemes for the Jubilee Hall short-listed by the GLC (top to bottom): John Laing Ltd, Tarmac Construction Holdings Ltd, and Capital & Counties Property Company.

© CGHP.

selection process. The JCF/CGCA plan was not among them. Officially, it was rejected on several grounds, including reservations about "financial shortcomings," but primarily because of its low ratio of housing-to-office provision. Mark Patterson offered a colourful elaboration: "The Jubilee Hall is a thoroughly nasty building. No one dissents from that view apart from a collection of eccentric gents in the art world, the Victorian Society, the TUC, and a couple of Labour MPs trying to make trouble for the GLC."

Norman Hyams was distressed, and wrote a long letter to Alan Greengross, Chairman of the GLC's Planning and Communications Policy Committee (PCPC), responsible for central planning, restating his case with embellishment: the cause was not sectarian, a prominent Catholic Bishop and an Islamic Mullah were on the point of joining the JCF "Senate", as well as the cultural attachés of the French, American, and Egyptian governments. Mrs Thatcher was also "studying a proposal to become the Foundation's first Honorary Patron."

The chosen contenders for the site were Capital & Counties Property Company (Architect: Sir Frederick Gibberd & Partners), Tarmac Construction Holdings Ltd (Architect: GMA International), John Laing Ltd (Architect: T.P. Bennett), and the Post Office Superannuation Fund Ltd (Architect: Llewellyn Davies Weeks), although the last withdrew its tender in January 1980.

Jim Monahan and Martin Dyke-Coomes were once again appalled by all four short-listed scheme designs, which they felt would blot the southern facade of the Piazza with completely inappropriate solutions. Also, all were predicated on the inclusion of expensive private flats rather than public-sector housing. However, the local community had achieved a partial success. Because so many of the submissions had included sports facilities, the politicians realised they had a battle on their hands. The PCPC decreed that sports facilities should be maximised, and in November 1979 the CGPC revised its brief to incorporate a replacement sports hall, erected to Sports Council standards, though less than half the size of the existing facility. The JHRC rejected this as inadequate. Nevertheless, by April 1980 this modification had been ratified by all senior committees, and was made a mandatory requirement in the second stage brief.

Meanwhile the members of the campaign committee pulled all the strings within their grasp. On 4 November 1979, Sir Hugh Casson, President of the Royal Academy of Arts, wrote to Alan Greengross, Chairman of the PCPC, urging him to renovate the building for public and cultural uses. It was, he said, "a vigorous building, evocative of its period." On the same day, Sir John Betjeman contributed his support: "We cannot afford to destroy the little we have left of familiar London."

The sponsors of the revised "Spuds to Sports" plan – the CGCA, the JHRC, and the JCF – complained that the GLC had never discussed their report, nor seriously considered the option of retaining the Jubilee Hall. It had, they complained, been "unreasonable and intransigent", and on 4 February 1980 the campaign committee pressured a somewhat reluctant JCF into submitting a planning application for their scheme, as a tactic to register their continued opposition. On 18 February, Lord Avebury spoke in the House of Lords to support the application, urging the government to call in an application for listed building consent. The JCF proposal soon ran into technical difficulties, because it had failed to comply with a 1977 regulation that schemes for new buildings higher than 20 metres had to be previously advertised in a local newspaper. The GLC took no action, and as soon as the statutory time limit of two months elapsed, the JCF formally appealed against the Council's failure to issue a decision.

In April, Marcus Binney, Chairman of SAVE Britain's Heritage, tabled before the campaign committee a report on possible legal action to safeguard the future of the Jubilee Hall. It had been prepared by George Allen, a barrister and influential member of SAVE. It was conceivable, he wrote, that there were grounds for action against the GLC. Its failure to re-examine the case for the retention of the building might be held to have contravened the standard of "natural justice" which applies to local authorities when considering their own proposals.

The Department of the Environment, he said, might also have a case to answer. This opportunity arose from a report which had appeared in the *Guardian* on 5 February 1980. Mr Geoffrey Finsberg was a junior government minister at the DoE, and a close associate of Alan Greengross, who had chaired the Covent Garden Committee which drew up the Jubilee Hall brief. According to the newspaper report, Finsberg's personal secretary had written to Hector Monroe, Finsberg's fellow minister responsible for historic buildings matters, about a report which had been submitted to Monroe by Lloyd Warburton, a senior DoE civil servant. In January 1980, Warburton had recommended that the Jubilee Hall should be listed, thus insuring a public inquiry into the GLC's resolution to destroy it. The intra-departmental communication stated: "Concerning the Jubilee Hall and Mr Warburton's report to Mr Monroe, I feel we should drop the issue or it will still be around and very tricky for the 1981 elections." Shortly after the receipt of this report, Monroe again refused to list the building.

The story had not been denied by the DoE. Barrister George Allen thought it offered only slender evidence of political interference, but that an order for discovery might turn up more. While he rated the chances of success against either the GLC or the DoE at no more than 15 per cent, the potential "political value might be very much greater."

Meanwhile, the approval procedures ground ahead. On 6 May 1980 the Team circulated detailed architectural designs and financial offers from the three remaining contenders to members of the CGPC for study. (Capital & Counties had proposed two variations, with a sports hall alternatively in the basement or on the first floor). A decision would be made at the next committee meeting on 30 June, but the resolve of the politicians against community protest was hardened by another item on the agenda, the attempt of the CGCA to quash GLC plans to redevelop 25–31 James Street and 8 Floral Street.

This was the cause for which, a year ago, Jim Monahan had dispatched a couple of busloads of protesters, including an unwitting Charlie Rossi, to demonstrate outside the suburban home of Dr Mark Patterson, Chairman of the CGPC. A few weeks previously, the CGCA had applied to the Divisional Court of the Queen's Bench Division of the High Court for a judicial review of the PCPC's decision to grant planning permission for the redevelopment of these buildings, on the grounds that this was a departure from the GLC's Action Area Plan. It was the last ditch of Monahan's dogged defence of the site for housing use. The application was dismissed by Mr Justice Wood because the CGCA had not succeeded in making out its case in law, and the CGPC, under Patterson, now recorded its victory.

On 14 May, the Royal Fine Arts Commission viewed presentations of the three invited tenders, plus the JCF scheme, which had been called in because it preserved the Jubilee Hall. The Commission had foreseen problems in developing the site when it had been asked to review the planning brief in November 1978. It was not to be disabused. When the three contenders favoured by the GLC were unveiled, there were gasps of dismay at their sheer size and bulk. The Tarmac and Laing proposals were judged "inappropriate for almost any location." The Capital & Counties scheme was thought "much too fussy." The Commission opined that "the buildings proposed would undoubtedly constitute gross overdevelopment of a relatively small and sensitive site…the result of a planning brief which asked for too much." It concluded that the JCF scheme demonstrated the merit of retaining the Jubilee Hall, while erecting a new building next to it, and urged the GLC to reopen the competition on this basis.

Apart from the support of the Royal Fine Arts Commission, the campaign to "Save the Jubilee Hall" could now count on such establishment organisations as the Victorian Society, the Civic Trust, the Sports Council, and SAVE Britain's Heritage, plus support from politicians within the influential policy-making committee of the GLC minority party known as Labour Group, the Westminster and Camden councils, and both local MPs, including active participation by Peter Brooke. The campaign committee lobbied intensively, choosing its targets with precision: on the GLC, apart from the Conservative chair of the CGPC, Mark Patterson, these included the Conservative Westminster Councillor Herbert "Sandy" Sandford, Chairman of the Central Area Planning Committee, which ratified CGPC decisions. At Cabinet level, as well as the Secretary of State for the Environment, they targeted Dennis Howell MP, Minister for Sport.

Patterson stonewalled. Of the members of the Royal Fine Arts Commission, he said, "their manners were only marginally better than their taste. They have exceeded their brief." He vowed again that he would not be deterred by the combined opposition of the Labour minority on the GLC, some dissident Conservatives, Westminster and Camden Councils and various national amenities societies. "Planning decisions should not be political," he said. "I cannot accept that just because there is an election around the corner, one should change one's policies."

Sherban Cantacuzino, Secretary of the Commission, thought this stance was disingenuous. "Does Patterson not realise," he wrote to the press, "that in every planning decision there are umpteen political and aesthetic implications? What's the point of the Commission commenting on such details as the shape of the windows when it's a matter of completely the wrong building for that site?"

On 24 June 1980, the Covent Garden Conservation Area Advisory Committee, under its Chairman, Revd John Arrowsmith, held a special meeting which condemned all three proposals. Its views were communicated the next day to Alan Greengross, Chairman of the PCPC.

Two days later the Covent Garden Forum rejected the CGPC's decision, but just barely. While accepting the Gibberd scheme as "the least unsatisfactory solution", it asked the GLC to request the Historic Buildings Division, in conjunction with the Team, to undertake development while preserving the Jubilee Hall. The vote was eight for and six against, with two abstentions.

This was all just the shouting after the fight had already been lost. The CGPC, meeting in special session, had made its choice amongst the surviving trio weeks ago. This was a decision influenced more by cock-up than conspiracy. The Covent Garden Team had strongly recommended the selection of Capital & Counties, which had advanced two versions of a development scheme, on the basis of the financial value of its offer. The Team expressed reservations about the timing of the premium payment offered by Laing, and about the complexity of the financial structure of the Laing proposal. Nevertheless, Laing seemed to be making the running in the rumours which circulated in GLC meeting rooms.

On 20 May 1980, in Room 180 at County Hall, after the usual pleasantries over tea and biscuits and glasses of wine, submissions were made by the rival developers. Mark Patterson, presiding for the Tories, dominated as usual. Because he had injured it, his leg, as well as the usual big cigar, intruded stiffly into the room, as the contenders ran through their well-rehearsed patter, and displayed detailed three-dimensional models of their creations.

Cllr Robin Young, with Charlie Rossi beside him, put up a barrage of beady questions on behalf of the minority party. The team representing John Laing Ltd made a superb presentation. Everything from the model to the pricing was spot-on. Young nudged his colleague Rossi and muttered, "This one's a sure winner." The presenter heard only another Labour interruption and seized on it to curry favour with the Conservative majority. "I'll get on with my presentation," he said, "but I don't hope to impress the brigade from Moscow."

He had misjudged the smudged line between political and professional loyalties, and his error invoked a heavy penalty. The Chairman was lighting another cigar, and at this comment he paused, squinting through the flame at the presenter.

"Is that model heavy?" he asked, mildly.

"Not really, sir," replied the presenter, mystified.

"Well, lift it and get the hell out of this room," Patterson commanded. "How dare you speak to my colleagues like that!"

For a dignified instant of cross-party solidarity, the Comrades had become "colleagues" of the Conservatives, and once again a random incident altered the fate of the Jubilee Hall site. The Committee backed the Capital & Counties proposals.

At its regularly scheduled meeting at County Hall on 30 June, observers John Wood, Robert Harris, and Simon Pembroke from the Covent Garden Forum saw their hopes dashed as the CGPC, by a vote of seven in favour and four against, publicly granted a building lease to one of the Capital & Counties schemes. It was a typical office development with private housing on top, plus a provision for a sports hall on the first floor.

The Planning Committee's recommendation was forwarded to the Central Area Planning Committee, chaired by Conservative "Sandy" Sandford, and was routinely approved by the politicians. The Jubilee Hall was doomed.

View from the Jubilee Market of the Central Market Building, shortly after its grand opening in June 1980.

Greater London Photograph Library.

CHAPTER EIGHT

A Pyrrhic Victory

1980–1981

The steps of County Hall, 7 September 1981: GLC Leader Ken Livingstone accepts a petition to save the Jubilee Hall, with nearly 125,000 signatures gathered by the Jubilee Market Traders Association.

TTENTION WAS DISTRACTED from the Jubilee Hall site while the drums of publicity began to roll for the grand opening of the Central Market Building. In June 1980, the six-year-old hoardings came down to expose the wonders the GLC architects had wrought. The cavernous halls, which had reverberated to the cries of vendors and the heavy thunder of iron-rimmed cartwheels on cobblestones, emerged from their chrysalis reborn as a modish and fanciful shopping centre. The new conception would, the press releases gushed, attract new custom and breathe new life into the centre of Covent Garden. The Jubilee Market traders shrugged – they had been making that happen for the past five years.

At the same time, the campaign of the Committee to Save the Jubilee Hall was mounting to a furious climax and attracting extensive press coverage. But the options for defeating the GLC decision had run out. Legally, only a listing could now save the building, and that had already been rejected.

A Cabinet change now took place in the national Tory government, and Michael Heseltine took over the reins of the Department of the Environment. Jim Monahan was frustrated: his renewed efforts to get the building listed had run into the sand. However, one day he received a curious telephone call from 'a well-wisher' within the DoE. This source claimed that the Department had actually made a recommendation that the building be listed, and that this had been turned down originally, not by the Conservative Minister, Peter Shore, but by Reg Freeson, who in 1974 had been Minister for Housing and Construction under the previous Labour national government. The matter had been referred to him because of the GLC's plans to include housing in the scheme.

The Covent Garden Community Association wrote to the former minister demanding an explanation. On 17 June, he replied that he had, in fact, agreed to a Grade II listing. During his administration Lloyd Warburton, of the Historic Buildings Division, had recommend listing based on the report of a DoE investigator who had examined the building inside and out (a thing not done earlier), and reported it "altogether more interesting than could be expected at first sight." But the Covent Garden Team leader, Geoffrey Holland, had written a strong letter to the DoE which claimed the conversion of the building was impractical and could lead to a "heavy loss of public funds." Holland was also dismissive of its architectural quality. The Jubilee Hall "sterilised the southern side of the market square," he said; it was "disruptive, with a squalid ground floor." Following this representation, said Freeson, the listing did not proceed, because he recognised that it would be a financial disaster for the GLC. Out of the total price of £6,050,000 which the GLC had paid to the Covent Garden Market Authority for the package of central market buildings, £1,350,000 had been apportioned to the Jubilee Hall. At that time it was understood that the Government had no intention of listing further buildings, and the council was thus obliged to pay the full 1974 development value. This could not be realised if the site were to be used for housing. When the CGCA showed him Martin Dyke-Coomes's plans for converting the building and redeveloping the adjacent site to recoup the GLC investment, Freeson obligingly wrote to Michael Heseltine to say he was now convinced his decision had been ill-founded.

And so it came about that, on 18 June 1980, when Horace Cutler, Conservative Chairman of the Greater London Council, came to Covent Garden proudly to open the Central Market Building, the adjacent Jubilee Hall site suddenly captured the headlines again. His public-relations advisers had prepared the usual confidential paper briefing him on how to respond to awkward questions from the press. Marked 'urgent and personal', this document arrived at County Hall after he had left. The envelope was opened by his personal staff, who, reading only as far as the heading, 'Jubilee Hall, Covent Garden', dutifully forwarded it to the CGCA. The Covent Garden *maquis*, always alert to a spot of sabotage, dutifully passed it on to the addressee, but not before gleefully making copies and distributing them generously to the press.

With its experience of the listing procedure, the CGCA knew it had found the wedge it was looking for. Legal precedents stated that financial constraints could have no bearing on whether a building might justifiably be listed. On 2 July 1980, solicitors acting for the constituent organisations of the campaign wrote to the Secretary of State for the Environment pointing out that the DoE had contravened the Planning Act by basing failure to list on financial grounds. They threatened to file a High Court action for a writ of mandamus requiring listing if the DoE did not respond within five days.

The response took only two days. On Friday 4 July, Michael Heseltine granted the Jubilee Hall a Grade II listing as a building of architectural and historic interest. It could not be demolished unless his specific permission was sought and obtained. The Jubilee Hall was saved – just days before the Covent Garden Planning Committee's decision to grant Capital & Counties a redevelopment lease to raze it was to have been ultimately ratified by the GLC's Planning and Communications Policy Committee.

The permission for the Capital & Counties development was consequently revoked. Any new plan would now require the retention of the Jubilee Hall. This changed the whole brief for the site and the basis of tendering. The big property developers who had been elbowing for position on the Jubilee Hall for years were chagrined; the potential development value of the site had been slashed at the stroke of a pen.

In terms of local *realpolitik*, it was back to square one. The future of the Jubilee Hall site was still unclear. The community of Covent Garden, represented by activists such as the CGCA leader John Toomey, architects Monahan and Dyke-Coomes, and the Revd Austen Williams, remained determined to preserve the recreational facility within any new plan for the area. In February 1981, the Jubilee Hall Recreation Centre, now entering the final year of its temporary GLC licence for the site, made a formal application for planning permission for permanent use of the first floor as a sports hall. As for the market traders on the site, although their temporary home was now a protected listed building, they still felt at risk. Rumours abounded and the Chairman of the CGPC, Mark Patterson, remained intransigent. Within days of the listing of the Jubilee Hall he had asked Brian Jolly, a director of Capital & Counties, to devise a smaller office scheme for the adjacent site. The Conservative Party was now in control of both the GLC and Westminster City Council, and the market traders felt that the Tories, with their interest in speculative business enterprise, were unlikely to leave the site empty for long. It was far too valuable. Before long someone was going to come up with another scheme.

Someone did. One day the traders discovered a planning application hanging on a lamp-post outside the market. It was a proposal to erect an eight-storey building on the site adjacent to the Jubilee Hall, creating a complex of shops, flats, and offices, and it came from a company they had never heard of, Speyhawk.

Speyhawk Land & Estates was, in fact, a formidable contender. A publicly quoted property development company established only in 1976, its primary interest was in commercial buildings in the City and West End of London. Significantly, Speyhawk had developed a particular reputation for the restoration of listed buildings and the execution of complex multi-use developments, particularly in inner-city areas, precisely as this site.

For the moment, though, the threat passed, as word got round that the Speyhawk project had been denied planning permission. Nevertheless, these fresh uncertainties stirred the traders out of their passivity. Local elections were forthcoming in May 1981. Horace Cutler was standing for re-election as the Conservative leader of the GLC. On the hustings he now promised to retain the Jubilee Market, but he didn't reveal what plans the Conservatives had in mind for the site; on the other hand, if Labour took control, it would undoubtedly want to change the development brief. The threats had come to the boil; it was time to get organised.

The traders first approached their landlords, Sherman & Waterman, with the idea of organising a bid for the site. S&W was furious. Apprehensive of losing its lease with the GLC, which had to be renewed annually, the market-operator again cautioned the traders not to make waves. Actually, Tony Sherman had already sounded out City institutions about the possibility of putting together a bid for the property, but he found no one was willing to put up the kind of serious money which was required. Financially, market traders were viewed as men of straw. They were not anchored by assets, and they came and went with the wind. Sherman argued that there had been traders before there were shops, and there always would be traders. But in the late 1970s the economy was perking up after the horrendous crash of the property market, and City minds focussed once more on building office property to cash in on the coming boom. Sherman reluctantly concluded that a market trading operation simply could not command the kind of financial clout to compete for the site.

Meanwhile, back at the cutting face, Ray Green had fastened onto the problem like a Jack Russell terrier. He decided it was time for the traders to band together and take matters into their own hands. In February 1981, they formed the

Jubilee Market Traders Association (JMTA). A committee of seven was elected: Ray Green was chosen as Chairman; Hymie Bomzer, Secretary; Mick Barron, Treasurer; and Simone Gold, Committee Secretary. Other members were Malcolm Landaw, Phil Diamond, and Butch Ansell. At their first meeting, on 10 April 1981, they decided to launch a campaign to "Save the Jubilee Market" by organising a massive public petition. To fund the expenses, each stall-holder would pay a levy of 50p per stall per day into the kitty.

But they had an organisational problem, because the membership of the different markets was quite distinct. The Monday antiques market and the weekend crafts market were under S&W's auspices, and the general market traders, who were not there on those days, didn't really know anyone from those markets. So, at first it was just the Tuesday–to–Friday stall-holders who got together. Approaches were made to Ron Vere-Field, manager of the crafts market, and Ian Whitfield, who managed the antiques market, but their employer, S&W, fearing that the market would slip from its grasp, put obstacles in the way. Ron Vere-Field forbade his stall-holders to join the general market traders' movement. The implied threat was that they would be thrown out of the market. Nevertheless, three brave crafts market traders took the risk of incurring the wrath of the market-operator. George Armstrong, Melvyn Taylor, and Steve Wilson joined the resistance.

The message got through. Within a few weeks, Tony Sherman came to a traders' meeting convened at the Bedford Head public house on 21 May 1981. He declared that S&W had applied to the GLC for permission to provide a permanent market hall on the site, but confirmed that, if this attempt were unsuccessful, he hoped another solution could be found which would permit the traders to stay. S&W thereafter dismantled its stone wall, contributed to the campaign funding, and encouraged the Monday antiques, and weekend crafts sections, to join in. Sherman was still concerned that protest activity would prejudice its position with regard to the lease, and therefore was happy to let the traders take the lead. However, once the traders got the bit between their jaws, S&W was to find itself ousted from pole position.

Every day of the week, visitors to the market now found traders standing by their barrows with scrolls of paper, inviting them to sign a petition. The traders' argument was that the traditional market should be preserved as a healthy counterbalance to the smart boutiques that had opened up in the Central Market Building and in the streets around the Piazza. It would create an island of normality, providing ordinary wares at affordable prices within a sea of expensive shops.

Unlike the battle-hardened veterans of the CGCA, the traders were innocent of the local political planning procedures. As far as they were aware, since the listing of their building, development seemed to have stalled. It was true that no further action had been taken towards selection of a scheme or developer. However, a great deal had been going on behind the scenes. Planning applications had been submitted by several organisations for the adjacent shed

The 'Campaign to Save the Jubilee Market', 1981.

site, registering their interest on the basis of a retained Jubilee Hall. As these parties had no legal claim on the site, the applications fell to the GLC to determine.

The Speyhawk application had, in fact, been rejected because it was found to be totally unacceptable on grounds of office provision policy. Capital & Counties had also returned to the scene, wanting to discuss two different approaches, with and without office content. The S&W application called only for a simple refurbishment of the market building.

The appeal lodged against the GLC because of its failure to decide on the planning application of the Jewish Cultural Foundation within the appropriate period, which had been filed before the Jubilee Hall had been listed, had not yet been heard. Rationalising its position, the CGPC had agreed at its meeting of 20 October 1980, on a vote of seven in favour and six against, that had the GLC been statutorily entitled to determine the application, permission would have been refused on the grounds that it was contrary to the intentions of the Action Area Plan. The net housing gain was only 48 persons, instead of 200, too small a contribution to justify the massive office content of 4,000 sq.m., and elements of the design had also failed to comply with the brief. Thereafter, a public inquiry scheduled for 16 March 1981 had been postponed at the request of the appellant. The ball was still in the court of the JCF, which could now either withdraw its application, require a new date for a public inquiry, or request a postponement in order to apply for planning permission for a revised scheme.

And there matters stood until the local elections of May 1981, which shifted all the goalposts. Control of the GLC was wrested back from the Tories by Labour and came under the leadership of Ken Livingstone. The CGPC was reconstituted as the Covent Garden Panel, and held its first meeting on 28 July 1981. It was comprised of three GLC members of the Labour majority party and two from the Tory minority, plus a representative each from Westminster and Camden councils. Labour's Ed Gouge took the chair, and the other members were George Nicholson, Charlie Rossi, Paul Rossi (no relation), H.H. "Sandy" Sandford, and John Major (no relation). The two community groups, the CGCA and the Covent Garden Forum, were also admitted to the Panel, which often met at the vestry of St Martin-in-the-Fields. However, only GLC members of the Panel could vote. Hence, owing to the weight of the Labour majority represented on the Committee their recommendations were, in fact, always decisions, because they were always ratified by the GLC.

With a new attitude at County Hall, the traders knew the brief for the Jubilee Hall site was certain to be redrawn. They had to make their pitch quickly, and with impact. The newly elected Chairman of the infant market traders' organisation had no experience of planning matters or local politics, so his first step was to get in touch with those who did. Alfred Calder-Brown, the retired Westminster Council planning officer who lived in Drury Lane and who had protested against the early development plan, had a profound knowledge of the local political machine. He introduced Ray Green to the Conservative GLC Councillor representing Westminster, "Sandy" Sandford. Although no longer representing the party in power, Sandford gave a valuable written pledge to support the future of the market traders on the Jubilee Hall site.

Ray Green also drew up a list of all the local consultative bodies and interested organisations, and wrote to them, introducing himself and asking for their support in the campaign to save the market. By early June he had made contact with all of them, but none could shed any additional light on the future of the site. The truth was, as seasoned veterans of community conflict like Martin Dyke-Coomes knew, that on the issue of the Jubilee Hall a white flag was waving over County Hall. GLC policy hung in tatters. It had been continuously battered by the CGCA and others, including ex-ministers and ministers. The coded message from the new Labour administration was "tell us what we want".

But the community, too, was in disarray. A chill had settled on the marriage of convenience between the CGCA and the JCF. After the listing of the Jubilee Hall on 4 July 1980, the JCF began to distance itself from the community campaigners, who felt their ally was procrastinating about future legal and financial arrangements. Neither side completely trusted the other's intentions, and a rift developed between the two architects on the project. While "Jim" Cadbury-Brown continued to work comfortably with Martin Landau, Martin Dyke-Coomes wanted to develop an alternative scheme. He began to realise he was becoming excluded from important meetings. Alan Tattersall, who now headed Jubilee Hall Recreation Centre Ltd, following the departure of Ian McNicol, also felt he was not being properly involved.

In April 1981, solicitors acting for the two community groups wrote to the JCF seeking prior assurance of an offer of a peppercorn rent. They received no answer, and by late spring they had come to the conclusion that the JCF was busily pursuing its own aims, and that they didn't know what was afoot. They had failed to extract a firm contractual assurance of a peppercorn rent for the community recreation facility, and they had seen no hard evidence of funding. Finally, Dyke-Coomes urged Cadbury-Brown to resign from the project. But the older architect remained keen on the architectural problem, and unconcerned about its implications. Dyke-Coomes felt unable to continue to give his support to the JCF proposal, Cadbury-Brown carried on with the project, and the unlikely coalition of the JCF and the CGCA fell apart.

This opened a door for the JMTA. The sports hall, after all, shared a building with the Jubilee Market, and the boisterous initiative of his next-door neighbours finally drew Alan Tattersall's attention to what had been under his nose all the time. It seemed inevitable that the two groups should pool resources. The CGCA, after all, had long ago sought to establish a street market in Drury Lane under the 1976 Draft Action Area Plan. Once both groups overcame initial suspicions, the traders found much common ground with the CGCA, which in turn saw in these shrewd, independent, but politically naïve entrepreneurs a possible source of commercial support for their community-focussed ideas.

The traders' worry was that, whilst approving the presence of a street market on the site, the GLC had not indicated how large it would be. Some stalls which had once been situated along the kerb line to the south had been relocated within the shed area adjacent to the Jubilee Hall when the cobbles were relaid. The market was popular, and there was a growing demand for space. The traders were determined it should be retained in entirety, including the shed space and the lost outdoor kerb area, and not reduced by one square metre.

During the critical summer of 1981, the Covent Garden Panel held monthly meetings to which the people of Covent Garden and all other interested parties were invited, to put forward fresh suggestions for the planning brief for the Jubilee Hall site to reflect the changed circumstances and priorities. The JMTA had no voice on the Panel, and thus sought a common interest with the local groups which did have non-voting representation, the CGCA or the Covent Garden Forum.

Alan Spence, a Marxist and the local Communist Party's candidate in the area, urged the JMTA to link up with the Forum, on which he was a representative. He was championing his own idea, which was to erect a separate structure on the site where the shed stood. The traders and sports hall would share the use of the basement and the ground floor, under a retail shopping gallery. However, there were snags. Because it contained no housing, Spence's plan failed to conform to the existing development brief, and because it contained no offices there was no way the GLC could get its money back on the scheme. Moreover, his thoughts on the eventual control of the market were sketchy. The dominant issue for the traders was their future security, and they were determined that their fate should lie in their own hands. In the end they cast in their lot with the CGCA. The community organisation agreed to support the traders' demand for fully restored market space, making it a condition of their representations to the Panel.

Meanwhile, the traders' organisation was getting into gear. Steve Wilson, George Armstrong, and Melvyn Taylor were co-opted onto the committee to represent the crafts market, Malcolm Landaw was elected Vice-Chairman, and a formal constitution was agreed.

The future of the Jubilee Hall was still murky. The traders made their first hard political contact with Labour's policy-makers when they achieved a meeting with Ed Gouge, Labour Chairman of the Covent Garden Panel, on 14 July 1981. He made favourable noises, expressing support for a mixed scheme which would

A sketch of the Alan Spence plan for the Jubilee Market, prepared in 1982.

J. Godfrey-Gilbert & Partners.

contain housing, sports and recreation facilities, and a market. The brief would be developed, he promised, in Panel meetings over the next few months, followed by public consultation, with the objective of putting it out for tender by developers by the end of the year. The traders remained distrustful. They feared that the GLC would eventually plump for a comprehensive development which would exclude any market activity, and they put out a press release demanding a public inquiry. To the familiar argument that an office block would destroy the old-world character of a historic area they added a new twist: it would also deprive local residents of a valuable shopping amenity and throw hundreds of market traders out of work. The newspapers took up the alliterative theme of "Barrow Boys v Bulldozers."

The timing was right for the traders to present their mass petition. In six months, over the spring and summer of 1981, they had accumulated nearly 125,000 signatures, including lords and ladies, Members of Parliament, film stars, ballet dancers, theatrical celebrities, and people, both prominent and ordinary, from all walks of life. Their public-relations instinct was to take to the streets. On 7 September 1981, the huge pile of petitions was tipped into a market barrow and trundled across Westminster Bridge. Representatives of the 400 stall-holders followed in a 1920s London Transport bus to the steps of County Hall, where GLC leader Ken Livingstone came out to receive the petitions in front of the television cameras. He referred the matter to his Chairman of Planning, Ed Gouge, whom the traders immediately invited, with his fellow committee members, to visit the Jubilee Market.

On 22 September the GLC issued a statement confirming that a street market would be included in any future development of the site. According to the GLC press release, the Jubilee Market had been saved.

CHAPTER NINE

Hilary Black's stall in the general market.
Photograph by Sean Sullivan.

How Can You Fight County Hall ?

1981–1982

*T*HE JUBILEE MARKET TRADERS had scored their first victory, but the war was just beginning. They had a pledge, but no plan. The Greater London Council had made no commitment about the size, style, or character of the market.

The Jubilee Market Traders Association continued to lobby effectively throughout the autumn. Both the Covent Garden Forum and John Wood, proprietor of *Rules* and Chairman of the Covent Garden Association, a group representing local business interests, wrote to Ed Gouge, Chairman of the Covent Garden Panel, expressing their support for a market on the site. Woods was himself on the Forum, and one of several members – the others being the Revd John Arrowsmith, Robert Harris, Simon Pembroke, David Bieda, Christina Smith, and Carole Woddis – who were entitled to substitute for the Revd Austen Williams as the official Forum non-voting representative at Panel meetings. The official Covent Garden Community Association delegate was John Toomey, who could choose from Jim Monahan, Martin Dyke-Coomes, Alec Kazantsis, and Jenny Vuglar as back-up. Camden Borough Council and Westminster City Council could also field one non-voting member apiece.

On 20 October 1981, the Panel met to consider the Covent Garden Team's report on the future of the site. This pointed out that times had changed since the original Action Area brief had been adopted. Architecturally, the requirement to retain the Jubilee Hall had dashed any hope of providing new buildings of a common scale, character, and design. Gone was the dream of creating a new architectural unity in place of the very varied collection of heights and bulks which over the centuries had intruded into Inigo Jones's original great classical design. There was no chance now of recreating his formal arcades on the south side of the Piazza. This would have repercussions for the extension of the Royal Opera House on the opposite side, which was foreseen, though not yet designed. The Team recommended, however, that at the very least any new building on the site should not exceed the height of the current structure.

The proposed usage pattern had also changed. The GLC's recently announced policy of opposition to offices now eliminated this use from the site; the upper floors of any new building could therefore be devoted almost entirely to housing. The recreational facility was to be retained, and in the meanwhile its temporary licence was extended. The immense popular support which had been generated by the "Save the Jubilee Market" campaign demonstrated that a market should also be included, under council management, in any future plans for development. However development should seek to heighten the desirable features of a market – colour, life, activity – and mitigate the undesirable features – uncontrolled parking by traders, congestion, visual untidiness, and rubbish disposal problems.

In view of these changes the Panel decided to amend the draft brief. The Team was instructed urgently to renew public consultation, and report on the response. It was also accepted that this plan would inevitably produce a smaller financial return to the council than other schemes, because of the retention of the

Jubilee Hall and the loss of offices.

The council was still receiving unsolicited approaches from developers, and this evidence of the continuing high profile of the Jubilee Hall site led the Team to suggest that the Panel should confront the question of whether the Jubilee Hall would now be redeveloped by the council itself, bearing in mind the substantial housing requirement, or by a public/private partnership, along the lines initiated by the previous Tory administration. If the latter course were to be adopted, the officers warned, "another publicly advertised competition will be essential, otherwise accusations of private deals, unfairness, and not safeguarding the council's best interest could be difficult to refute."

The Panel left that question open, but approved a fresh draft planning brief. This proposed that the maximum height for new buildings should not exceed that of the existing Jubilee Hall. The stipulated uses included housing (20 to 24 flats, total 1,200 sq.m. minimum), a street market (850 sq.m. minimum), a community sports facility (951 sq.m., as existing), and the remaining space (1,800 sq.m. maximum) to be allocated to commercial, retail, or cultural uses. A major office development was excluded – only a few small office suites would be considered. The Panel invited comment by circulating this brief to 36 organisations and individuals known to be concerned with Covent Garden in general, and who had responded in the past to consultation documents, or who had a special interest in the Jubilee Hall. Eighteen replies were received, ranging from the Metropolitan Police to the local Communist Party. Responses were predictably varied.

In its letter to the JMTA, the Panel also requested the traders to provide evidence of the financial viability of a market, and this brought the latent division between the traders and Sherman & Waterman to the surface. Ray Green raised the issue at a meeting of his traders' committee on 17 November 1981. Suppose the S&W bid for the landlord's lease on the market were rejected. What then? "We traders," he declared, "must be prepared to take care of our own future." With the assistance of Alfred Calder-Brown, the ex-Westminster Council planning officer, the JMTA came up with a radical new idea: a traders' co-operative, which could take over the lease from the GLC. The JMTA wrote to Team leader Geoffrey Holland, supporting the S&W application for a longer tenure of lease, but suggesting that if this were refused, the traders themselves should be granted the lease. When it came to the crunch, however, the street traders backed another option, which called for direct GLC management of the market.

Surprisingly, in its reply to the Panel the CGCA executed a complete volte-face in its historic opposition to new offices, suggesting that both the height limitation and the exclusion of offices should be dropped. Its Executive Committee at that time included the two activist architects, Jim Monahan and Martin Dyke-Coomes, and they successfully argued that these restrictions would cripple the commercial viability of the scheme. They felt that there should be as few restrictions as possible, in order to attract a variety of architectural treatments, in partnership with developers, through open competitions.

Jubilee Hall Recreation Centre Ltd pointed out that, four years after its creation, the sports hall was operating at 85 per cent capacity, and was probably the most intensively used leisure centre in the United Kingdom. However, at peak periods, it was now having to turn away 20 bookings a day – 15 badminton courts and 5 football courts – because of lack of space. This amounted to 500 people per week, or a potential 30 per cent increase of current usage. The JHRC needed more space and therefore, it too opposed the height limitation. It favoured an open tender on the site, but stressed that any future development should continue to provide a lease for a community-based facility at a peppercorn rent, not a commercial operation. It pointed out that local councils throughout the UK commonly provided massively subsidised leisure centres for the local community, and that these paid neither rent nor rates.

Both Camden and Westminster Councils welcomed the retention of the building. However, Paul Velluet, of the WCC planning office, was concerned about car parking. He appreciated that, as the building was now listed, it was no longer feasible to provide the 200–250 public car parking spaces originally required, but believed there should be some spaces, particularly to cater for the residential units. Aesthetically, he suggested that the height limitation should not be determined solely with reference to the height of the Jubilee Hall; the appearance of the new construction should be influenced by the style of the six neo-Renaissance stone-and-brick blocks erected around the Piazza between 1876 and 1890 and designed or inspired by Henry Clutton. These were Bedford Chambers, Russell Chambers, Lloyds Bank Chambers, 1–4 and 41–42 King Street, 1–2 Henrietta Street/25 Southampton Street, and 34–37 Henrietta Street.

The local Communist Party Secretary, R.T. Gandy, wanted to limit the site to its two existing main uses, the sports hall and the market, and form a public trust from the area's statutory bodies and voluntary organisations to administer it.

Nathaniel Lichfield, a planning consultant hired by the Jewish Cultural Foundation, said that no architectural competition was needed, and disputed the GLC's ruling that the JCF scheme designed by "Jim" Cadbury-Brown contained too high an office content relative to the housing gain. The Royal Fine Arts Commission, he wrote, supported this plan, and "vigorously condemned" the designs of the developers which had been favoured prior to the listing of the building.

Earlier, a curious meeting held on 24 September revealed how keen the JCF was to re-establish its credentials with the community. The CGCA and JHRC had finally received an answer to their letter of the previous spring asking the JCF to provide contractual assurance of a peppercorn rent. The reply was useless, merely a vague letter of intent. JHRC directors Ian McNicol and Alan Tattersall now found themselves summoned to a meeting with Norman Hyams, co-Chairman of the JCF, executive director Martin Landau, and the architect Cadbury-Brown, at which they were pressed to persuade the CGCA to rejoin the JCF scheme. The JHRC directors pointed out that the CGCA was a separate body, and they were in no position to direct its thinking. The sponsors of the JCF proposal claimed they wished to work in close co-operation with the sports hall, and wanted all the directors of the JHRC to exert influence against any other possible alternate scheme for the site. McNicol and Tattersall were prudently non-committal.

Cadbury-Brown himself replied to the GLC's draft brief in his capacity as Chairman of the Covent Garden Conservation Area Advisory Committee. He agreed with the CGCA that the brief should be as open as possible, and opposed the height restriction.

The Forum supported the retention of the Jubilee Hall and both of its existing facilities. It suggested that a joint charitable trust be set up by the GLC to administer both facilities and take over responsibility for the building site. However, in spite of its leading role in formulating policy for increased housing in the area, the Forum opposed the housing provision. This site, the members of the Forum felt, was inappropriate for housing; there was too much noise and not enough sunlight.

To solve the financial conundrum, the Forum suggested that the site, which, with interest calculated in, had risen in book value from £1.35 million to £2.8 million, should be revalued, since listing had reduced its development potential. Compensation could then be sought from central government, thereby reducing the charges for development. Any new building on the site, the Forum felt, should not exceed the height of the Jubilee Hall, but could be linked to it, and it too was in favour of a competition to solve the design problem.

While the process of community consultation was under way, the Panel had instructed the Team to consider the implications of retaining the street market within the Jubilee Hall. In June 1981, Mike Pargiter, who had joined the Covent Garden Team at the moment of its agonising reorientation in 1977, had been appointed Deputy to Geoffrey Holland (who also had another role as the GLC's Chief Transport Planner), and he took over most of the responsibility for providing the Panel with estate management advice. A case could still be made for the total redevelopment of the site – only in this way could all the objectives of the Action Area Plan be achieved, and it would provide maximum housing gain. However the Team recognised that public opinion was against it, and prepared a feasibility study and costed outline scheme which was presented to the Panel on 1 December 1981. It postulated three options for the retention of the Jubilee Hall and its facilities. The first two called for only modest repair and renovation. Under the first, the recreational and market activities would remain under their present managements, respectively the community-based JHRC and the commercial operators S&W, while under the second the GLC would take over direct control of the market. These options would create estimated capital values, respectively, of £1.38 million and £1.91 million. The third option called for the full implementation of the programme envisioned in the Action Area Plan, including a council-operated market, and would produce an estimated capital value of £3.39 million. Appended to this report were memoranda from the GLC's Head of Legal Branch and the Comptroller of Finance, both reminding the Panel of the financial desirability of the wholesale demolition and commercial redevelopment of the site. This would realise an estimated capital value of at least £4.5–5.0 million, provided that the Secretary of State for the Environment could be persuaded to give his permission.

This paper had also been circulated to the community organisations by the Panel. Jim Monahan, working with the JHRC co-ordinator, Alan Tattersall, and Jim O'Connor, who now managed the sports hall, had already engaged Alan Prichard, of the architectural practice MacCormac & Jamieson, to draw up three feasibility studies for the site based on these options. At the Panel meeting of 1 December, the CGCA (now led by Chairwoman Grace Cook, local resident and a former publicity and promotions manager for IPC Women's Magazines Division) expressed its support for option three – refurbishment of the Jubilee Hall and complete redevelopment of the adjacent shed site. This worried the market traders, who saw option two, calling only for modest renovation, as less disruptive to their activities.

In what proved to be a seminal meeting, the two groups discussed the issue on 17 December. The CGCA explained that it supported a new development adjoining the site because that was the only option which would result in housing gain as well as retaining the sports hall. But the locals assured the stall-holders that they were also keen to retain a market, of an extent to be determined. They stressed that it was vital for the two groups to work together, so that the GLC could not divide the current users of the site. Both sides agreed that the GLC should not manage the market: in preference it should be the traders themselves. And so, a combined strategy was finally agreed between the three organisations to support redevelopment under option three. The CGCA wanted housing on the site, the JHRC wanted more practice space and improved facilities, particularly changing and

Stalls on the Piazza by the Jubilee Hall, 1981.
Greater London Photograph Library.

storage room, and the JMTA wanted a long lease which would offer security of tenure for the market. S&W, the current market licence-holder under the renewable short-term lease, also supported this union of interests, as it was the traders' intention to take the company on as the management agents for the day-to-day running of the market. They all agreed to make a joint representation so that the GLC would realise it was not dealing with a variety of disparate groups using the Jubilee Hall, but a group of organisations working together.

After consultation and discussions with the GLC and the Forum, on 11 January 1982 this group, known as the Jubilee Hall Consortium, met Ed Gouge at County Hall to inform him that they were prepared to develop an overall scheme that would suit all interests, and four days later they submitted their joint plan to Team Leader Geoffrey Holland. It was signed by Martin Dyke-Coomes, Treasurer of the CGCA; by Ray Green for the JMTA, which was now in the process of setting itself up as a traders' co-operative and Limited company; and by Jim O'Connor and

Sue Biggar, acting for the JHRC.

Their plan contained four essential conditions: a minimum of 24 dwellings; a community-based sports facility not less than existing and with the possibility of expansion; a street market with the same capacity as existing and an improved environment; and "an additional commercial element" which would be compatible with a mixed-use site. By 21 January 1982, preliminary sketches had been developed by the practice of MacCormac & Jamieson, now working together with Jim Monahan and Martin Dyke-Coomes, in order to assess the commercial viability of the idea.

This joint scheme encountered opposition from elements within the community, for all sorts of reasons. Communist Party member Alan Spence of the CGCA was fiercely opposed to what he saw as Monahan's sell-out to commercial interests. So was another influential member, Tudor Gates, former Chairman of the CGCA, a writer who also ran a local club. He complained that half of the elected members of the CGCA Executive Committee did not live in Covent Garden, and the two architects had a vested interest in the scheme. On the other hand, Chris Gittings, a member of the Forum, who owned the eccentric novelty shop, *Knutz*, in nearby Russell Street, feared that housing on the site would transform the prestigious shopping area into a downmarket *Costa del Sol*, with washing hanging out on lines. The Forum stayed its support for the Consortium scheme for another year; until then it remained bound by its rebuff to the GLC's planning brief – no offices, no flats, no noise.

Undeterred, the Consortium announced its intention to make a bid for the development of the site, with the aid of a commercial developer, following the forthcoming GLC Panel meeting on 2 February 1982. That meeting, chaired by Ed Gouge in the Vestry Hall of St Martin-in-the-Fields, considered the three options which had been put forward by the Team. Conservative Councillor "Sandy" Sandford argued strongly for the Consortium's plan, under option three. He was certain that it was a financially viable proposition, and he secured agreement to a request for financial estimates to be produced. He also suggested a feasibility study for GLC control of the market. During the meeting a great deal of support was expressed for option two, option one was not mentioned at all, and option three – calling for development – was carried by an absolute majority, largely because of the potential housing gain. The Panel endorsed the Consortium's ideas: a minimum of 24 dwellings, the community-based sports facilities on the first floor to be retained, and a street market. The remaining space might include commercial, retail, cultural, or workshop space. Only marginal office use was considered suitable – a few small suites, perhaps. Most importantly for the traders, it was agreed that the present size of the market should be retained. Any space taken from the present area of the site should be compensated by an overspill into the south side of the Piazza. The need for flexibility was recognised, and the Team's draft development brief was modified to remove all restrictions of size and measurement. The GLC itself would undertake the development of the site.

It looked as though the traders might be, quite literally, home and dry in the shelter of a new market, and the mood was buoyant at the general meeting of the JMTA on 19 February. Their major concern was whether the Panel would permit them to trade in the Piazza during the redevelopment period. The traders recognised that the JMTA would have to evolve into a more formal corporate structure in order to become involved in any tender or lease. There had been internal clashes. The crafts and general market traders were of different temperaments, the latter often feeling that the craftsmen valued ideals of craft purity over the practical imperatives necessary to get the scheme off the ground. Differences were patched up at this meeting by inviting S&W to join the traders' Executive Committee. The original craft market representatives withdrew from the leadership, and a new election was scheduled.

On 31 March, the Panel decided to hold a competition within the council's own architecture and civic design department to find a suitable scheme. The draft brief would meanwhile be the subject of further urgent public consultation. The traders and the local residents reacted by resolving to produce their own development proposal. While the CGCA had suggested there should be a general architectural competition, the GLC had responded with an internal contest. Time was running out, and the Consortium feared that the GLC plan would never emerge from the bureaucratic machinery. By putting its own scheme together now, the Consortium reckoned that, even if it were to be rejected by the GLC, its ideas might force the council's hand in the right direction. Martin Dyke-Coomes of the Covent Garden Housing Project dusted off his plans and set to work designing again, while the working arrangement between the local groups was formalised as the Jubilee Hall Development Consortium (JHDC). This was a Limited company banding together the JMTA, CGCA, JHRC, and S&W, still the temporary lease-holder of the site. Tony Sherman, Ray Green, David Taylor, and Grace Cook were the first directors. Andrew Westcott of the Soho Housing Association joined later.

Meanwhile the JMTA was also reorganising. On 1 April 1982, a new elected committee of 14 took their seats on its Executive Committee. There were seven representatives each from the general market and the crafts market, the latter group including Ron Vere-Field, representing S&W. Ray Green was re-confirmed as Chairman. Malcolm Landaw and Ron Vere-Field were voted co-Vice-Chairmen, Hymie Bomzer became Secretary, and Butch Ansell, Treasurer. Other committee members were, from the general market, Brian Bromley, Phil Diamond, and Norman Walmsley, and, from the crafts market, Mick Aldridge, Duncan Browning, Alan Dowsett, Bill Horn, Amanda Ryder, and Steve Wilson (the only one of the original crafts market trio to retain his seat). Their first business was to work up an outline development scheme for the use of the site by the JMTA, as a member of the JHDC, for submission to the GLC. They decided to take steps to form a Jubilee Market traders' co-operative.

Then someone raised another point. There was talk that the JCF was back on the scene, lobbying the GLC to allow it to build a cultural centre on the site. Was it yet another distraction, or a potential bombshell?

CHAPTER TEN

Mr Livingstone Presumes

1982

The GLC meets the market traders in the Jubilee Hall, 16 June 1982: (left to right at table) Cllr Charlie Rossi, Ray Green, GLC Leader Ken Livingstone, and Malcolm Landaw.

*I*T WAS A BOMBSHELL. The Jewish Cultural Foundation had resurfaced, with a new proposal giving a Jewish cultural centre pride of place within a large office building, in spite of the veto on office space. Moreover, the traders heard that this plan was fervently backed by the GLC leader of the majority party, Ken Livingstone. He had simply pulled the rug out from under the whole planning brief which had been carefully worked out by the Covent Garden Team and approved by the Covent Garden Panel and the full GLC Central Planning Committee. Within a week of the Panel's decision to approve the new planning brief, on 9 February 1982, the JCF had met with the Team to protest that its cultural centre had not been included, and this was the result.

Events had taken a sudden unpredictable turn. Somehow the JCF had won the ear of the GLC's Policy Co-ordinating Committee (PCC), a powerful body known as the "Labour Group" and made up of 23 majority party members. Though devoid of executive powers, it effectively determined Labour policy. On 24 February 1982, this body had received the situation report on the Jubilee Hall, indicating that the Panel and the Central Planning Committee had decided that the GLC should implement the newly agreed brief in preference to partnership with any development agency. At that meeting, Labour's policy-makers arbitrarily insisted that the claims of the JCF also be considered. In its report to the Panel on 11 March, the Team pointed out that this requirement could cause a conflict with the other agreed uses, but at its meeting of 16 March, whilst once again extending the sports hall licence for another year, the Panel had dutifully instructed the Team to carry out "an urgent feasibility study on the accommodation of all the major interests proposed for the Jubilee Hall site, *including space for cultural facilities*," and to seek the views of the potential users and various consultative bodies on the proposal. This directive had been confirmed by the full GLC Planning Committee on 31 March, when it had resolved for an internal architectural competition.

At County Hall Martin Landau suddenly had great credibility. Cllr Charlie Rossi, for one, was unhappy about it. Although he was now Vice-Chairman of the GLC, he was unaware of any behind-the-scenes moves until, out of the blue, the JCF reappeared in committee papers. He asked the Labour Chief Whip, Harvey Hinds, about it. With a perfectly straight face, Hinds told him "The JCF are the leading contenders for this site. They were instrumental in saving this site from being awarded to Laing or the others." Charlie Rossi had a different memory of events: he recalled that the JCF had not had the money to back their ideas. From that moment he began to fall out with the party leadership.

While the JCF widely circulated a document entitled "The Case for Siting the Cultural Centre of the JCF in the Jubilee Hall", the Team did its homework. It consulted the other users of the site and interested parties. All of them objected to the plan to accommodate the JCF. The Team nevertheless produced four options for its inclusion, as instructed. However, it took pains to point out that, if the JCF were forced into the development at this stage, and no other competition were mounted apart from the JCF's bid, the obligatory legal procedures for ensuring "best consideration", under the provisions of the Local Government Act 1972 would not be properly observed. This report was never presented to the Panel, but was considered by the Labour Group on 19 May. In the confidential section of its meeting, after the Team officers had departed, the Labour Group vetoed all four proposals, and decided to adopt instead a fifth option which had been separately prepared by the JCF architect, "Jim" Cadbury-Brown.

The political will of the highly placed members of the GLC Labour Group was clearly being frustrated by the considered recommendations of its Team of professional advisers. The Chairman of the Panel, Ed Gouge, therefore requested that further discussions with the JCF be handled by other departments of the council. To the dismay of Deputy Team Leader Mike Pargiter, his group was debarred from further work on the project, and its role was taken over by the GLC's Finance Department. The Comptroller of Finance, Maurice Stonefrost, thenceforth took the lead in negotiations.

When the JCF option five was made public on 14 May, Ray Green was outraged to find that it consigned half the market to the basement of the building – an impossible site for street trading. He objected to it on the grounds that it gave priority to the JCF rather than to the existing users. Jim Monahan had deeper suspicions, viewing Martin Landau's community commitments as merely vague promises; he too came down strongly against Livingstone's plans.

Once again, a great deal of stress was being generated in the committee rooms of County Hall and on the streets of Covent Garden. The former allies of the JCF, the Covent Garden Community Association and Jubilee Hall Recreation Centre Ltd, were now their bitter opponents. "Jim" Cadbury-Brown resented the fact that his former collaborator on the JCF project, Martin Dyke-Coomes, was now drawing up proposals alternative to his own. The latter felt he had given his former colleague fair warning that a more community-orientated scheme could be created with other partners. Alan Tattersall, for the JHRC, explained its position in a representation to County Hall: "Since then, the nature of the brief has changed. Only after the public consultation process had been completed has the JCF been introduced on to the site, to the obvious detriment of one, if not all of the already agreed uses." He also underlined his concern about the future financial security of JHRC under this proposal.

Nevertheless, it became apparent that the leader of the GLC Labour Group, Ken Livingstone, was insistent that the JCF be included in the development scheme. The CGCA was outraged when Ed Gouge put the architectural competition for the site on the back burner until the brief was finalised. Ray Green and his traders were angered and mystified. This impasse ushered in a series of meetings over the next five months, in which the architects from Covent Garden Housing Project and Ray Green, acting for the Jubilee Hall Development Consortium, met with the architects employed by the JCF to try to reconcile the uses agreed in the brief with the requirements of their plan. The commitment to accommodate a market was a key snag.

Jim Monahan and Ray Green formed a complementary and extremely effective team. Thrown up by events as the natural leader of the traders, Ray was a fierce bundle of energy. Jim was a cooler, more experienced advocate. Without him, the traders' leader might have dashed about Covent Garden like a Chinese firecracker. Monahan was the rifle barrel which guided this human explosive.

Green now gained further helpful orientation from Ron Vere-Field, Sherman & Waterman's crafts market "toby", who also ran a co-operative craft centre in Rotherhithe. This was funded by the GLC, and Vere-Field knew several of the councillors, including Charlie Rossi and George Nicholson, who was soon to take over the Chair of the GLC Central Planning Committee from Ed Gouge. Rossi was going to open the annual crafts fair in Rotherhithe. Green went down to introduce himself, but there wasn't much opportunity to talk, so he asked Rossi to come down to his stall at Wembley Market the next day. Fortunately, the invitation was reinforced when Rossi's wife, Margaret, heard a radio commercial extolling the market, and the councillor found himself shopping there that weekend. After Green filled him in on the Jubilee Hall situation, Rossi suggested an opportunity should be arranged for Ken Livingstone to meet the traders, so that they could put their case directly to him. Green found the perfect occasion. He had been sponsored by all the traders to run in a half-marathon to raise money to buy vital equipment for the children's ward of the Shaftesbury Hospital. The traders had purchased it and invited the surgeons and representatives of the St Peter's Research Trust to attend a reception at the Jubilee Hall in a few weeks time to accept their gift. Green secured Livingstone's agreement to make the presentation on the traders' behalf.

In the mean time, two nagging worries surfaced in Ray Green's mind. First, the funding for the JCF scheme seemed elusive. Like the members of the CGCA, he began to wonder who was supposed to provide it. Second, he was himself active in Jewish community affairs. For four years he had been Vice-Chairman of the Executive Committee of the largest Jewish youth club in Europe, the Brady Maccabi Youth and Community Centre at Edgware. Many activities in the Jewish community naturally came to his notice, but he had never heard of anything being promoted by the Jewish Cultural Foundation. It was headed by Martin Landau with the sonorous title of Executive Director of the Board of Management, and its letterhead was studded with the names of highly eminent members of the Jewish community who had lent their reputation to the project. Among them were Daniel Barenboim, Yehudi Menuhin, and the Chief Rabbi, Sir Immanuel Jakobovits, as well as the Archbishops of York and Southwark. There were also two members of a distinguished Jewish family of politicians: the Rt Hon Lord Janner, and his son, the Rt Hon Greville Janner, QC, MP, and President of the Board of Deputies for British Jews. Was it possible that these people were not fully aware of what was going on in their names?

On 2 June Ray Green sat down and wrote a five-page letter to the Rt Hon. Greville Janner, in his capacity as a Member of Parliament. Green pointed out that it was the apparent intention of the GLC Labour Group to revise the development brief, in cavalier disregard of community opinion. The users of the site were being forced to negotiate with the JCF on the basis of option five. He expressed his fears that the bid to secure the Covent Garden property would discredit the Jewish community, and he questioned the origins of the organisation.

On 16 June, Ken Livingstone came to the Jubilee Market to present the traders' gift to Lady Morrison Bell, representing the trustees of the Shaftesbury Hospital. The traders also presented Livingstone with a crystal decanter. Charlie Rossi was there, too. He felt he had recently been deprived of the post of GLC Chairman when Livingstone arranged a deal with right-wing elements within the GLC, whereby six leftists were returned to their posts unopposed in return for voting for Sir Ashley Bramall as Chairman. Rossi's comment to *Time Out* was: "So much for friendship and loyalty to the left." Rossi now seized this occasion to test his party leader in a debate on his Jubilee Hall policy and vigorous argument arose from the floor. Feelings ran high, the Leader of the GLC majority party was booed by some unruly elements, and he and his decanter left in a hurry. Before his departure, however, Livingstone agreed to convene a discussion at the GLC on the following evening, to be chaired by Rossi and attended by all interested

GLC Leader Ken Livingstone (right) presents the JMTA donation to Mr Philip Ramsley and the Children's Ward Sister of Shaftesbury Hospital, as Ray Green (centre) looks on, at the Jubilee Hall on 16 June 1982.

parties. The next day the JHRC contributed its own letter of protest to County Hall. That night, all the members of the Consortium – the traders, the CGCA, and the JHRC – arrived for the meeting, but only a couple of Labour councillors put in an appearance. The meeting was a flop, and the traders suspected a deliberate boycott had been inspired by the Leader of the GLC or his Chief Whip. However, one man who did turn up was GLC Labour Councillor George Nicholson. He listened to the traders' complaints and promised to help. This was to prove influential later, when he took over from Ed Gouge as Chair of the GLC Central Planning Committee, to which the Panel reported.

A reply now came from Greville Janner. Dated 21 June, it was not on the stationery of the Houses of Parliament; Janner had answered in his capacity as President of the Board of Deputies of British Jews, and his response, while anodyne, was revealing. The JCF, he said, had not previously been active in Jewish affairs; it had been formed for the single purpose of building a cultural centre.

Rossi now alerted Ray Green that the Jubilee Hall was on the agenda of a GLC Labour Group meeting scheduled for 29 June, and promised to speak for the traders to try to derail Livingstone's initiative. Ray wrote to every Labour councillor on the GLC, asking them to think very carefully before voting on whether to allow the JCF proposal into the brief.

Another letter, which he directed to the man who had listed the Jubilee Hall two years previously, Minister of the Environment Michael Heseltine, went out the day before that meeting, and summarised the traders' position. Green advised Heseltine that, just four months previously, after a year of bitter campaigning, a draft brief for redevelopment of the site had been agreed with the Panel. It had called for the provision of a street market offering daily shopping facilities, partly within the site and partly in the Piazza, with the same capacity as existing, and a guarantee that no stall-holder would lose his pitch. He expressed the traders' concern that the new JCF proposal enjoyed the public support of the leader of GLC. The GLC, after all, owned the site and therefore was empowered to grant itself planning permission for a development without consideration to other persons or users. It seemed to be ignoring public opinion, and this could lead to the loss of the promised shopping facilities, and the livelihoods of some 400 traders. He therefore asked the minister to overrule any planning applications not in the interest of the community.

At the crucial GLC Labour Group meeting on 29 June, events took a decisive turn. Ray Green returned to County Hall, where less than ten months ago the traders had won their reprieve by handing their petition with 125,000 signatures to the Leader of the GLC. This time he was accompanied by Jim Monahan of the CGCA and two Forum members, Alan Spence and Vice-Chairman Bob Harris. This little group stood outside the door of the meeting room to lobby the councillors as they came in to attend the session of the policy-making group. Ray Green tried to speak to Livingstone, but didn't get a word in. "No chance!" barked the leader of the GLC, and swept past him. Some of the lobbyists repaired to the next room, which was empty, and resonant. By pressing their ears to the wall, they could hear what was being said.

Cllr Gerry Ross, member for Hackney, attacked the letter Ray Green had written objecting to the JCF proposal. He used the familiar "outsider" tactic, complaining, "This letter of objection from Ray Green is on notepaper headed with an address in Edgware, Middlesex. What has Edgware, Middlesex got to do with Covent Garden?"

Ken Livingstone defended the JCF scheme as the best potential use of the site, and Charlie Rossi found it difficult to attack the proposal without appearing to be anti-semitic. A vote was called and the JCF proposal squeaked through, 13 votes to 11.

Rossi felt he had been stitched up again by a clever political manoeuvre. Coming out of the meeting, he met the dejected lobbyists.

"What do we do now?" asked Ray Green.

"Don't worry," Rossi, replied, "we've only just started to fight."

Ray Green could see that his answer contained more hope than sincerity. "You really think so?" he asked.

The councillor invited him to his office for some solace, and over a drink they came up with another idea. A direct appeal to the public, the traders' petition, had helped to focus Livingstone's political instincts before. They decided to invoke the power of publicity once again. They placed a full-page advertisement in the next week's issue of the *Camden New Journal*, a local paper which had supported their campaign, explaining what was happening to the Jubilee Hall site, and expressing their fears that it might fall into the wrong hands for the wrong reasons. Readers who agreed with their arguments were invited to sign and return a coupon addressed to Cllr Rossi at County Hall.

When the advertisement appeared, Hymie Bomzer, Secretary of the JMTA, resourcefully sent a copy of it to every member of the "Senate" of the JCF, with a letter asking them if they realised they were associated with this project, and explaining what was being attempted in their name. Plastic bin-liners full of tiny coupons and indignant letters of support were filling up Rossi's office by the end of the week, and this time the response from the Jewish Board of Deputies was also swift.

On Friday evening, 9 July 1982, the phone rang at Charlie Rossi's home in Camden Town. Dr Jacob Gewirtz introduced himself. He explained that he was the Executive Director of the Defence and Group Relations Department of the Board of Deputies of British Jews, which was responsible for monitoring anti-semitic activities throughout Europe.

"I don't know quite how to put this to a good left-wing councillor," he opened, "but how can you be so racist?"

"Now you are talking serious," replied Rossi. "How do you mean, racist?"

"Your advertisement in the *Camden New Journal.*"

"Actually, it's not my advertisement," said Rossi.

"I see your name in it."

"Have you got it in front of you?"

"Yes. Your name is in the bottom right-hand corner."

"That's a coupon, asking people to sign and return to me. But do you also see a signature there?"

"Yes, Ray Green."

"That is the man who has placed that advertisement. He is Vice-Chairman of the Executive Committee of the Brady Maccabi Youth Centre in Edgware. As a matter of fact, if it wasn't after five o'clock I would give you his phone number, but he's so orthodox he won't even answer the phone on Friday night!"

Rossi exaggerated. Ray Green is not orthodox, but he made his point. The initial misunderstanding was quickly sorted out, and the Labour GLC councillor offered Green and Dr Gewirtz his office at County Hall as a meeting venue on Monday morning. Rossi was invited to listen while Ray expressed his doubts about the JCF.

When he had finished, Rossi added, "I wouldn't want to do anything to upset the Jewish people, or any other ethnic minority. Some people have been trying to deflect the main opposition to the JCF proposal down false avenues." Dr Gewirtz asked to visit the site, and Ray Green escorted him on a tour the same day. Before he left, Gewirtz said he wanted to hear the other side of the story, and promised to investigate the position of the JCF. That same afternoon, at a meeting of the Panel, Martin Dyke-Coomes tried to push a resolution through putting that body on record as rejecting the JCF's option five. Although that scheme was universally resisted, Vice-Chairman Rossi, who chaired the meeting, felt he could not accept the motion at that moment.

The battle continued in the media. *Time Out* had quoted a furious Jim Monahan on the decision taken by the Labour Policy Group on an issue which had never been debated by the Panel, on which both the CGCA and the Forum were represented: "Livingstone is totally ignorant of local views. He has been stupid, to say the least. He is following the lead of the Chief Whip, Harvey Hinds and totally underestimating the strength of the opposition."

In an interview given to *City Limits* Hinds replied, "I gave a personal commitment that if anything could be done to help the JCF in central London I would support them." Ken Livingstone complained about GLC officials and members of his own party: "The officers worked us into a position in which the JCF were frozen out of the site. We imposed them, after consultation, because we were not going to be put upon." He confirmed that support for the JCF stemmed from commitments given prior to the GLC election: "They were not in writing. They were more of an understanding than an agreement, but we feel bound to honour them. The JCF is working very closely with Labour Group on this issue. All we have decided is that JCF be included in the site. I believe if all the interested parties would sit down and talk this over something would be worked out."

Meanwhile the *Jewish Chronicle* published an article which signalled that Reg Freeson, the sitting Labour MP for Brent East, was fighting for his political life. According to this piece, the dominant left-wing faction within his own party was fighting a determined campaign to replace him with Livingstone in a parliamentary reselection battle anticipated in September. Freeson was a committed Zionist with a strong power base in the Jewish community of North London. Livingstone's supporters were quoted as saying that the GLC leader would agree to stand only if he saw an excellent chance of winning. The JCF scheme was not mentioned, but those who opposed it puzzled over a possible connection.

On 19 July, Green and Dyke-Coomes laid their own plan, termed option six, before Panel Chairman Ed Gouge. Livingstone invited Green to a meeting on 22 July in another attempt to try to get the users of the site to back the JCF scheme. Green had not yet heard the opinion of the Jewish Board of Deputies, so he rang its Woburn House headquarters. However, Dr Gewirtz had not yet been able to interview the two prime movers behind the JCF scheme, Martin Landau and Norman Hyams. Green asked for the other members of the Consortium to be involved in the meeting, and Livingstone agreed. The representatives of the JCF were ranged on the other side of the table. The GLC Leader chaired the meeting, which was also attended by Gouge and Rossi. During one heated exchange, Rossi asked the JCF's consultants where, in their proposed plan, the market traders would go. "They can go down below in the basement," was the reply. Rossi found this a dusty answer, and said so. "They can go to hell, if they don't take it or leave it," was the rejoinder. Rossi turned to his colleagues on the GLC, commenting, "That's the kind of people you're dealing with. This isn't good enough."

His complaint appeared to register with the GLC Leader. Ray Green then stepped in with a report which questioned the viability of option five and presented the Consortium's alternative option six. Livingstone told him this proposal was out of the question, because it would require the council's decision to award the site to the JCF to be overturned. Ray Green promised he would orchestrate that. Livingstone replied, "It's never been done before, and it can't be done, because you would need a two-thirds majority of the Labour Group." He suggested it would be far more sensible to work out a compromise between options five and six. The Consortium agreed to enter into negotiations, but only on the basis that the traders would be permitted to retain the 2,226 sq.m. of ground floor space they already enjoyed. On this understanding a meeting was arranged between both sets of architects, Monahan and Dyke-Coomes across the table from Cadbury-Brown and his partner John Metcalfe, to be attended by Green, on 27 July.

Another fly had been attracted to the ointment at the meeting of 22 July. A representative of the firm of Nathaniel Lichfield and Partners, employed as planning consultants to the JCF, threatened that, if the Jubilee Market traders wouldn't take on the basement site, he knew others who would. He claimed that two of his clients were interested in tendering for the management of the Jubilee Market under option five. These were the well-known private market-operators, *Wendy Fair* and *Country Wide*. The next day, a troubled Ray Green was on the phone to Ken Livingstone. "We are going to constitute ourselves as a co-operative and we intend to ask for the lease of the market in any redevelopment," he told the GLC leader. "We didn't think it was Labour Group policy to bring in outside market-operators." Livingstone agreed, and stated that he had no objection to a co-operative running the market, provided the traders dealt with the architects behind option five in good faith.

At the first meeting of the two teams of architects on 27 July, Metcalfe, acting for the JCF, revealed that his clients did not actually intend to develop the site themselves. They wanted to be tenants and lessees, so development funds would have to come from elsewhere. Ray Green dug his heels in over the traders' space requirements, and continued to refuse to allow half of them to be shuffled into a basement, as shown in the option five plan. Little progress was made, but it was agreed to produce minutes to demonstrate to the GLC leader that negotiations were under way.

In the mean time, Green and Rossi were determined to overturn the GLC Leader's juggernaut. They launched a vigorous lobbying campaign directed at every Labour member of the GLC, writing, phoning, and racing full-pelt through the corridors of power. Each night Green would sit down to catch breath and add up the putative votes for and against Livingstone; but the two-thirds majority remained out of his grasp.

Early in August, Green received the anxiously awaited call from Dr Gewirtz. It was good news. He reported that the Board of Deputies of British Jews had serious misgivings about the JCF's development proposal, because it could require the allocation of about £3 million of public money from the GLC. The Board feared this could reflect on the Jewish community, and therefore official Jewish support for the proposal should be withdrawn. He concluded by offering the traders his best wishes for success in their application and promised that an official statement would be prepared for the press.

On 6 August 1982, the *Jewish Chronicle* published an eyebrow-raising account of the JCF bid for the Jubilee Hall under the headline "Here's the culture, but where's the cash?" It reported that the Chief Rabbi, Sir Immanuel Jakobovits, had resigned from the JCF because of the controversy now surrounding the project. On another page in the same issue was the news that the President of the Board of Deputies, Greville Janner, MP, had swiftly followed his example. And on 27 August, in the same newspaper, Norman Hyams, co-chairman of the foundation, announced that the eminent "Senate" of the JCF had been dissolved. The official letter from Dr Jacob Gewirtz explaining the judgment of the Board of Deputies of British Jews did not arrive until 7 October 1982:

> Concern for the livelihood of the hundreds of market traders who would be affected is most certainly a major factor in our thinking. We would therefore refrain from supporting any plan which affected adversely the economic security of so many individuals, Jewish or Gentile.
>
> Without commenting on the *bona fides* of the Jewish Cultural Foundation itself, I am of the opinion that in these days of economic hardship, when our hospitals, schools, and social welfare institutions are suffering from insufficient funding, it would be most inopportune for our community to be at the receiving end of a public grant to support our cultural and leisure needs.
>
> It was in this sense that the word "controversial" was used in explaining the decision of the Chief Rabbi and the President of the Board of Deputies in announcing their dissociation from the Foundation.

Dr Gewirtz also referred to press reports that this stand was simply "a reaction to the position of certain members of the GLC regarding the conflict in the Middle East."

> While deeply deploring the racialist views of the extreme Left and Right who would deny to Jews the right of self determination in their homeland, I state categorically that this factor was not the reason for our decision. We are naturally dismayed that ethnic minorities should be used as political cannon-fodder to advance the political fortunes of politicians. That many people will see the extension of financial aid to minority groups in these difficulty days as a flagrant example of political patronage is something which we could not, in good conscience, ignore.

Ray Green was jubilant, and he and the other key movers in the Consortium felt they now had the ammunition to scuttle the JCF initiative. But Charlie Rossi warned that they would have to take the opposition by surprise, so that there would be no time to prepare a plausible alternative defence of the JCF bid.

A meeting of the Strategic Purposes Committee was scheduled for 11 October 1982, when the decision to grant the Jubilee Hall site to the JCF was on the agenda for final ratification. In the interests of promoting a sense of fair dealing, Ken Livingstone had created this group, comprising the Chairmen of all the GLC Committees, and it had the power to reject or endorse policies for virtually automatic approval by the Labour Group. This meeting was chosen as the site of the ambush. Ray Green provided documents on the JCF affair which Jim Monahan and Martin Dyke-Coomes assembled into a dossier.

Charlie Rossi was entitled to attend the meetings of this group, but had no vote. He would not even be able to speak at the meeting without the permission of its Chairman, the GLC leader, and did not expect to get a word in. As he cast about for allies, he could not count many friends among its members. One member, for example, was Michael Ward, one of three hopefuls whom Rossi had defeated in the contest for selection as Labour's GLC candidate in 1979, thereby setting back Ward's political career at least a couple of years. He was now one of Livingstone's key aides.

However, not everyone was in the Leader's camp. Tom Jenkinson and John McDonnell agreed to help. McDonnell, member for Hillingdon, Hayes, and Harlington, was Chairman of the Finance and General Purposes Committee; and the Comptroller of Finance, Maurice Stonefrost, had contributed an agenda paper which, though neutral in tone, was dubious of the ability of the JCF to finance the capital construction costs. As Livingstone rose to reaffirm the JCF decision, Cllr McDonnell interrupted, seeking leave to present further information. Livingstone, surprised but unsuspecting, agreed. Tom Jenkinson swiftly distributed Ray Green's documents around the table, while McDonnell secured the Chair's permission for a few minutes' interval for the members to read them. Somehow the GLC Leader was the last to receive his papers. They consisted of a copy of Dr Gewirtz's letter from the Board of Deputies of British Jews, and cuttings from the *Jewish Chronicle* reporting on the collapse of the JCF. He leapt to his feet, shouting, "This is a propaganda tactic worthy of Goebbels!"

Rossi nudged Tom Jenkinson to speak, but he whispered, "Say no more, you've done it." The members of the Strategic Purposes Committee read the documents and referred the issue back to the Labour Group for reconsideration the following week. At that meeting, on 19 October 1982, Rossi put forward a resolution to overturn the initial 13–11 decision in favour of the Livingstone-backed proposal. It was seconded by Gerry Ross, the councillor who had previously spoken against "the protest from Edgware, Middlesex." The other members joined their support, and the Labour Group decided that the resolution in favour of the JCF project should be withdrawn, a face-saving device which did not require a two-thirds majority. The leader of the GLC had challenged both Charlie Rossi and Ray Green to do the undoable, and they had done it.

In Britain the planning process is very strong and exerts a powerful influence on the value of land. The only way a local community can get a site developed the way it wants is to intrude into the political process. Once again the market traders and the local community, by working hand-in-hand with the local political representatives, had persevered, with astonishing success, to get their ideas adopted. In the end it turned out to be a helpful coincidence that the GLC both owned the site and was the regulatory body. The local politicians could see capital in preserving it from yet more commercial development and granting these other community uses.

The GLC leader put no further obstacles in the way of the Consortium, but has never revealed the reasons for his dogged commitment to the JCF. Today he will say only, "Unfortunately, I have the dimmest recollection of the issue, and so I would be completely unreliable as a source…but I think I recall the issue of anti-Semitism hovering in the background, and disputes within the Jewish community." Illtyd Harrington's remark on Livingstone's political savvy, quoted in a 1992 profile of Ken Livingstone in the *Sunday Independent*, may provide a key to his actions: "He has the benefit of not believing in anything."

In October 1982, a permanent sports hall and market remained as elusive as ever. During the political wrangling of the past couple of years, it had become patent that the GLC was in any case not in a position to fund the redevelopment and there was no well-heeled white knight on the horizon.

CHAPTER ELEVEN

Getting the Act Together

1982–1983

Martin Dyke-Coomes, architect of the Jubilee Hall redevelopment, on site as his building nears completion in 1987.

*T*HE INFORMAL APPLICATION of the Jubilee Hall Development Consortium, option six, was still on the table. And, though deprived of official council support, the proposal from the Jewish Cultural Foundation was also still in the running. At that stormy Labour Group meeting chaired by Ken Livingstone on 19 October 1982, it was agreed that both of these contestants should be given an equal chance to work up their schemes. The revised brief included all the agreed provisions that had been presented to the Greater London Council: the listed Jubilee Hall would be refurbished, and a sympathetically designed new building erected on the adjacent site to include a street market with the same capacity as existing, 28 fair-rent dwellings, a community-based sports facility at least two-thirds larger than that already existing, and new public toilets. The candidates would have to demonstrate an independent funding capability; the GLC had no budget for it.

At this stage the normal local government procedure would have been to issue yet another invitation tender to all interested parties, based upon the revised brief. Instead, in a decision which was later to earn a rebuke from the Local Ombudsman, the GLC had approved both the Consortium scheme and the rival JCF proposal in principle, and in November 1982, Comptroller of Finance Maurice Stonefrost asked each to make a financial submission. In December, he had to report to the GLC Labour Group that he did not consider that either had the money to execute their scheme. GLC Leader Ken Livingstone thereupon gave both candidates eight weeks in which to put forward a viable financial plan for concrete bids for the development of the Jubilee Hall site, including costing, valuations, and finance.

Ray Green's Jubilee Market Traders Association and the market-operator Sherman & Waterman were now working closely together within the Consortium on separate but parallel paths. Though both organisations wanted a financial share, Tony Sherman realised he could not stump up the millions of pounds which were required for complete control of the market. The JMTA had registered as a workers' co-operative on 25 August 1982 and funding continued by the 50p per day, per stall contribution. In a fluid situation, many bets remained open. Ray Green sought support from the GLC to guarantee the traders, should they take up a direct lease, while at the same time S&W was negotiating with the GLC for the extension of its annual lease into 1983–4.

What the Consortium now needed most was a sympathetic financial partner. But the Covent Garden Community Association professionals on the team knew that, if they went a-begging with a capful of dreams but no practical financial strategy, they would be easy prey for a self-interested developer. Experience had taught them how difficult it was for a community group to retain control of a development process if it did not have the means to control the money as well. In this instance, though, the CGCA reckoned it did have some financial clout – the market, which was a major beneficiary, could fund its share and more.

The rest would have to come from the commercial world, and the scheme devised by the Covent Garden Housing Project included an office provision to attract private investment. This drew a great deal of flak from the local community; many of those who had long campaigned with Jim Monahan and Martin Dyke-Coomes were aggrieved. It was difficult to raise money for public housing in choice central London property, because you could put no commercial valuation on it. The CGHP would have to negotiate a deal with a developer which would include the housing as a non-profit element; moreover, the developer would have to provide a deck to build it on. Many loyal Covent Garden activists feared that the project would not be able to subsidise housing – if any at all appeared on this choice Piazza location, it would turn out to be private luxury flats.

If only for their own self-esteem, Monahan and Dyke-Coomes would have to prove these second-guessers wrong. They were totally committed to including low-cost housing on the site and, for the sake of their reputations, could not proceed otherwise. There was no chance of the council putting up money. The only agencies which could effectively achieve inner-city housing were the publicly funded housing associations.

They knew Andrew Westcott, development director of the Soho Housing Assocation (SHA), a vigorous grass-roots operation which had been started by people living in Soho in 1973 to improve local housing conditions and ensure that the local community was not overwhelmed by development. The CGHP put the problem on Andrew Westcott's plate, and he undertook to bully the Housing Corporation into coming up with the cash to fund most of the building cost of the housing element in the Jubilee Hall project. Flats would be earmarked for existing SHA tenants and others on the Westminster City Council waiting list who were in dire housing need.

The two architects lined up Robert T. Horne & Partners as structural engineers and E.C. Harris & Co as prospective quantity surveyors. Simon Kolesar and Richard Darrant of the latter firm put them in touch with David Bond, a partner with Weatherall, Green & Smith, commercial property agents. A connection of this calibre would lend the project credibility within the commercial market, and Bond's firm was engaged to value the property and work out a viable financial plan which could attract funding from a developer or a pension fund. Bond had his work cut out for him. It was a complex scheme, and most of the members of the Consortium were amateurs, with no track record as developers. On the face of it the scheme was not viable. The GLC wanted a premium for the land. The vastly greater part of the expenditure was going to be required for the market and the sports hall, and it was difficult to place a value on any of that. The potential income from a street market would be highly volatile. The merchant bankers to whom Weatherall, Green & Smith would normally turn as sources of long-term finance would require a very high yield on capital to compensate for the risk, and the interest charges would make the project economically unworkable.

At that time, the SHA was sponsoring a mixed development of offices and housing, Richmond Buildings, backing on to St Anne's Court in the heart of Soho. Andrew Westcott suggested that the Consortium might talk to the commercial developer who was handling it. Derek Parkes was the joint managing director of Speyhawk Land and Estates Ltd (later Speyhawk plc), the company which had made a speculative planning application for an office block on the Jubilee Hall site in 1980. Monahan was unaware of that connection, otherwise he would probably have never agreed to the contact; in his view the Speyhawk application had been a typically insensitive, blockbusting office development proposal, displaying consummate ignorance of the complexities of the site.

But in 1980 the GLC, which was in the singular position of both owning the site and approving planning applications for it, had settled on demolition without agreeing a development plan, and Speyhawk, like others, had put in an application as a way of stirring the pot to see what might come out of it. Now the GLC had adopted a specific community-based plan, and in terms of awareness of cultural values in Covent Garden, 1983 was already a long way distant from 1980.

ON ITS RECORD, Speyhawk appeared to be a company very far from the caricature of the freebooting developer. Only seven years old, the Speyhawk Group now comprised a development arm, Speyhawk Land & Estates, and L. Tellings, a construction company. It had enlarged its reputation for the relatively painless resolution of difficult infill situations, working with several local authorities to redevelop publicly owned property by providing a viable mix of social uses supported by income from commercial lettings. While restoring a church in Leadenhall Street in the City of London for ecumenical use and grafting on income-producing office space, Speyhawk discovered the ruins of the base of a twelfth-century chapel, and managed to preserve them within the construction. In Windsor, the company had converted a police station and magistrate's hall into offices and a community theatre.

Like the two architects, Derek Parkes was young and enthusiastic, and for good measure he sported a dark beard. He was keen to involve his ambitious company in the high profile Jubilee Hall site. He could also see it was a potential heartbreak, because of the need to reconcile so many different community interests. But he was intrigued by the challenge of resolving those issues. He saw the developer's role as one of counsellor and conciliator between those people who were completely opposed to development of any kind, and those who agreed it was necessary. Instead of a single-minded, money-grasping developer the Consortium had found a man with a highly flexible attitude who was actually stimulated by the process of working with people to find a solution which had something in it for everyone, and was prepared to earn his profit by putting a lot of sweat into the process.

The CGHP partners invited him to attend a meeting of the Consortium in the office of Weatherall, Green & Smith. Around a table with David Bond were all of the prime movers – Ray Green of the JMTA, Andrew Westcott of the SHA, both Tony Sherman and Cyril Waterman of S&W, Grace Cook, Chairwoman of the CGCA, and David Taylor, representing the JHRC. Derek Parkes was impressed by the dedication of the people he met and by what they had already achieved:

One often hears people complain "Why was this development allowed here and why was that allowed there?" In fact all planning is referred to the community. There are Structure Plans drawn up for every area of the country, which are subject to public scrutiny and discussion. But the action tends to go on up there at council level, and unless it affects their own homes, ordinary people don't notice. But these people got together because they thought here was something worth fighting for. They took on this site and tackled it as an entity outside of the Structure Plan and said to the planning authorities, "Here is what we want. We want a sports hall, and we want a street market, and we want public housing, and all of this should not be swept aside by redevelopment."

What's more, they did it the right way. They prepared their own development brief for the land, they commissioned an architect who designed a scheme which put back on the site the uses they wanted to protect there, and included offices to make it attractive to commercial developers. And then they got that adopted by the GLC as the approved planning scheme for the site.

Before he was able to analyse the factors carefully, Derek Parkes heard himself making verbal commitments. Ray Green insisted that CGHP be retained as architects, at least up to "stage three" of the project, when development capital would be required. Although the young architects had never before been involved in a project of this magnitude, he felt the whole-hearted commitment they had demonstrated would be of enormous value. Derek Parkes readily agreed to give the project his support on these terms. "There they were, all needing this scheme to go ahead, having moved mountains already. So there was no saying no. I thought Speyhawk would make a profit somehow, but we were probably ignoring the really difficult problem, which was, how do you finance a street market?"

That issue was deferred while the Consortium obtained detailed planning permission and agreed the price to be paid for the land with the GLC. This entailed a complex structure whereby the GLC retained the freehold but sold a long lease to Speyhawk. The developers agreed simultaneously to lease back the sports hall to the GLC, which would in turn sublet it to the JHRC. Speyhawk also entered into an agreement with the SHA to build its housing up from the deck that would be erected over an extended sports hall. The developers would be left with a corner site where an office block would also rise over the covered market, plus a mezzanine restaurant in the covered market and a basement area for workshops and storage. The financial risk for the developer was intimidating. If Speyhawk made any mistake in co-ordinating the whole project, it would lead to a cost overrun, which would have to come out of its slice, as everyone else was on a fixed contract.

Speyhawk and the SHA agreed to provide initial funding, and the Consortium now formally instructed CGHP to bring the outline scheme as far as "stage three". While Monahan remained politically active, Dyke-Coomes took over the project as architect, setting up a design team which included structural engineer Bryn Bird and the quantity surveyors E.C. Harris & Co, to work out an approximation of the likely building costs.

With all that planning in place, the Consortium had still not begun to confront the most intractable problem. The scheme was estimated to cost a daunting £6.5 million. Of that, £3 million would be needed to create the market and sports hall. Where was the money to come from? There was only the vague notion that Speyhawk might somehow be persuaded to invest in and collect rent from the stalls, in effect becoming market-operators.

A brainstorming idea which had hatched when the Consortium members first started working together now resurfaced – that the traders themselves could be an important source of funding. The market was a very valuable asset. One hundred and eighty stall-keepers were unlikely to go belly-up on the same day, whereas an office developer might. Bond was unimpressed; he couldn't see how nomadic traders could be persuaded to provide capital investment. How much money would a bank advance against a street market? As he did the rounds of the pension funds, he quickly confirmed what he suspected and what Tony Sherman had already found out: the traditional sources of finance were simply not interested.

After the slump of the mid-1970s, the property market was picking up again. Everyone wanted to build offices now. And shops. But not markets. Apart from the hassle of dealing with 400 separate traders, the financiers said, what happens if the market fails? The counter-argument was that there had been street markets before there ever was a *Marks & Spencer* or *Boots*; and there would be street markets after they were gone. No retailing chain has the flexibility and quick response to changing fashion that a street trader has. By and large he carries his inventory in his van, and if jeans stop selling one week, he will switch to another line the next. Or another trader will take his place.

The traditional sources of finance lacked this kind of vision. They would contemplate a market only on condition that, if the whole thing didn't pan out, it could be converted into shops. Dyke-Coomes therefore started wrestling with different potential shop layouts, as if the market were not in the plan. He started to divide it into various units. And then the penny dropped. "Maybe," said David Bond, "we could split the financing up too."

He was thinking about time-sharing, whereby various owners own a fortnight or so of a specific holiday flat. Why not sell the stalls to the traders on a time-share basis? A street market, after all, is an ideal vehicle for time-sharing. Unlike a holiday home, there is relatively little upkeep. It has to be cleaned and supervised, but basically you are merely providing an empty space and the right to sell certain commodities. If you could keep the initial purchase figure low enough, you could say to a market trader, "This area is where your stall will be, every Tuesday, to sell clothing for the next 125 years." Suddenly the trader becomes a property owner, with a stake in the future of the market. And it would substantially reduce the risk for the developer. With part of the property pre-sold he could use the cash to develop the rest of it.

David Bond is a modest man who works in a conservative-minded profession. At first he thought his own inspiration was a daft notion. "The important thing," he claims, "is that others grabbed it and said it was not so daft. Derek Parkes was always receptive and responsive to creative ideas." The more the group turned the idea over, the more promising it looked. The market was the key. No developer could see sufficient profit in funding a low-cost community sports hall and cost-rent housing to offset the high risks implicit in the scheme. But the market generated cash. Effectively, the market could fund those other community uses which institutional investors shied away from.

A complex three-pronged financial strategy now began to take shape. Bond revised his view of the financial muscle of the market traders when he worked out that they might raise nearly half of the total £6.5 million investment themselves through a time-sharing scheme. Could they stump up £3,600 to buy the use of one stall for one stipulated day per week for the next 125 years? That would raise £3 million, enough to provide for the rebuilding of the market and the extension and refurbishment of the sports hall. He asked Ray Green, "Can the traders raise that kind of money?"

It was a tall order. Ray Green was being asked to sell commercial real estate to people who had little notion of the concept of ownership. Few owned their own homes, and their instinct was to live day by day, without much heed to the future. Not only would he have to extract millions of pounds from them, it was unthinkable to contemplate writing to several hundred cash-dealing nomads every month, asking for payment of their percentage of building costs incurred. He had to get all the money before a brick was laid.

Ray's response was instant and positive. He didn't think then about how it could be done, but having got this far, he wasn't about to say no. He approached Ivor Mylcrest, the manager of the local branch of Lloyds Bank just across the road. Many of the traders banked there, so he reckoned it might come as less of a shock to Mylcrest to be asked to covenant for a loan against which no assets could be pledged until the building went up. It was a propitious visit. At the time Lloyds was particularly keen to demonstrate its support for small businesses, and Mylcrest was sufficiently comfortable with the philosophy of market trading to favourably recommend the forward funding proposal upward to his head office.

The Consortium reckoned that for a contribution of £3 million the market traders, organised as a limited company, could receive a 125-year underlease on the market premises at a peppercorn rent, and the GLC would be given a 125-year leaseback for the community sports hall, also at a peppercorn. A second tranche of cash would come from the Housing Corporation, to give the SHA a 125-year underlease for the 28-unit housing block at a peppercorn, which was to be fair-rented. With these important chunks of the funding in place the developer would then find it attractive to finance the office block, restaurants, and studios and storage in the basement – all of which would be productive of rental income. There was also a thoughtful provision for public toilets, to be leased to Westminster City Council at a peppercorn.

In a scenario of this novelty and complexity the developer's role was critical. Speyhawk had a good record of profitability, and Derek Parkes had the rare flexibility of mind and manner needed to master this innovatory project. The banks felt he could deliver.

The Consortium met the Comptroller's deadline, submitting an outline feasibility study to the GLC Comptroller of Finance on 15 February 1983. Maurice Stonefrost reported favourably on this imaginative funding scheme to the GLC Labour Group, and on 7 March it agreed to negotiate with the Consortium. That same night the proposal was revealed to the market traders at a general meeting at the *Bedford Head* public house, attended by the representatives of the Consortium. It was illustrated in a glossy brochure devised by Martin Dyke-Coomes, which showed the disposition of the leases on the site, to be touted around to potential investment funds. Derek Parkes reassured the traders that it was not they but the banks which were taking on the risk. Ray Green's eloquence and fervour was not to be denied. The audience was enthusiastic, and trader Harry Cohen's motion to double the stall-holders' weekly fund contributions to continue to finance the scheme was carried easily.

The GLC later objected to the stark architectural treatment of the proposed building adjacent to the Jubilee Hall, which was clad in glass and steel, and the exterior was to be substantially altered. But internally the scheme conformed to the brief. The plan was to separate the commercial and non-commercial areas vertically within two new adjacent structures, because funding institutions are wary of independent uses outside their control which are situated above or below their own property. Public-sector housing for 28 flats and 1,100 sq.m. of office space would be provided separately in two adjacent new structures rising five storeys above the ground-floor frontage on the Piazza, and increasing to seven storeys along part of Southampton Street and Tavistock Street. The sports hall on the first floor of the Jubilee Hall gained a substantial extension for additional facilities within the new structure. The existing market on the ground floor would be preserved within the refurbished Jubilee

Artist's conception of the initial CGHP plan for redevelopment (not built), looking east towards the new building on the corner of Southampton Street and the Piazza.
© CGHP.

Looking west towards the refurbished Jubilee Hall on the Piazza.
© CGHP.

Hall and the new structure with a double height, 6.2-metre ceiling, permitting the inclusion of a mezzanine balcony for restaurants or cafés. There would be 150 demountable stalls, to enable different layouts, plus 20 lock-up units. Also provided were space for light industrial workshop studios or an exhibition hall, traders' storage facilities, new public toilets, and a London Electricity Board substation. It would cost an estimated £5,120,000.

From the GLC's point of view the deal was attractive. It had bought the site for £1.35 million in 1974. With accrued interest, the ratepayers had paid out around £2 million. So what would they get for their money? First, while retaining the freehold value of the site, the GLC would receive a £1 million cash premium for the right to develop it, plus a 125-year lease at a peppercorn for a refurbished sports hall, extended to 1,500 sq.m. This would permit the GLC to continue to honour the JHRC lease of the original premises at a peppercorn, while charging a market rental for a 60-year lease on the extension. Moreover, the site would be developed as the GLC wanted it, with all the public facilities in place, as the consultative brief required. There was to be no need for a GLC funding exercise, and the GLC internal architects' competition was also no longer required.

Moreover, for the first time in many years, no alternative seemed handy. The JCF had failed to respond on the question of funding, and sank out of sight.

With the JCF no longer on the scene, the Covent Garden Team was recalled from the wilderness and asked to vet the proposal. Deputy Team Leader Mike Pargiter was at first sight worried that the unconventional funding scheme might lead the financial institutions to look to the GLC as freeholder to supply guaranteeing covenants in case of default, whilst it would lose out on long-term equity. However, he was surprised and encouraged to hear of the attitude of the CGCA, in backing a more substantial office content for the project, a pragmatic decision which could attract development funding.

In April 1983, the CGHP, acting for the Consortium, made formal application to bid for a lease to develop the site. On 11 May, the Team reported to the GLC Labour Group that the scheme was attractive to the council because, although it would require substantial revenue funding, there was no need for additional capital input. The Team's valuation surveyors were still mindful of the need to justify their endorsement as "best consideration" for the GLC. But they rationalised that it was already well into 1983, nothing had started, and loan charges on the original acquisition cost were mounting steadily. In a report to the Panel on 17 June, the GLC Comptroller of Finance stressed the need for an urgent firm decision to avoid unreasonable debt charges.

Responding to these pressures on 21 June 1983, in the Vestry Hall of St Martin-in-the-Fields, the Panel formally abandoned its previous resolution for an internal architect's competition and instructed the Team to proceed to negotiate with the Consortium to develop its plan. The Covent Garden Forum still favoured an open competition for the site, and put in an objection to the planning application. However, it was approved by Ed Gouge, as Chairman of the Panel, with the authorisation of the GLC's Central Planning Committee, on 20 July. The proposed uses of the site were: market, 2,302 sq.m., workshops, 515 sq.m., offices, 1,378 sq.m., residential 1,702 sq.m., and sports facilities, 1,639 sq.m.

George Nicholson, who had now taken over leadership of the Central Planning Committee from Ed Gouge (though the latter still held the Covent Garden Panel Chair), convened a Working Party Committee to steer the proposal. Its role was to work towards signing a building lease for the site between the Consortium and the GLC by the end of 1984 and to negotiate the financial structure of the scheme. As Chairman, he selected Cllr Charlie Rossi. The bones of the financial package were laid before him. The GLC would be paid back for the money they had put out for the land, 28 modern flats would be created in the heart of Covent Garden for council tenants, and the traders would fund a community sports hall by investing in their own stalls. The canny politician from Glasgow thought it over and then nodded, "It's a bloody good deal."

Recognising that both parties had experienced disappointed hopes with regard to the Jubilee Hall site, Rossi felt that the Tories had a significant role to play in finally resolving the issues, and he chose the membership of his Working Party carefully. He invited two Conservatives to sit on it, "Sandy" Sandford, a long-term supporter of the market traders, and David Avery (who was to become Mayor of Westminster in 1990). Although Ed Gouge was nominally on the Committee, he never attended, and it looked as though Rossi had given the minority party a voting edge against himself – a full mandate in recognition of its past involvement. In effect, he was throwing party dogma out the window. However, he felt he could count on the support of the lay members of the team, drawn from Consortium members: Grace Cook for the CGCA, Ray Green for the JMTA, Andrew Westcott for the SHA, architect Martin Dyke-Coomes, and Derek Parkes of Speyhawk. Deputy Team Leader Mike Pargiter was also well-disposed. It was not a high-risk strategy, as Ed Gouge could always have been summoned to vote in a pinch, but it was an effective gesture. The Tories worked hard, and were able to exert influence at the national level of government, too. Rossi had discovered that a bi-partisan approach held the solution to the Jubilee Hall site.

Throughout 1983, Alan Spence, representing the local Communist Party, continued his gadfly role, posing an alternative solution which would provide neither offices nor housing on the site. The Chairman of the Working Party paid little attention to him. But Mike Pargiter was keenly aware that, even at this late stage any alternative bid which might land on the table, if it held out the promise of a higher financial return, would have to be considered on its merits. On the contentious issue of the development of the Jubilee Hall site, which had vexed the good burghers of Covent Garden for the past ten years, Spence, in fact, was to demand the last word.

CHAPTER TWELVE

Raising the Dosh

1983–1984

Ray Green (left) and Frank Ferris making the rounds of stall-holders at the Jubilee Market.

*R*AY GREEN IS A LONG-DISTANCE RUNNER. From his fabric shop in Electric Avenue in Brixton, at the end of the day he would often run home to Edgware, fifteen miles on a gradually rising incline all the way. It was good practice for the uphill struggle which lay ahead of him now, as the elements of David Bond's financial jigsaw began to fall into place.

Under the leadership of the Working Party, intensive discussions took place between all members of the Consortium over the ensuing months to refine details of an acceptable scheme, secure funding, negotiate leases, and ensure full implementation of the agreed brief. By June 1983, the Executive Committee of the Jubilee Market Traders Association included Ray Green as Chairman, the late Malcolm Landaw as co-Vice-Chairman, and Norman Walmsley (who had also been elected Vice-Chairman of the CGCA), Treasurer. All of these were drawn from the general market. Other general market traders serving on the committee were Brian Bromley, Phil Diamond, Andy Graham, and Lionel Amron. The seven crafts market representatives were now Amanda Ryder, Mick Aldridge, Steve Wilson, Carole Wright, Julian Williams, Bo Carter, and Jean Robson. In July, Ron Vere-Field resigned and left Sherman & Waterman, and in November he was replaced as crafts co-Vice Chairman by Amanda Ryder. At the end of August, the committee was able to inform the traders that the Consortium scheme was now the only one in the running for the development of the Jubilee Hall site. Negotiations were in hand with the Greater London Council to allow the traders to move their pitches out onto the Piazza during the rebuilding.

Anticipating a fixed-price contract to pay for the erection of the main floor and mezzanine area of the market hall, and the refurbishment and extension of the sports hall, Ray Green's task now was to produce the £3 million from the traders. It was a strictly cash-up-front deal; the money had to be in the bank before construction started. Speyhawk would proceed as head leaseholders and developers only if Ray managed to confirm that a target of £2.35 million was 'in the bank' by its option date in June 1984. He kicked off by hiring the Empire Rooms in the Tottenham Court Road for a huge meeting on 15 September 1983, where he presented the plan to his 400 traders. No outsider, however knowledgeable and eloquent, could have persuaded this naturally sceptical community to support an untried scheme. But Ray Green put it to them in his own terms, which they could understand. He was, after all, doing it himself. He was putting his own money, his own future, and his own family at risk. His question was simple: did they want to know? And the answer came back a resounding "Yes".

Significantly, Derek Parkes of Speyhawk was on hand as an observer. A few days later, the Consortium reached agreement with Speyhawk to act as developer for the site. Speyhawk was introduced to the Working Party on 21 October 1983, and its partnership with the Consortium was approved in principle by the GLC.

In November 1983, Charlie Rossi's Working Party reported on progress to the GLC Central Planning Committee. The total finance of £6.75 million was seen to be in place as follows. The developer, Speyhawk, would pay a premium to the

GLC for the grant of a 125-year headlease at a peppercorn rent, and would put up the cash to develop the rest of the building. Speyhawk would grant an underlease of the sports hall back to the council for 125 years at a peppercorn, while leasing the office building at a commercial rent. The large financial surplus generated by the offices offset the less remunerative uses and would increase the attraction of this unusual mixed development to funding institutions. The traders would put up the cash to convert the market and the sports hall in exchange for a 125-year underlease on the market hall at a peppercorn. The idea of a traders' co-operative was dropped; the traders would form a limited company instead. The Soho Housing Association would pay for the housing accommodation on an at-cost basis in return for an underlease for 125 years at a peppercorn. Speyhawk would retain and manage the café, workshop and storage space, as well as the main office building.

The total funding, including Speyhawk's contribution, would eventually work out as follows:

		£ million
From Hackney Borough Council Pension Fund,		
against guarantees from Speyhawk, for an office building:		
Premium to GLC	*1.250*	
Development costs	*2.900*	
		4.150
From Speyhawk:		
Contribution towards sports hall and deck for housing	*1.050*	
Two restaurants, basement studios, storage and market office	*2.080*	
Cost overrun on housing	*.022*	
		3.152
From the Housing Corporation, via SHA, for housing		1.130
From the market traders for the sports hall and market		3.075
	Total:	11.507

On the morning of 28 November 1983, at a meeting of the JMTA Executive Committee, a crafts market representative, Steve Wilson, objected that the Consortium had taken on Speyhawk as a development partner without the prior agreement of the JMTA Committee. Ray Green apologised, but pointed out that, as the JMTA was only one organisation out of the group of five making up the Consortium, the objection was largely academic. Moreover, he said, he could see no reason why the JMTA would oppose the agreed structure. He then repaired the technical oversight, and his formal resolution to accept Speyhawk as a partner was carried.

This resolution was an important preliminary to a definitive meeting which was held on the afternoon of the same day at the Charing Cross Hotel between the JMTA, its bankers, Lloyds, and Speyhawk. The discussion outlined the terms under which the developers, as head leaseholders, would offer a 125-year underlease to the company to be formed by the traders. The JMTA would be restructured as a limited company, Jubilee Market Hall Ltd (JMHL) and would grant sub-underleases to individual traders. Stringent covenants restricting types of trading use would be affixed to these sub-underleases; and, to ensure stability of the market community, Derek Parkes insisted that individual traders could not assign their sub-underleases for the first three years.

The original structure of leases was as follows:

Freeholder	GLC
Head Leaseholder	Speyhawk
Sports Hall	125-year leaseback to the GLC
	60-year underlease to the JHRC
Housing	125-year underlease to the SHA
Office Block	125-year underlease to the Hackney Borough Council Pension Fund
Market Hall	125-year underlease to Jubilee Market Hall Ltd
	125-year sub-underleases to individual traders
Other underleases	Mezzanine restaurant
	Basement studios
	Basement storage
	WCC toilets

On 12 December 1983, a revised scheme was shown to the Covent Garden Team, the Architect of Historic Buildings, and the Westminster City Council, and this went some way towards satisfying the original criticisms regarding the massing of the buildings and the detail of the designs. On 4 January 1984, Derek Parkes and Martin Dyke-Coomes presented the Consortium plan to two Covent Garden Forum groups, its Planning Filter Committee and the Conservation Advisory Area Committee. These were not appeased, and reported to the Forum: "while approving the uses to which the building is being put, the design submitted is totally unacceptable visually and architecturally. This important site demands a more positive and convincing architectural treatment." At its meeting of 10 January, by a vote of 12 to three, with four abstentions, the Forum in its advisory role recommended in principle a grant of the lease to the Consortium, subject to a satisfactory planning position, but echoed the aesthetic views of its Committees, "and therefore [we] look forward to a further submission of drawings…at an early date."

These objections went unsatisfied. The Team submitted a full report with proposed content and financial details to the Covent Garden Panel and on 31 January 1984 it instructed the Team to finalise a building agreement and lease with Speyhawk to secure the development of the site, inviting the company to submit the scheme for planning permission. The Consortium proposal was now widely expected to become Labour Group policy, but WCC approval was still needed. Behind the bi-partisan leadership of Cllrs "Sandy" Sandford and Charlie Rossi, the Consortium made a presentation to the WCC Planning Committee on the tenth floor of City Hall, Westminster on 1 February 1984 and secured that approval.

The rest was routine. A full report was made to the Panel on 8 February. A motion by Charlie Rossi, seconded by Ed Gouge, was passed to authorise Speyhawk to grant a 125-year underlease on the street market accommodation to the JMTA on terms to be agreed. Speyhawk was to pay a premium of £1.25 million to the GLC for the use of the site, upon the granting of building agreement. Having first received the blessing of the Labour Group, on the 15th the GLC Central Planning Committee approved the Consortium's plan to undertake the refurbishment and development of the site, and granted a building agreement and ground lease of the site to Speyhawk.

There were dissenting voices; the angriest belonged to Alan Spence. The ambitious project designed by the Dyke-Coomes and Monahan Covent Garden Housing Project practice was much grander than anything the two architects had attempted before. Alan Spence thought it was over-scale, like "trying to get a pint into a half-pint pot." His antagonism was rooted in the successful intervention of the Covent Garden Community Association to include offices in the final brief, at the instigation of the two architects. Like them, Spence was a persistent and altruistic Covent Garden gadfly. He sat on the Forum, the GLC-financed representative body which the CGCA had inspired in 1974, but from which it later withdrew. He recycled all the old resentment about Executive Committee members of the CGCA who were not residents of Covent Garden, and argued that the two architects, who were still members of that committee, had a vested interest in an architectural commission which they themselves had manufactured. It was his purist socialist view that no offices should be allowed on the site. He disagreed with the more pragmatic viewpoint at which Dyke-Coomes and Monahan, after a long journey, had eventually arrived: that it was better to have achieved some housing gain than none, and that none would be achieved without the acceptance of offices and the injection of capital they would bring.

Alan Spence had been attempting to jam a spanner in the works at least since May 1983, when he sought a meeting with the GLC's Chairman of Housing. This was denied him on the grounds of the recent decision of the Labour Group that negotiations should proceed with the Consortium. In late October 1983, he had brought his own far more modest scheme to the Team. It involved the erection of a single-storey cast-iron frame building on the site adjacent to the existing Jubilee Hall. His idea was that the the market and the sports hall could share the same accommodation, the stalls being cleared away to make room for evening sports activities and set up again in the early morning. He proposed to meet the housing-gain provision of the brief by an ingenious sleight-of-hand, namely by building somewhere else altogether. The Bedfordbury site in Covent Garden, owned by the Peabody Trust, had originally been purchased from the Metropolitan Board of Works, progenitor of the London County Council and its successor, the GLC. Jim Monahan had once discovered a restrictive covenant on the sale dating from the nineteenth century which stipulated that, if the land were not used solely for "artisans' dwellings", the Peabody Trust was obliged to sell it back to the Board of Works at the original price, about £5,000. (Whether the GLC could have enjoyed the benefit of these old covenants against the Peabody Trust's inevitable resistance in the courts was never tested. Ultimately the quandary fell into the lap of the authority which disposed of the GLC-owned properties when that authority was later dissolved, the London Residuary Body. This institution had no statutory planning function, and was solely concerned with maximising financial return to the boroughs. It released the Peabody Trust from the potentially disastrous obligation for an agreed payment).

The Team rejected Spence's ideas on the grounds that they did not conform to the planning brief and were financially unsustainable. This rebuttal only fed his energies. His further volley of complaints throughout the early months of 1984 to the GLC's respective Chairmen of Housing, Finance, Arts & Recreation, and Planning were ignored. Finally, at the end of March, the Chairman of Housing wrote to him rejecting his scheme on two grounds: it contained no housing, and it would not tie up the site tightly and quickly enough, therefore leaving it open once again to the possibility of a major office development. Spence retorted that the site was being overdeveloped, that office provision was counter to the Action Area Plan, and that it was impossible to include public housing on it. In May 1984 he made an independent application for planning permission to develop the site for his own scheme. He also filed a complaint accusing the GLC of stonewalling his proposals in favour of the Consortium plan, and citing the CGHP architects for conflict of interest. This was referred to the Local Ombudsman for his consideration.

The Consortium had quickly lodged a strong protest against this last-minute diversion. On 6 February 1984, Ray Green wrote to Revd Austen Williams, Chairman of the Forum, rejecting the Spence plan on several grounds. The space-sharing idea, he said, was impractical. Moreover, while the Consortium plan offered 465 sq.m. of traders' storage space to ease traffic problems, there was none in the Spence scheme. Most importantly, it would provide only a temporary structure. The uses might be changed during the tenure, which did not extend to the full period of the 125-year ground lease. This would put the future at risk. The Consortium considered Spence's proposals "dictatorial"; they did not consider the wants and needs of the traders and the JHRC, who intended to use the Jubilee Hall site, and had been prepared without consulting them. In contrast, the Consortium scheme had been carefully developed in a series of meetings with the GLC Comptroller of Finance, Maurice Stonefrost, who had then recommended to the majority group that it proceed with these proposals. The Consortium had gone through all the correct procedures, including public consultation, before making its planning application, and had received the official blessing of the Forum.

In March, there was to be a second meeting of all the traders, this time at the Conference Hall at County Hall, where Ray Green would reveal the final details of how the finance was to be arranged. To prepare for it, he worked daily at the Isleworth headquarters of Speyhawk with Derek Parkes to price up the stalls and prepare his flip-chart presentation. Ray had no experience of selling real estate, and it was clear that he would need specialist help to convert the traders' interest into hard sales contracts. Derek Parkes introduced him to Frank Ferris, a specialist commercial property agent who had worked with Speyhawk on many occasions in the past. The two hit it off at once, and Frank came on board to mastermind the sales effort. His experience was invaluable to the marketing exercise, and he and Ray Green still share an office today.

On 24 March 1984, before the sale was formally completed, Speyhawk took over the headlease of the site, and began preliminary investigations. Simultaneously, management of the market passed from S&W to the traders they had managed for the past nine years. A detailed planning application was submitted by Speyhawk on 18 April 1984, and in the Covent Garden Team's annual report to the Panel on 29 May, Geoffrey Holland anticipated that work on the site would start in January 1985.

In April 1984, the traders reorganised as a limited company, Jubilee Market Hall Ltd (JMHL). The time-sharing idea was exquisitely simple, but the structure required to put it into effect was extremely complicated. The legal complexities were unprecedented. To sort them out the traders appointed the firm of Hudson Freeman Berg as the company's solicitors, and Ray Green relied heavily on senior partner Keith Hudson in devising the unusual scheme.

There was a need to determine how many stalls could sell each type of goods, and how many shares one person could own. Consequently, the company's Memorandum and Articles of Association was an exhaustive document. It included stipulations to keep the initiative in the hands of the traders, and avoid being taken over. Only those traders who had bought leases on stalls could become directors. On 14 April 1984, the first board meeting of the new company was held, and the traders who had served the longest on the committee of the JMTA were appointed as the first directors of the company: Ray Green, Malcolm Landaw, and Norman Walmsley from the general market, and Steve Wilson, Amanda Ryder, and Mick Aldridge from the crafts market. George Armstrong was appointed Secretary.

The GLC insisted that, to provide stability of leadership during what might prove to be a turbulent period, the directors' term of office should be six years, until the AGM of 1990, to span the building period and the first three years of operation. Moreover, the company could not trade until the Jubilee Market Hall opened in 1987. Meanwhile, Ray Green was appointed official Trustee by the GLC, Speyhawk, the market traders, and the others with a legal interest in the site. In this role he would be responsible to all parties for seeing the project through with the developer, and for the control of a non-profit-making Jubilee Market development fund, which was to handle the entire exercise until the building works were completed. Lloyds Bank Trust acted as fund-holders, and would pay out the traders' £3 million against the architect's certificates as the building went up.

Both the sports hall and the market were to continue to operate throughout the building period. Alan Tattersall, the sports hall Co-ordinator, set about organising support for the project from the Sports Council. Operating at 90 per cent capacity, the community recreation centre was now the most intensively used in the UK, according to a report by the Recreation Management Department of the North London Polytechnic. It attracted 2,500 users every week. Fifty per cent of its customers were local residents, 40 per cent met the standard ILEA "youth usage" classification, and it had the highest proportion of female usage in the country. This vital facility continued to operate on the first floor of the Jubilee Hall throughout the construction period.

At the market next door, Ray Green now took over as Trustee to administer the market where he had first set up his own fabric stall eight years previously. For the past three years, that stall had also been his office, the hub of the "Save the Jubilee Market" campaign. Now he left it in charge of his partner, John Povey, and, for the first time in his business career, began to spend more time inside a proper office than on the stall. Tracey Allen joined him as PA, and he was also assisted by S&W. The company was to be retained as contracted market management until the building works were completed, for the benefit of its management expertise, and also to help soften the blow of losing its lease on the market.

On April Fools' Day 1984, Ray Green and Frank Ferris opened their sales office in a small room suspended from the ceiling of the old Jubilee Market Hall, and started selling stall leases on a time-sharing basis. Their task was to persuade hard-headed traders to risk several thousand pounds to buy 125-year leases on stall spaces which they would not be able to occupy for more than three years. Loans could be arranged through a bank, but the traders would have to put up some collateral.

Their stall sales plan was complicated, because there were three different markets on the Jubilee site in any one week, the Monday antiques and flea market, the weekend crafts market, and the general market during the rest of the week. They set the price by simple division. Approximately 140 pitches were available each day. Sunday trading fell into a grey area of the law, so the six-day total was 840 stalls. Ray Green figured that even in the best case he would be unlikely to sell more than about 80 per cent of the available time-shares. He set a target of 700 day-units, and an average price of £3,600 per stall per day for a 125-year leasehold. That would produce approximately £2.5 million, and the rest would be provided by the interest that sum would earn while it sat in the bank, before being dispensed in stages as the building works progressed over the next three years.

Ray Green offered the Monday antiques market in its entirety to the original landlord, S&W, because it had founded the market and had treated the traders reasonably. If S&W came up with £577,500, it could acquire the lease of the market for Mondays at a peppercorn rent for the next 125 years. S&W bit his hand off, and at a stroke Green had a fifth of the money he needed.

The remaining units were available on a single or multiple unit basis, on the appropriate days, i.e. a craft trader could only subscribe for a weekend lease, and general traders for Tuesdays to Fridays. The 140 unsold units which Ray Green

Left:

Steven Hebbard of the crafts market.

Right:

Potter John Watts at his crafts stall.

Left:

Jean Sinclair and her decorative mirrors.

Centre:

June Wheatley at her dried-flowers stall.

Right:

Olivia Barnard-Firth with her lace parasols.

Amanda Ryder at her jewellery stall.

All photographs by Sean Sullivan.

had allowed for actually proved to be one of the great attractions of the scheme, because these were lettable. For each day-unit which a trader bought, he also received a share certificate. If only 700 day-units were sold, each share would entitle him to 1/700th of the letting income which would be derived from the units which had been unsold. Moreover, this rental income would be applied against the general expenses of the company, thereby significantly reducing the stall-holder's annual service charge for the operation of the market. As Ray Green put it to his prospects, "It's a sort of miracle deal, isn't it? In buying a stall, you are also buying a subsidy for your service charges."

Frank Ferris expected his assignment would last four weeks, but seven months later he and Ray Green were still pitching hard. At the bottom line, they were asking hard-nosed traders to give them £3 million, without getting anything in return for three years. Frank Ferris, however, was a down-to-earth operator who had no trouble talking the kind of language the traders understood, and Ray Green at his side believed in the idea so strongly that success shone out of him.

About 160 traders eventually signed up for agreements to sub-underlease from JMHL. While there was no limit to the number of units which could be subscribed for, voting rights in the company were limited to the first 16 shares owned by any individual or group. Many traders bought four day-units so they could trade Tuesday to Friday. Some put in for three or four pitches on the four days and therefore had to find tens of thousands of pounds. Usually they had a few quid stashed away somewhere, but most of them had to borrow, and Frank and Ray arranged about three-quarters of the mortgages through Lloyds Bank.

When the June option date arrived, they were still below target, but the bandwagon was rolling with sufficient momentum to encourage Speyhawk to grant an extension until the autumn. The agreement to underlease the market to JMHL was approved, but not yet signed. The exact cost was determined at £2,970,000, comprising £2,470,000 in building costs and £500,000 in professional fees.

Meanwhile, Alan Spence had not given up. Ignoring the categorical rejection his proposal had already received, he wrote to JMHL on 15 July 1984, again trying to interest it in his ideas for the site. This was hardly likely. It looked as though the traders would soon be set fair. Planning permission had not yet been granted, but that was expected to be rubber-stamped at a GLC Planning Committee meeting set for 18 November.

However, another set of politicians, this time in the Houses of Parliament, had been brewing up further troubles. Very suddenly, another thunderhead appeared on the horizon.

In its 1979 election manifesto Margaret Thatcher's Conservative Party had declared that London did not need a capital-wide layer of government, habitually controlled by Labour, inserted between it and the local authorities. The GLC was to be abolished. The GLC had responded with a heavy advertising campaign, seeking voter support to preserve its future. It had failed to carry the day, however, and now its doom was ordained. Seeking to draw the teeth of the dying entity, the national Tory government voted through a "Paving Act" which gave it wide powers to restrain the GLC. The Act would receive Royal Assent on 31 July 1984, when Secretary of State for the Environment Patrick Jenkin would set about its enforcement. It forbade the GLC to dispose of land or licences without the minister's approval.

So the GLC worked day and night to push a great flood of disposals through the approval mechanisms before the deadline. On this conveyor belt, moving in speeded-up action with the sword of Damocles hanging overhead, was the application for the Jubilee Hall site. If it failed to achieve planning approval before the end of July, it was back to square one.

Fortunately, the market traders had always enjoyed bi-partisan support. Tory GLC Cllr "Sandy" Sandford had given Ray Green unwavering assistance since 1981, and he kept his party behind the proposal. On the other side of the chamber, Cllr Charlie Rossi, Chairman of the Working Party, continued to champion the scheme with the Labour Party. When the proposal came up on the planning agenda on 18 July, the GLC Central Planning Committee broke precedent by graciously inviting Grace Cook, Chairwoman of the CGCA, and the late John Arrowsmith, Vicar of St Paul's, Covent Garden, and a representative of the Forum, to make a presentation to the full committee. With this fair wind, the project sailed through. Planning permission was granted on 20 July, with the blessing of both political parties. Preliminary work would start on site in January 1985.

Predictably, Alan Spence, who had not yet heard from the Local Ombudsman on his recent complaint against the GLC, reacted by filing an Appeal in the law courts against the GLC's failure to come to a decision on his application for planning permission. Another snag surfaced when the SHA failed to extract its financial contribution from the Housing Corporation in time to exercise its option. Technically, the developer was now entitled to substitute funding for private housing, and as the weeks dragged by it became a tempting prospect for Speyhawk. Derek Parkes, who had to balance commercial pressures against his emotional dedication to the project, was continually cajoled by Ray Green, convincing him to keep on waiting. The SHA funds eventually came through, two months after option date.

Joe Mitchell by his fruit and flower stand.

While the market itself was managed by S&W until the completion of the building contract, JMHL was busy progressing legal documentation, planning consent, and matters affecting the allocation of stalls. Ray Green was determined to keep the three markets just as they were, antiques on Monday, crafts on Saturday, and a traditional market during the week, and specific usages were written into the sub-underleases and the Articles of Association approved by the GLC. Throughout the summer, as the message got across, stalls sold like umbrellas in a rainstorm. Ray was pleased that basic services could be retained in the new market mix, including two greengrocers, a health food enterprise, a baker providing rolls, cakes and doughnuts, a sweet shop, and Len Bassett, the butcher. As autumn began Ray Green and

Frank Ferris had sold leases totalling £2.1 million, only a quarter of a million pounds shy of their goal.

But as the final days before the option ticked away, the sales drive ran into the sand. A dozen units had been allocated within a purpose-built food hall, and apart from two taken by a greengrocer, and one by the butcher, they could not be shifted. The traders said these spaces were just too small. If Green and Ferris failed to find takers, the whole deal was off. The community dream of the Jubilee Market, the sports hall, and the public housing would be a dead letter filed under the familiar heading of Covent Garden Lost Causes.

At the eleventh hour Ray Green found salvation, when a consortium of buyers agreed to purchase the unsold food hall section, with the intention of installing a mini-supermarket. On 30 October, he was able to report to the board of JMHL that he and Frank Ferris had pre-sold enough stalls to guarantee the continuation of the market in its traditional form. The option figure of £2,350,000 had been exceeded by £20, while another £300,000 was still under negotiation. His five colleagues on the board breathed a collective sigh of relief, and authorised him to exercise the option to agree the underlease with Speyhawk. By 17 November, the sum lodged on deposit in Lloyd's Bank Trust in the City had mounted to £2.4 million. Reckoning on interest, the deal was secured. The GLC gave the nod, and on 19 November 1984, agreements to lease were exchanged.

There was one unfortunate final hiccup. The Memorandum and Articles of the Company provided that, with the single exception of the S&W representative, only stall-holders who had bought leases could serve as directors. The only sitting director who had failed to do so was Steve Wilson, and on 27 November, by a vote of five for removal and one (his own) against, he was dismissed from office. Ray Green was reconfirmed in the office of Trustee during the building period. Jean Robson, Tony Sherman, and George Armstrong were appointed directors, bringing the full board strength to eight.

Two weeks into the New Year, JMHL closed its order books. The maximum target for stall leases had been achieved, and no more would be offered for sale. The train had left the station.

Reconstruction

1985–1987

Her Majesty Queen Elizabeth II at the opening of the Jubilee Hall on 5 August 1987, with (left to right) Ray Green, Tony Sherman, Derek Parkes, and Trevor Osborne, Chairman of Speyhawk.

© Stan Strangeway.

S UDDENLY EVERYTHING was happening at once. The builders arrived early in the New Year and started boarding up the site. On 28 March 1985, jugglers, unicyclists, and acrobats on stilts converged on the south side of the Piazza in an exuberant carnival atmosphere reminiscent of the opening of the Sherman & Waterman market a decade previously, for the grand unveiling of the decorated construction hoardings which now surrounded the Jubilee Hall site. These were 440 feet long and painted with the iconography of the vanished Covent Garden Market, bowler-hatted porters with towers of baskets on their heads, and carts loaded with fruit and vegetables. The politicians on stage, such as Cllr Charlie Rossi, were keen to point out to the press that the celebrations, like the Jubilee Hall redevelopment itself, would not cost ratepayers a penny. Speyhawk had authorised an expenditure of £20,000 for the murals, designed by the Free Form Art Trust, which won an 'Art at Work' award that year as an outstanding example of "art in a working environment."

The next week the traders were back where they had been nearly 350 years before, at open-air pitches in the Piazza. Through the Covent Garden Team, Rossi had secured a two-and-a-half-year trading licence from the Greater London Council for the duration of the reconstruction. The plan was for both the sports hall and the market to continue operating while the works went on. In part, this problem was solved by building around the traders. Half of the existing market site remained in use while works proceeded in the other half, the traders switching to the new half when it was finished.

Once again constructive attitudes turned a problem into an opportunity. Some of the temporary stalls in the Piazza were sited opposite the entrance to Russell Street, and Chris Gittings, proprietor of *Knutz,* the jokey novelty shop nearby, became concerned about the effect of these on his own trade. While registering an objection with Jubilee Market Hall Limited, he also helpfully proposed a solution. He pointed out that there was a disused corner of land where James Street entered the north side of the Piazza, where hoardings concealed an exposed basement. It was owned by the Royal Opera House Land Development Trust, a body composed of the ROH and the Arts Council, and would be included in that institution's own plans for building expansion. Chris Gittings and Ray Green together approached the ROH, pointing out that it was deriving no current benefit from that property. Green offered to create a concrete and steel floor over the yawning hole in the ground and apply for temporary planning permission for a street market from September 1985 until August 1987, which would provide the Trust with an annual income. The ROH, in chronic need of financial support, was delighted with the idea, which was endorsed by its Director, Sir John Tooley. The ROH obligingly granted JMHL a year's rent holiday so that it could pay for the building works. The traders moved in, and are still there in 1992, on their third temporary planning permission, while the plans for the ROH expansion remain on hold pending a financial solution.

The traders return to the Piazza during reconstruction.

Photograph by Sean Sullivan.

Celebration of the unveiling of the building boardings, March 1985.

Left:

Street entertainments.

Right:

(Left to right) Lara Rebecca Green, sports hall manager Jim O'Connor, and Ian Todd staff the vegetable stand inside the Jubilee Market.

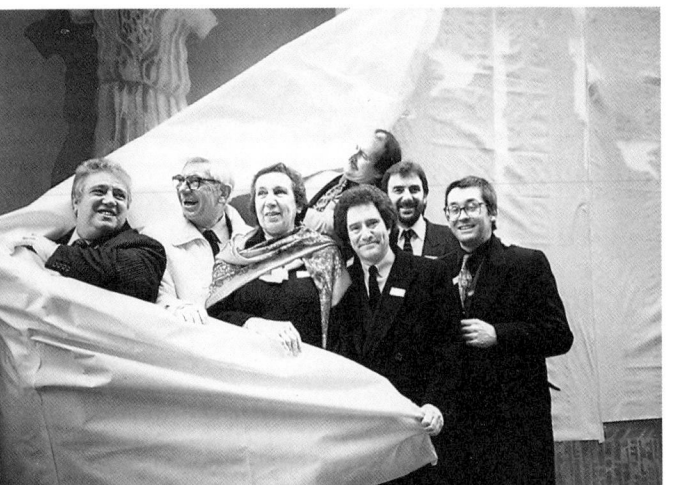

Left:

(Front, left to right) Cllrs Charlie Rossi and "Sandy" Sandford, Grace Cook, Ray Green, Derek Parkes, and Alan Rossiter of Free Form Artworks Ltd with Martin Goodrich, also of Free Form, in the rear.

Right:

GLC Councillors Ed Gouge and Charlie Rossi are introduced by the town crier.

The boarding around the Jubilee Hall construction site, with entrance to the street market.

© Free Form Artworks Ltd.

On 26 March 1984, Speyhawk took over control of the site from S&W, and Ray Green, as Trustee, took on the management of the market. His first task was to install order into the market-place, though not without some misgivings. He had to improve the chaotic stall layout that had existed until then, together with some of the "special favours". While the public likes the jumbled disorder of "character market-places", they do not work for all traders, as it is impossible for the organising body to maintain fairness under these conditions. Green and his colleagues had to reorganise the market, but tried to minimise the loss of the colour, bustle, and local charm that bring people to a market in the first place.

The temporary Jubilee Hall market extension next to the Royal Opera House.

Photograph by Sean Sullivan.

At the same time the reconstruction created its own imperatives. Stalls were erected in the Piazza, and a floor laid over the basement opening on the site behind the ROH. The ground floor of the Jubilee Hall was gutted. Internal walls were demolished, the remaining walls painted, and lighting installed to create a temporary trading area. The construction team meanwhile started demolishing the old shed next door. When they cut through the concrete base which had been installed some decades previously, there was a surprise in store. The red-brick vaults of the eighteenth century houses were discovered underneath, filled with soft earth.

It was just the kind of nightmare Derek Parkes had feared. The plans for the new building called for it to be erected on pilings driven into the London clay, so from day one his building costs had escalated. Moreover, there was no planning permission for a basement, and no use envisaged for one. The GLC gave interim permission to proceed, pending a revised planning application, while everyone pondered what to do with the void they had discovered.

Meanwhile, the diggers kept digging. When they got down to 15 feet, they found another surprise – a human skeleton and other Saxon remains more than a millennium old. It was not the first skeleton uncovered in a Speyhawk basement; archaeologists had removed others from their Leadenhall street scheme in the City. Derek Parkes sighed and redrew his critical path analysis, allowing a week for Robert Whytehead and his team from the London Museum, who had been maintaining a watch on the site, to excavate the relics without serious disruption to the building timetable.

Another event threatened to hold up the works permanently. Amazingly, despite his setbacks, the dogged Alan Spence had still not given up. By July 1985, work on the site was well under way. Nevertheless, on the 23rd of that month, a public inquiry opened, in the meeting-hall of the Africa Centre in King Street, into two appeals by Alan Spence on the failure of the GLC to give notice of its decision on his applications for outline planning permission and listed building consent for

*The Jubilee Hall dig,
May 1985.*

Department of Greater London
Archaeology at the Museum of
London.

his own development proposal for the site. He conducted his own appeal. The Department of the Environment eventually ruled against him on 14 October 1985, but not only because the rival proposal was already in progress. The Inspector referred back to the 1978 approved Action Area Plan, pointing out that it aimed to safeguard and increase the housing stock in the Covent Garden area, and articulated a specific policy to include a housing element on the Jubilee Hall site. Spence received more satisfaction from the Local Ombudsman, Dr David Yardley. His report, published on 4 December 1985, concluded that the GLC had indeed been guilty of procedural irregularities which "amount to maladministration." These arose from the intervention of the Labour Group, in February 1982, to force the inclusion of the Jewish Cultural Foundation into the new brief which had just been agreed by the Covent Garden Panel. "The council was sidetracked into dealing solely with the JCF…and regrettably a year was lost." He questioned the powers of the Labour Group to do this, but also its contrary decision, a year later, to reverse its position in favour of the Consortium. "Again, nothing in the Panel's earlier conclusions allowed for this." While the latter oversight was repaired when the Panel and the Central Planning Committee approved the continued relationship with the Consortium in June 1983, the Ombudsman was concerned that from that time "it would have been unlikely for any other interested parties to be given detailed consideration." He declared:

> for the avoidance of all doubt…it would have been better if a public competition had taken place; and yet I accept that there was a difficulty because by the time it had become clear that the council would not carry out the development many months had passed, and so there was pressure to proceed. Perhaps with hindsight the council's real error was in not identifying sooner that it would not carry out the development after all, and in not considering the ramifications of this.

He found that, although the GLC had not dealt particularly well with Alan Spence's representations, its final decision to award the site to the Consortium was properly considered, and he saw no reason to believe that, had the council handled the matter any differently, Spence's scheme would have been preferred. With that judgment, Alan Spence's robust opposition to the construction work which was now proceeding apace on the south side of the Piazza finally withered.

Meanwhile, on site, faced with the practical realities of redevelopment, the ambitious coalition between community and commerce, which had saved the Jubilee Hall, showed signs of stress, and even crack-up. Derek Parkes had to maintain a delicate balance. He was carrying out a large and complicated commercial development with the community, and though all parties were in general agreement, there would inevitably be occasions when he would want to do something that elements within the community might find objectionable. All the members of the Consortium had a first loyalty to their individual constituencies rather than to their development partner. Increasingly, he found it a struggle to keep the scheme economically viable.

The two architects, particularly, were in a cleft stick. Jim Monahan and

Construction goes up from the new rooftop platform above the market hall, April 1986.
© CGHP.

Martin Dyke-Coomes had been personally involved from the very beginning in the Covent Garden Community Association project to save the Jubilee Hall as a recreation centre, and their motivation remained very strongly community-directed. They had compromised with commerce but had driven a bargain which they felt would guarantee the survival of the sports hall, housing, and shopping facilities, important for local residents in an area where few traditional corner-shops existed. On the other hand, they had accepted a commercial architectural commission from Speyhawk and JMHL.

Dyke-Coomes was struggling with a very difficult design project. Within the Consortium he had to serve a number of different clients who had just embarked upon a steep learning curve. In the community at large, there was wide debate, and some sceptics who wanted the whole scheme to fail anyway. Internally and externally, most of those with a view to contribute had never been anywhere near a multi-million pound development. They were unschooled in architecture and ignorant of the complexities of the development process. But they knew what they wanted.

The objectives of the various groups in the Consortium, though mutual, did not overlap exactly, and interpretations sometimes differed. The latent division came to a head dramatically half-way through construction, when Speyhawk applied for a change of use on a section of the scheme which would yield a higher development value. In the south-west corner of the new building, where an entrance for the mezzanine restaurants had originally been planned, a small office would be fitted in on two floors to house Ray Green's market administration, site

The Driscoll House flats nearing completion, above the office on the corner of Southampton and Tavistock Streets, 1987.

management for Speyhawk, and an estate agency. Derek Parkes felt that the alteration was trivial. In any event, the entrance to an upstairs restaurant could never have been a subdued affair, so he reasoned that a light, glassed-in two storey office unit on the corner would be an improvement from the point of view of appropriate urban use. It fell to his architects, Covent Garden Housing Project, to put in the amended planning application. The revision to the planning application came up at the next meeting of the CGCA. Martin Dyke-Coomes had prudently resigned from its Executive Committee when he took on the commission for the Jubilee Hall, because he felt there was a clear conflict of interest in identifying himself with one member of the Consortium. Jim Monahan, however, and another CGHP architect, David Tomkinson, remained on the CGCA Executive Committee, which Ray Green of the JMTA and his PA, Tracey Allen, had also joined.

Dyke-Coomes went to the CGCA meeting well aware that his practice was now deeply enmeshed in the critical conflict of interest he had feared. Though he was personally strongly opposed to the change of use, he felt CGHP could make no comment on it. He resolved to keep mum, but when the matter came up and Monahan got to his feet, he realised with a sinking heart that he had neglected to gag his partner. Ray Green listened open-mouthed to the architect complaining about his own firm's planning application. Monahan urged the CGCA to oppose the small office provision. It was a change from retail to office space, something the CGCA had fought for 15 years, and which the Consortium had not agreed to. Because of their involvement in the project, all five principals were asked to leave the room, while the remaining members of the committee debated the issue. They voted to recommend refusal of this part of the application.

Feelings ran high on both sides. The next day Derek Parkes rang Jim Monahan to complain that he had acted unprofessionally and without prior consultation. For a few anxious days the CGHP architectural partnership fully expected it would have to resign or be fired from its most prestigious assignment. However Parkes took the pragmatic view that at this stage they all really had little choice but to continue to work together, and everyone got on with the job.

The CGCA objection was ignored by the GLC, which approved the new application *in toto*, including various other modifications which had been introduced during construction. The economic viability of the scheme was also assisted by a decision to move the workshop studios to the basement which had been added beneath the new building, replacing them with a 735 sq.m. restaurant in the basement of the old Jubilee Hall, plus space for boiler-rooms and storage and toilets for the traders.

In the light of the GLC's objections to the original steel-and-glass conception, the exterior had been redesigned. About the only architectural point that all parties were now agreed upon was that the new building should not present itself as a dominating, homogenous street block, but should somehow be reconciled with the Inigo Jones inheritance, as interpreted by Henry Clutton. The Piazza now

Location of the Jubilee Hall redevelopment.
© CGHP.

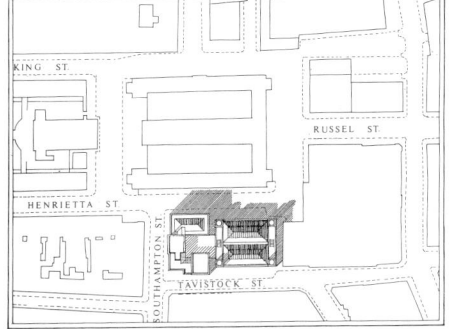

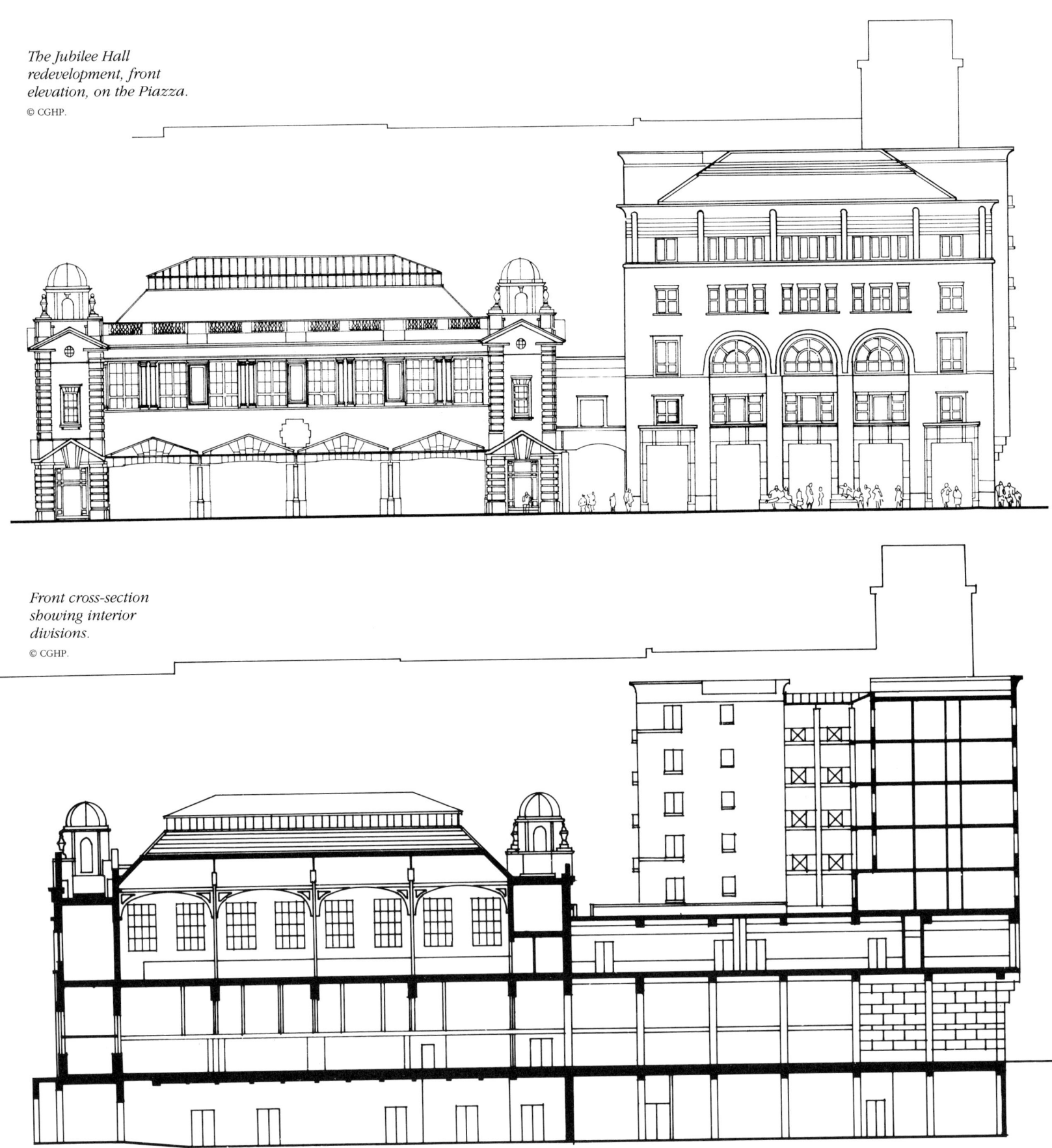

The Jubilee Hall redevelopment, front elevation, on the Piazza.
© CGHP.

Front cross-section showing interior divisions.
© CGHP.

comprised a number of isolated blocks designed in various Italianate modes, set amongst Victorian market hall buildings. To harmonise with these surroundings, the Piazza elevation of the new building, where the office premises rise above the covered market, was faced principally in red brick and stone. Halfway down Southampton Street the construction juts out and extends two stories higher. It appears to be an entirely separate building, giving relief to the eye, and a change to yellow brick at this point underlines change of use from offices to housing. A lighter-colour stock was used on the rear elevation, because the buildings opposite on Tavistock Street enjoy ancient rights of light.

The multiplicity and intensity of uses on the site presented a formidable design challenge. Martin Dyke-Coomes devoted the entire ground floor of the site to the double-height market, and built a deck above it for the sports hall extension, connecting straight through to the existing facility. On top of that he placed a three-storey block containing 1,110 sq.m. of air-conditioned office space on the Piazza corner, with a separate entrance in Southampton Street. Behind it he erected a five-storey tower of 28 flats, also with separate access and occupying 600 sq.m. It's deceptive, because as you wander through the street market it's not apparent whether you're standing in the old Jubilee Hall or the new building, or beneath the sports hall, the offices, or the housing.

Internally, the composite building provided space for 150 stalls, including a food-hall and 19 lock-up stalls, and a 370 sq.m. café on a newly constructed mezzanine overlooking the market. In addition to the huge restaurant, the basement area allocated 510 sq.m. to studio space and 270 sq.m. to traders' storage, plus 45 sq.m. for an electricity substation and 90 sq.m for plant.

The sports hall was vastly improved. Today, the great iron girders of the old Victorian building arch over a spacious main hall, two studios, and a massive gymnasium. The extension of the sports hall into the new building above the market hall provided aerobic exercise and ballet practice rooms, weight training and changing rooms. There was a gain of 620 sq.m., producing a total area of 1,540 sq.m.

Drawing of the new building, with the original Jubilee Hall to the left, from the Piazza. © CGHP.

A final complication emerged regarding the sports hall. This had been leased back to the GLC for 125 years, which provided it to the Jubilee Hall Recreation Centre (JHRC) for a peppercorn. But the GLC now proposed to charge the JHRC for the new extension which had been added to its facilities through a 60-year underlease. Alan Tattersall knew this would make it difficult, if not impossible, to continue to run the centre in the community-inspired way that had always been intended. It could not be funded out of revenue because, to give community needs priority, you could not always fill up the courts with profitable uses.

With the help of Charlie Rossi, another 'miracle deal' was set up to cover the market rental of the sports hall premises. The GLC also owned a large basement area beneath the redeveloped

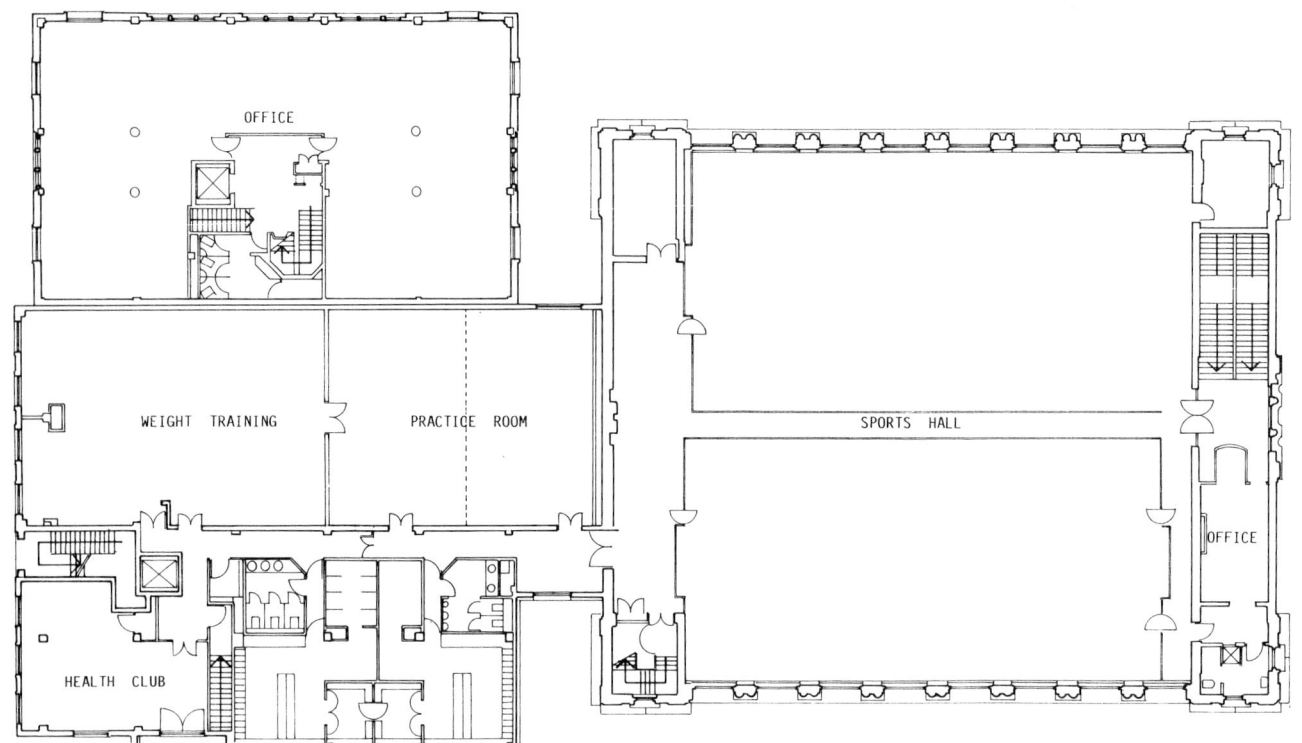

OFFICE

WEIGHT TRAINING

PRACTICE ROOM

SPORTS HALL

OFFICE

HEALTH CLUB

Plan of the first floor of the Jubilee Hall redevelopment, showing the large extension added to the sports hall, from Tavistock Street.
© CGHP.

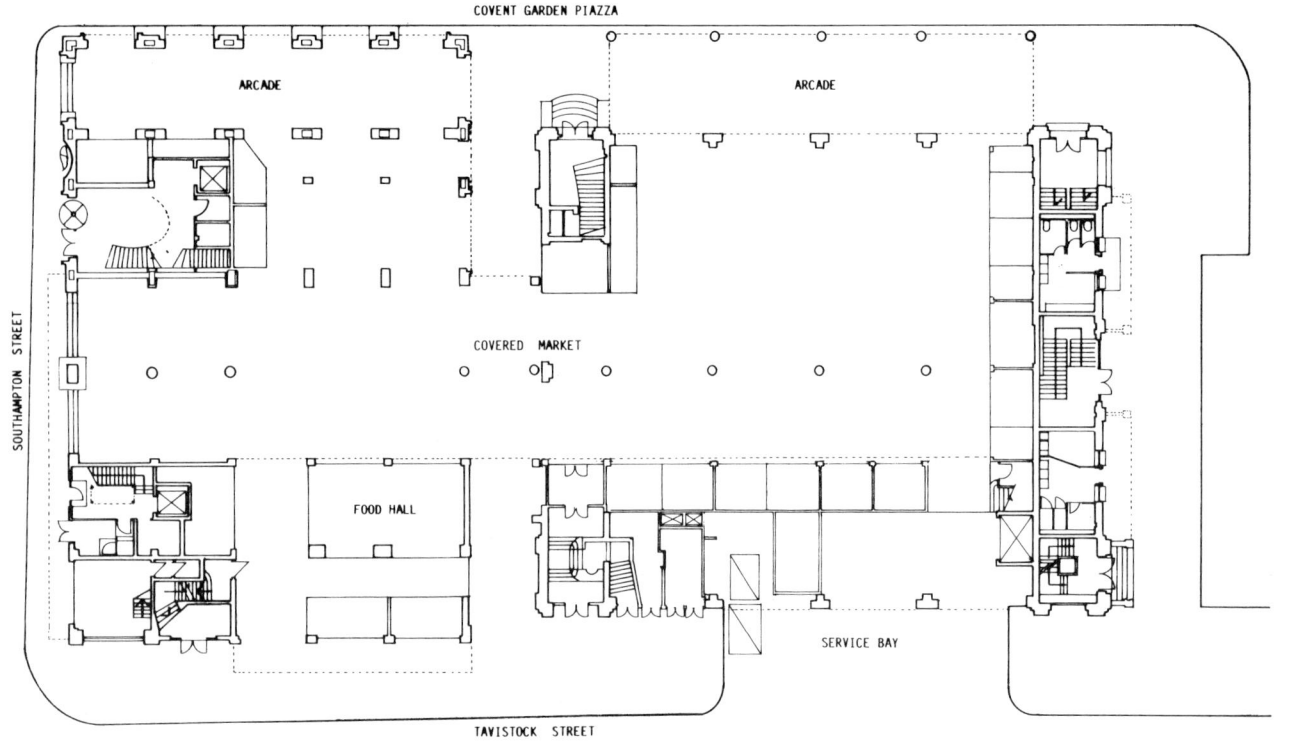

COVENT GARDEN PIAZZA

ARCADE

ARCADE

SOUTHAMPTON STREET

COVERED MARKET

FOOD HALL

SERVICE BAY

TAVISTOCK STREET

Plan of the ground floor of the Jubilee Hall redevelopment, devoted to the Jubilee Market, from Tavistock Street.
© CGHP.

block where the *Odhams* printing works had once stood, in the rectangle bordered by Long Acre and Neal, Endell, and Shelton Streets. It was persuaded to grant a conditional 60-year agreement to lease this basement to a company set up by the JHRC, called Covent Garden Health & Squash Club Ltd. The idea was that the basement could be developed as a commercial health, squash, and fitness club, and the profit used to subsidise the rental of the community recreational facility at Jubilee Hall. At a meeting of the Panel on 11 September 1984, the GLC agreed to guarantee a loan to the company for the conversion of the *Odhams* basement.

Alan Tattersall left the JHRC, to be replaced as Co-ordinator by Jim O'Connor, ex-GLC Labour Councillor Alec Kazantsis remaining as Chairman. With the death of the GLC on 1 April 1986, an interim entity called the London Residuary Body (LRB) was set up under Sir Godfrey Taylor to wind up the GLC and liquidate its remaining assets. Amongst those in Covent Garden were the basement of the *Odhams* site, the freehold of the Jubilee Hall site, and the 125-year headlease of the Jubilee Hall sports centre above the market. The GLC's Covent Garden Team gained a reprieve to conduct this business, and Mike Pargiter became Team Leader in place of Geoffrey Holland, who was elevated to a post with the LRB. (Ironically, it was just three weeks after the abolition of the GLC that the jewel in its crown received royal recognition when an informal walkabout around the Central Market Building was included in Her Majesty the Queen's 60th birthday celebrations. Members of the Team, at least, led by Mike Pargiter, were still on hand to greet her on this glittering occasion).

It was not until January 1989 that the LRB disposed of the freehold of the Jubilee Hall. It was taken up by Speyhawk, the head leaseholder, to strengthen its legal hold on the site and enhance the capital value of its investment. The benefits to Speyhawk were largely psychological; as freeholder it would still be bound by

The Jubilee Hall in July 1987, just prior to the official opening.
Photograph by Richard Mildenhall,
© The Observer Ltd.

Ray Green escorts Her Majesty the Queen through the Piazza.

© Stan Strangeway.

Her Majesty the Queen accepts flowers from well-wishers.

© Stan Strangeway.

Ray Green, with Grace Cook just behind, escorting Her Majesty the Queen through the Jubilee Market.

© Stan Strangeway.

Her Majesty the Queen chats with a group of stall-holders. Behind her, (left to right) are Derek Parkes, Martin Dyke-Coomes, and Ray Green.

© Stan Strangeway.

The principals of Speyhawk, Derek Parkes (left) and Trevor Osborne (right), show Her Majesty the Queen through the flats at Driscoll House. Martin Dyke-Coomes stands behind her.

© Stan Strangeway.

David Jockelson, Chairman of the Soho Housing Association, and residents of Driscoll House greet Her Majesty the Queen on the rooftop terrace.

© Stan Strangeway.

Aerobic dancing, a
T'ai Chi demonstration,
and a trampoline artist
compete with the
reception line for the
attention of Her Majesty
the Queen in the sports
hall.

© Stan Strangeway.

Ray Green, GLC Cllr
Charlie Rossi, and Grace
Cook, Chairwoman of the
CGCA, on the great day.

© Stan Strangeway.

covenants to the lease. It was one of the last official acts of the Team. Having disposed of the last of the GLC assets, it had put itself out of a job, and the doors at 1–4 King Street were locked for the last time on 31 March 1989.

Speyhawk transferred the freehold of the office block to Hackney Borough Council Pension Fund (later passed on to Fenchurch Nominees, a subsidiary of Kleinwort Benson), subject to a leaseback to the traders for the market area. Thinking very far ahead indeed, the local community leaders found one final trick in the pack to play. They persuaded the LRB to attach a covenant to the freehold which was sold to Speyhawk. This tightly binds the uses of the site for 150 years. In theory, therefore, when the JMHL 125-year underlease expires in September 2109, the traders of the twenty-second century can apply for a 25-year extension, should they have the ability to plan and fund it. Ray Green says, "We hope that those who follow us are as determined as we were to make the future secure."

With the conclusion of the building works in sight, Ray Green invited Her Majesty the Queen to visit the Jubilee Hall redevelopment, and to his great delight she accepted. On 5 August 1987, Queen Elizabeth II opened the first new building in the Piazza since the completion of the original Jubilee Hall in 1903, which had commemorated her great-great-grandmother's Jubilee.

Her Majesty was greeted by the Lord Mayor of Westminster and the Lady Mayoress. The housing project had been named Driscoll House, in honour of community leader Sam Driscoll, who died in 1976, and his sister, Miss Kitty Driscoll, presented a bouquet. Her Majesty then unveiled the commemorative plaque, formally opening the 1,860 sq.m. Jubilee Market Hall. The Chairman of the JHRC, Alex Kazantsis, conducted Her Majesty into the Jubilee sports hall for a demonstration of *T'ai Chi*, dance, and children's games and trampolining. John Toomey, Life Chairman of the CGCA, guided her through an exhibition of its work

The Jubilee Market traders committee is honoured by fellow traders at a ceremony in September, 1987. Second row, left to right, are George Armstrong, Norman Walmsley, Ray Green, and Malcolm Landaw. Next to the Pearly King on the left in the row behind is Tracey Allen, the first Co-ordinator of the Jubilee Market, and on the extreme right of that row is Eve Buskin, the oldest female trader, standing next to stall-holder Olivia Barnard-Firth.

on behalf of the community over the past 16 years. David Jockelson, Chairman of the Soho Housing Association, then conveyed Her Majesty to the top floor of the fair-rent housing project to see the magnificent view from the roof garden enjoyed by the residents at £29 per week for a one-bedroom flat, £35 for a two-bedroom unit. Down on the second-floor garden area, the tenants gathered to meet Her Majesty, accompanied by Ray Green and Grace Cook, representing the Consortium. After the Queen left, there was a celebratory afternoon tea and knees-up in the Jubilee Hall, to the music of the Pasadena Roof Orchestra, Mark One.

On 8 December 1987, the various underleases were granted and the market traders officially took possession of their new home. For Speyhawk, which had taken a chance on a very difficult project with a low profit potential, the costs of the scheme had risen in every respect. But property values had continued to grow steeply in London while the building was going up, and the developers were baled out by being able to achieve higher rentals than anticipated for the office building, the serendipitous bonus of the basement restaurant, and the mezzanine, where several fast-food outlets have been squeezed in.

The traders' Committee Members had spent six years with no financial reward in securing the future of the market for at least 125 years. Ray Green had been Chairman of JMTA since it was started in 1981 and of JMHL since its inception in 1984. To show their appreciation for the work that their committee had accomplished, the 400 market traders whose livelihood had been preserved in Covent Garden dedicated a polished black granite plaque in the front arcade of the Jubilee Market Hall, where it fronts the Piazza. It is set into the wall of the Jubilee Hall about 20 yards from the spot where Ray Green set up his stall when he came to Covent Garden 12 years previously, to sell fabrics.

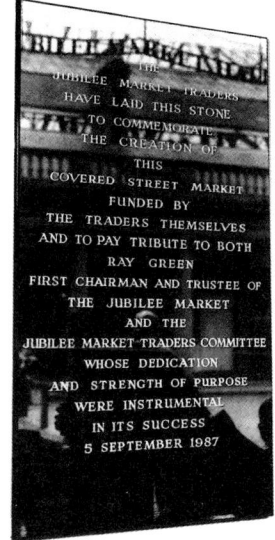

The commemorative plaque.
Photograph by Ketan Patel.

Market stalls return to the Piazza.

© CGHP and private collection, Ray Green.

Construction starts behind the hoardings.

© CGHP

JUBILEE HALL SITE·REDEVELOPMENT

A COMMUNITY INITIATIVE.

1978· H.R.H. The Duke of Edinburgh opened the Jubilee Hall as a community sports & recreation centre

An original G.L.C. plan proposed the demolition of Jubilee Hall to make way for commercial development.

1980· Jubilee Hall was listed to save it from demolition

1981· The G.L.C. guaranteed the continuity of the market following the presentation of 125,000 signatures collected by the market traders.

The G.L.C. initiated public consultation to formulate a brief for the redevelopment of the Jubilee Hall site.

1982· A G.L.C. brief was agreed & The Covent Garden Community Association. The Jubilee Hall Sports & Recreation Centre, The Market Traders Association & Sherman & Waterman formed the Jubilee Hall Development Consortium Ltd. to put forward proposals. The Soho Housing Association were also invited to join the Consortium.

Inset:

The cellars discovered under the Jubilee Hall site.

*The new building
goes up.*

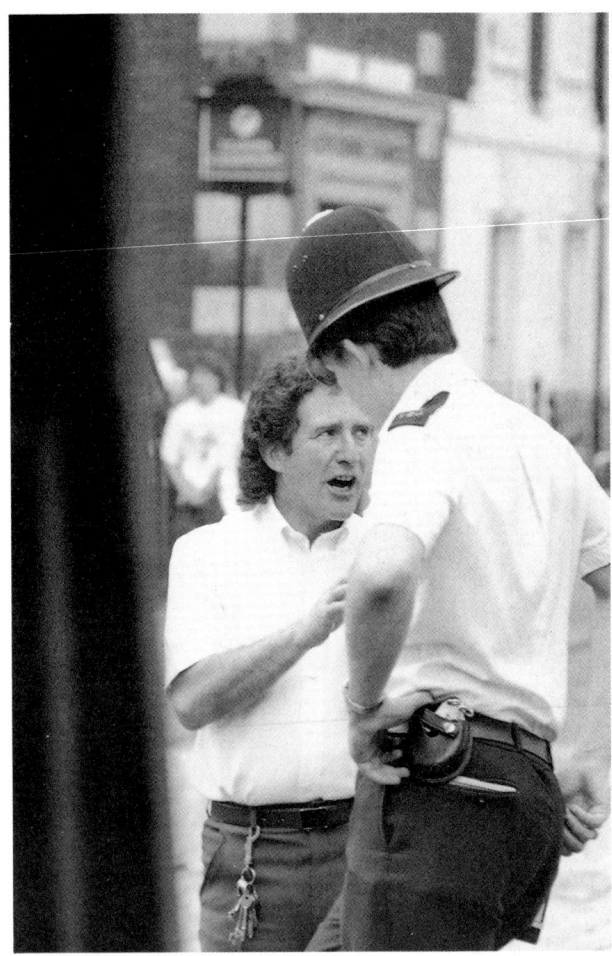

Life in the Piazza market during reconstruction.

Photographs by Sean Sullivan.

Stalls under the portico of the new Jubilee Market Hall.
© CGHP.

Today and Tomorrow

1992–2109

*T*HE ARCHITECTURAL PROFESSION tends to judge its creations in terms of their appearance, and how they compare to whatever shapes, styles, and materials happen to be in fashion at the moment. To the layman who must use it however, the central question about any new building should be: "Does it work?"

The Jubilee Hall is a bustling microcosm of city life which exists today only because of the goodwill, energy, and inspiration of a great many dedicated people. To persuade a commercial developer to build 28 rent-controlled flats, a sports hall, a street market, restaurants, cafés, and workrooms, plus offices, on an inner-city site was a magnificent achievement. This was recognised when the building won the Community Enterprise Scheme Award, sponsored by *The Times* and the Royal Institute of British Architects in 1988.

Inevitably, the result is a product of compromise. Developer Derek Parkes admits that the architecture of the office building and the flats could have benefited from the application of more thought, and from a longer time-scale, but, he insists, the miracle is that it happened at all. There was much sniping from various quarters throughout the planning process. Many in the Covent Garden Forum were opposed to the architectural solution. Others fought for alternative community uses, or were adamantly opposed to the inclusion of offices. Every faction of this highly participative community wanted its particular dream to be fulfilled, so every statement, every letter, every planning alteration aroused hostilities aimed at defeating an opposing force which thought differently. Issues blurred in the frenzy which accompanied this warfare. But, with enormous determination by a handful of people, a scheme of considerable merit was devised. The dream materialised.

Many of those who worked very hard to create this unique resource are less than satisfied with the result. Martin Dyke-Coomes, who led the design team, says, "It was an absolute nightmare to build. As an architect I think we were crazy to ever take it on. But we drew up the brief for it ourselves. And at least we did it. We set out to save the Jubilee Hall as a building and retain the sports hall, which we did. We set out to maintain the market, and we set out to build new publicly funded housing acceptable to local people. We achieved all that admirably." The change-of-use application which created the small corner office still rankles, but otherwise his only reservations are aesthetic. He would have preferred something more in tune with the time, rather than historically based, but he accepts that the Consortium and Speyhawk had little room for manœuvre. The political complexities were difficult enough without the added complication of trying to argue a more avant-garde design through the Greater London Council.

No one has more right to express an opinion than Jim Monahan, who was involved in every phase of the development of Jubilee Hall. He was one of the early 'squatters' who, in 1975, occupied the old building and converted it for temporary use. As a leading figure in the Covent Garden Community Association, he helped establish the sports hall, then led the campaign to preserve it by getting the building listed. He worked with the market traders to plan and fund an

Detail of original skylights preserved in the sports hall.
© CGHP.

Interior entrance of the new office building.
© CGHP.

alternative scheme, which his own architectural practice designed and built. But in the end, control of the project slipped out of his personal grasp.

In some respects he thinks the building is a monument to a lost opportunity for creative urban neighbourhood renewal. Ideally, he wishes the architectural competition had gone ahead as planned. The architecture would have been better, he believes, if the design brief had been fixed, and the terms on which the land was going to be transferred had been ironed out. He remains bitterly disappointed about the way the site is used. On the positive side, he appreciates that there is fair-rent housing on the site, and a sports facility. But he believes the latter has moved far away from the original educational concept which sprang from David Bieda's commitment to local kids. In the pursuit of money the charity has, he feels, moved too far from the locals and the schoolyard with the trend to pumping iron and other adult keep-fit activities.

But, as Brian Anson foresaw when he quit the campaign in 1973, the old neighbourhood was doomed to change. The Jubilee Hall Recreation Centre is not the kind of playground romp Jim Monahan first helped create. Westminster City Council is not a generous funder of community groups, and the JHRC management has chosen to engage the commercial realities of the leisure centre market in the 1990s. In those terms the centre is a tremendous success, packing in 6,000 visitors every week at relatively economical charges.

The rooftop courtyard enjoyed by the residents of Driscoll House.
© CGHP.

New badminton courts in the original Jubilee Hall building.
© CGHP.

The entrance leading to the sports hall on the first floor of the Jubilee Hall.
© CGHP.

The main hall of the Jubilee sports centre on the first floor was refurbished with a new roof and floor, and the extension provided three fully mirrored exercise studios with semi-sprung floors, and new male and female changing rooms. Today, under the management of Sue Biggar, fifty different sports and keep-fit activities are on offer seven days a week. Natural daylight floods through the twin peaked runs of roof lights, supported by the original iron girders, to illuminate a 465 sq.m. gymnasium panelled with mirrors.

The Jubilee sports hall has evolved into a large, state-of-the-art fitness centre, with all the funky bells and whistles. It is an important London centre for martial arts, offering 11 different disciplines. There is a great emphasis on body-building, circuit-training, and fitness assessment, and all the sophisticated equipment that goes with it. Less frenetic keep-fit activities include sauna, whirlpool baths and yoga. It is still the venue for organised local indoor sports teams; children get a look in with classes in ballet, karate, and football, and special holiday programmes and workshops in circus and gymnastic skills. A treatment centre offers alternative therapies, including osteopathy, acupuncture, aromatherapy and shiatsu. There's also a small vegetarian café.

As the sports hall expanded its keep-fit programme, the new extension turned out to be insufficiently sound-proofed for the activities which are now held there, and this created a problem for the residents in the Driscoll House flats above. The JHRC has proposed to relocate its exercise studios, constructing a half mezzanine floor in the main hall of the Jubilee Hall building, which will provide sound insulation as well as extra space, and is now seeking approval for this alteration.

A registered charity, the JHRC declares that it has remained faithful to the principle of providing low-cost recreation to the surrounding communities. However, unlike most public leisure provision in the UK, it is no longer council-financed. By balancing popularity and pricing, it is now entirely self-funding. Alec Kazantsis remains as Chairman of the Board and David Guy is still a prime mover, as well as a mix of other politicians and notables such as Frank Dobson MP, Joe and Pearl Dennis, Christabel Russell-Bick, Eugene Lamb, Caroline Keen, and Alan Morgan, formerly manager of the local corner branch of Lloyds, the bank which helped the market traders to fund the Jubilee Hall redevelopment.

With regard to the market hall, aesthetically Monahan's primary concern, as always, is community-orientated. He regrets that the Jubilee Market bears faint resemblance to a traditional street market. Apart from oranges and apples, snacks and sweets, there is little fresh produce available. The stalls no longer sell vegetables or fish, nor, by and large, ordinary household needs. These uses were fundamental, he says, to the idea which the traders first put to the CGCA and the GLC. They were lost sight of, he feels, in the drive to raise funding. His model is the historic Berwick Street market in Soho, a bountiful shopping ground where all the best restaurants as well as the local community find high-quality fresh produce at good value.

He is perhaps, regretting a more fundamental change. Though Covent

Garden was saved, at least in part, as a place for people to live in, it is no longer the neighbourhood it was when Brian Anson, Sam Driscoll, Jim Monahan, and all the other activists first set out to save it in the early 1970s. It is tourists who dominate the area now, and in a changing social landscape you cannot freeze the culture of a street market. There is now baking on site, where there was not before, but the products are snacks, rather than staples. The Jubilee Market, like any other, can only respond to demand, and it is its capacity to adapt which will guarantee its survival.

Ray Green's fabric stall, during the rebuilding of the Jubilee Hall.

THE PERMANENT TRADITION of market trading in Covent Garden has evolved with the times for three-and-a-half centuries. Today it contains one of the biggest covered markets in the country. The Jubilee Market Hall still houses three different markets on different days of the week, but the traders are now a tightly knit and well-organised community. And they are here to stay.

The building changes character by the day. Very early each Monday morning, over 200 dealers assemble here to create the Jubilee Market Hall antique and flea market, still managed by Sherman & Waterman. It is now the prime dealers' market in London, with a long waiting list for casuals. One hundred and sixty-five stalls offer antiques, memorabilia and bric-a-brac, but the serious business is still done between 5 and 7 a.m. amongst the traders themselves. The general market takes over Tuesday to Friday. It still sells some fresh food, flowers, plants, and herbs, as it did 350 years ago, but most of the emphasis is on good cheap clothes and shoes, toys, costume jewellery, household goods, cut-price books, and track suits – almost everything you can find at posher places and higher prices elsewhere in the Garden, and there's no charge for the genuine London accents. On weekends craftspeople from all over the southern half of the country flock here to display their wares at the Jubilee Hall crafts market. There is a fascinating variety on offer, from fine crocheting to glass decorations made from old bottles. There are engravers, locksmiths, wood-carvers, frame-makers, pottery, toys, leather, knitwear, lingerie, and gift items. The emphasis is on British-made goods, and you are buying direct from the craftsmen themselves.

A busy row of instant eateries perches on the mezzanine balcony overlooking the bustle of the market hall. The large restaurant in the basement, despite its superb central location, has had its ups and downs and changed hands a couple of times. Now it seems to be in the right hands. Brian Stein, who started the *Brahms & Liszt* wine bar in Russell Street in the early 1970s, and later the popular brasserie, *Maxwells,* around the corner, has long supported CGCA initiatives affecting the area. In April 1992, he opened *The Roadhouse* in the

Jubilee Hall, serving live music as an additional relish for the American-style food.

The temporary outdoor outpost of the Jubilee Market still perches on the Royal Opera House redevelopment site in the north-east corner of the Piazza. Forty stalls trade here throughout the week in antiques, old jewellery, prints, *objets d'art*, coins, medals, ephemera, atticana, and other bits and pieces every day of the year.

Some of the stalls in the Jubilee Market are available for letting to casuals, so there is a changing mix of fresh attractions on sale all the time. You can rent a stall cheaply by the day, and if you're a 'regular casual' you get it at a discount. Rents are adjusted regularly to keep pace with inflation. The company's leases do not allow stall-holders to sublet. If they don't want to work, they have to ask the traders' company to let their stalls. Some stall-holders have left, assigning their time-share leases to newcomers; these must be approved by the company, though permission will not be unreasonably withheld. To maintain trading standards, all new applicants for stalls are vetted by the Board of Directors of Jubilee Market Hall Limited. Demonstrators are prohibited. While they can add colour to a market, the crowd a good demonstrator will attract overlaps other stalls, and can stop his fellow traders from earning a fair living. But Ray Green encourages his traders to 'flash' their goods properly, displaying them well to put on a good presentation for the punter.

The general character of the market has been shaped by the times, and some losses are regretted. Tony Sherman feels some of the buzz has gone out of the market. Because it is indoors, sanitary regulations have tidied it up. Veg no longer spills out on to the pavements, and Len Bassett, the butcher who once

Scott Harris brings on the clowns.

Photograph by Ketan Patel.

Doreen Pickard hand-painting her pottery cats.
Photograph by Ketan Patel.

auctioned his cuts of meat off the back of a lorry, now serves his customers from a fully integrated, tiled and refrigerated unit. A few traders have used their market stall as a springboard to owning their own shop, in Covent Garden or elsewhere. But the majority stay. No one gets forced out of the market by rising rents. So, while the area all around has been subject to regularly increasing rents, the leaseholders in the Jubilee Market have bought themselves an oasis of exemption from exploitation by market forces that will last for 125 years.

One of the reasons that you will continue to find bargains at the Jubilee Market is that the finances have worked out well for the traders. It was at the time a plunge into the unknown. No other group of traders had ever co-operatively financed its own operation on such a scale. It may have been a unique situation which can never be repeated elsewhere. Certainly it required an extraordinary degree of organisational initiative and political skill. Even then, the campaign to save the Jubilee Hall ran into dead-ends again and again, before the traders found their way through the obstacles.

Yuki Yamaguchi at her earrings stall.
Photograph by Sean Sullivan.

There are many other indoor markets in Great Britain, but no other market, indoors or out, is owned by its own traders. If others were able to follow this example, in theory the implications for the market trade would be immense. It could mean that market traders would be able to initiate the development of new shopping centres. Property developers could look to the markets to form the basis of their centres with the finance being provided

Selling commemorative mugs, 1987.

by selling the stalls in advance, as Ray Green and Frank Ferris did, through mortgages. It would offer market traders, who habitually carry their business in their van or on their backs, a form of secure asset.

Owners and operators of market sites from all over Britain make pilgrimages here to wonder. In practice, however, the Jubilee Market success story is likely to remain a one-off. It was the product of a unique set of circumstances. Trading conditions were buoyant, and there was a strong political will to make it work. At the time the GLC was fighting a lone battle against Thatcherism, but the Jubilee Hall was special. Through the constant badgering of the highly skilled and articulate lay leaders of the CGCA and the dogged persistence of Ray Green and his pack of terriers, it gained strong bi-partisan support. Both parties eventually became keen to be identified with this prime example of a successful community initiative, so the battlegrounds where planning applications are often put to the sword by political opposition did not exist. Discussions about the final scheme were always positive and planning consent was readily granted.

The pioneers have reaped the reward of their foresight. To achieve initial commitment early on, Derek Parkes had insisted that traders could not transfer their holdings during the first three years. Now, they can be sold under agreed conditions, and stalls have appreciated dramatically in value. Many of the original traders who purchased their sub-underleases in 1984 have now become "market multiples", extending their interests to other markets throughout London and Southern England.

However, the traders at the Jubilee Market are not without long-term problems. Variety is what attracts shoppers to a market. In the pursuit of profit, private operators sometimes forget this, and end up overloading a market with certain lines – racks and racks of identical T-shirts and jeans, for instance. Shopping becomes boring and the whole enterprise suffers.

Ray Green believes passionately in variety, and determined to preserve it by building clearly defined 'use clauses' into the traders' sub-underleases. These determine what goods traders can and cannot sell, and they are a source of potential aggravation in any market-place, even amongst retailers in a large modern shopping centre. Market traders are particularly sensitive to anyone attempting to intrude on their business, perhaps because any such attempt is highly visible.

Ray Green says:

> We tried to make these clauses as fair as possible, so we wouldn't have traders arguing about it. But we didn't have the battalions of experts to do it for us, as a shopping centre does. We were a group of amateurs putting together hundreds of leases as well as we knew how. We did well, probably better than the GLC managed at the Central Market Building, because they experienced bigger problems than we did. But, in retrospect, we could have drawn the rules tighter if we'd had the time. We had only six months to sell £3 million worth of stalls, each with specific use clauses written into the agreement. It is very hard to define categories of goods sometimes, and it's a constant source of aggravation. My managers have a policing role and where we have the legal powers to stop transgressions, we do so.

Like any retailers, the traders also have to anticipate changing market trends. While the tradition of market trading seems robust and secure enough after 350 years on this site, will the specialist aspects of the antiques and crafts sections prove to be of lasting attraction, or simply passing fancies?

The traders can adapt to these challenges. But the major threat is out of their control, and that is the general economic appeal of Covent Garden. Will people continue to be drawn to the Piazza, as they have through the centuries, or will its special quality succumb to the pressures of mass retailing? All the buildings that occupy and surround Inigo Jones's noble rectangle are now in private ownership, and once again subject to market forces. How will these pressures change the character of the area?

THE OPENING of the Central Market Building in 1980 had a dramatic effect. Though big companies relocated out of the area, decreasing the number of working commuters, new, smaller service businesses sprang up to replace them. Today, over 5,000 people live in Covent Garden, up from 2,000 before the restoration of the market. Both schools then were half-empty. Now they are flourishing again, with a mixed ethnic population, which was always the case. Traces of the village atmosphere remain, particularly north of Long Acre and around the Wild Street estate on the eastern boundary, where old Covent Garden families have lived for generations. The best news for the locals, who mourn the passing long ago of the Civil Service Stores in Bedford Street, the original Sainsbury's supermarket on Drury Lane, and Woolworth's on the Strand, was the opening of a Tesco supermarket within Covent Garden in 1992. But whereas the wholesale fruit and vegetable market dominated their lives for so many years, now it is the tourist industry which prevails. In the peak seasons, summer and pre-Christmas, and sunny days any time of year, visitors are attracted to the Piazza at the rate of up to a million a week. This has driven commercial rents up to levels most easily afforded by large retail chains or fast-moving merchants of shoddy tourist paraphernalia, and discourage the local artisans and quirky speciality shops which had made the area a magnet in the first place.

With the restoration of the Jubilee Hall as the final piece in the game, many thought the battle of Covent Garden was finally over, but it is still going on. John Toomey, Life Chairman of the CGCA, a native son who has struggled against the entire gentrification process, says, "The building of Covent Garden was three hundred years of accident. Finally, the people of Covent Garden got together and saved the fabric of the area, but today there is a more insidious threat, which most people don't see. Rising rents will destroy the character of the specialised shops. The fish-and-chip shop on the corner cannot survive if its rent is suddenly raised from £28,000 to £70,000."

The attitude of the GLC towards Covent Garden, at first visionary and cavalier, was bent by the force of popular protest into a more sensitive and responsive posture. At the meetings of the Covent Garden Panel, the deliberations of the GLC members and their officers were attended by representatives of the Westminster City Council, Camden Council, the Forum, and the CGCA, who were able to contribute their views before final ratification by the GLC Central Planning Committee. This structure of consultation, which had created order and stability out of turmoil, came to an abrupt end with the abolition of the GLC, producing a string of events which in turn have created enormous problems now, and for the future. One of the first casualties was the Forum, which collapsed when the WCC refused to underwrite the support of this GLC creation.

In 1985, the Tory Central Government under Margaret Thatcher set April Fools Day 1986 as the date for the demise of the GLC. Amongst the thousands of questions this created about the future provision of GLC services was the practical problem of how to deal with the properties it owned. The response of the Department of Environment was to create the London Residuary Body, a quango led by single-minded surveyors and accountants, with the mission of disposing of all GLC assets in London. Amongst these were some of the choicest commercial properties in Europe, the buildings in and around Covent Garden's Piazza. By now the restored Central Market Building, with its unique and carefully safeguarded mix of speciality shops, was an outstanding success, attracting 12 million visitors a year.

WCC asked for these properties to be passed into its possession. The DoE refused, insisting that the properties had to be sold to the highest bidders, and the proceeds returned to the London boroughs, as appropriate. (Had the original 1981 proposal for the GLC to manage the Jubilee Market been adopted, this too would now have passed into the hands of commercial interests).

The community leaders who had fought to bend the GLC in the direction of conservation were alarmed. Who would ensure that these policies would continue in the future? If the properties were sold to the highest bidder, unrestrained commercial pressures would determine the mix of the market. The high volumes of traffic were irresistible bait to the multiple retailers and fast-food outlets that dominate every provincial High Street in Britain, and the sex shops that continue to proliferate like mushrooms in nearby Soho, despite repeated attempts at suppression by the WCC. All these popular services had the means and the motivation to bid higher than any speciality shop. They would swamp the area, and, collectively, quickly destroy its unique character.

The DoE planned to market the portfolio in two phases, the first closed, the second open. In the first stage, 35 public companies and institutions were invited to apply to purchase the main 'core' properties located south of Long Acre – the Central Market Building, the blocks on James Street, and the properties bordering Russell Street/Wellington Street. Of these, 24 expressed interest and 12 potential buyers were short-listed. The 'non-core' properties, mainly located to the north of Long Acre, were to be advertised openly and sold to the highest bidder.

This was a carve-up. Although the powers of the GLC would devolve upon the two local authorities, no longer would there be a specific, concerned, statutory guardian for the area. Essentially, it would leave the heart of Covent Garden deregulated, its conservation and future development at the mercies of dozens of external powers with conflicting interests, a return to the days when control first slipped from the hands of the earls of Bedford. Who would see that the precepts of the Action Area Plan, the statutory document conceived jointly by the GLC, the two local authorities, and the local community, a policy which had controlled the area since 1978, would be enforced in the future?

Once again, it was the CGCA which rode to the rescue, with Jim Monahan and Grace Cook to the fore. It was their inspiration to galvanise local interests into forming a registered charity called the Covent Garden Area Trust (CGAT). They recognised that to negotiate with the huge economic interests which are represented in this area, they needed more than advisory powers. The core of central Covent Garden could not be left at the mercies of a freeholder with the objective of maximising rents to satisfy its shareholders. They required a statutory body, free of day-to-day commercial considerations, with the power to exercise legally binding and enforceable restraints. Once again a union of local community interests, including David Bieda and Revd Austen Williams, applied pressure to the government, now represented by Sir Godfrey Taylor, Chairman of the LRB. They had no power base and no money and they wanted to control the freehold of some of the most expensive properties in London. The DoE was keen to be seen to be acting in the public interest, but this had to be balanced against the statutory duty of the LRB to obtain the best price for its property, and any restrictive covenants would reduce that value.

Fortunately, the locals had well-tuned connections. They secured excellent advice from the senior partners of Clifford Chance, one of Britain's largest firms of legal advisers, accountants Peat Marwick, and from Lord Carnock, a leading expert on Trust Law. Eventually the DoE was persuaded to accept the Trust as the holder of a 150-year headlease on all the properties in the 'core' area of the liquidated portfolio. Its charter enshrines the concept of restraint, and its covenants can curb any ultimate purchaser who might want to introduce an undesirable change to the character of the area or to its building fabric. Its constitution is tightly determined, and its constituency broadly drawn, to frustrate takeover attempts by dedicated and manipulative minority groups. Any resident of Covent Garden, anyone who runs a business there, or simply any person who expresses a legitimate interest in the area, can apply to join the Trust for a token annual fee. Its management committee, or Council, of 18–20 trustees, is structured to reflect the mix of residential, business, and entertainment uses of this special area of London. The two local authorities, Westminster and Camden, nominate two each, and another represents the CGCA. Five further trustees are chosen by other worthy institutions with a common interest in preserving the historical and architectural character of the area and its special qualities – English Heritage, the Civic Trust, the London Tourist Board, the Theatres Trust, and the Westminster Chamber of Commerce. The remainder are elected annually from the general membership, apart from the Chairman, who is nominated by the Secretary of State for the Environment.

Fittingly, the man who signed the preservation order on Covent Garden in 1973 as Secretary of the Environment, Geoffrey (later Lord Geoffrey) Rippon, was invited by the DoE to become the first Chairman in 1988, while Grace Cook, formerly CGCA Chairwoman, fulfilled the deputy executive role. Effectively, she was the executive leader, presiding over the bi-monthly meetings and co-ordinating the working parties which deal with lease applications and particular issues. Other familiar names from the early days of the struggle – Jim Monahan, David Bieda, Robert Harris, John Toomey, and Revd Austen Williams – were repeatedly elected to membership. At the 1991 AGM, however, change was in the wind; Grace Cook stood down, as did Robert Harris, who had sold his venerable stage make-up business, and Lord Rippon retired.

Once again, the wheels of progress turned full circle in Covent Garden. The man appointed by the DoE to occupy Lord Rippon's Chair of the CGAT in 1992 was Geoffrey R. Holland (now OBE), recently retired from his appointment at the LRB. The former Covent Garden Team Leader, once Brian Anson's boss, was one of the originators of the discredited 1968 plan against which Anson raged. As a professional adviser, he was borne on all the tides of political and social change which have swept through the area since. Now it is he who is charged with the guardianship of Covent Garden, and few can be more qualified by personal experience. He is likely to take a far more hands-on role than his predecessor.

While any community or conservation issue affecting the quality of life in Covent Garden is theoretically within the remit of the CGAT, its role in most of the area is merely advisory. The northern part of the GLC portfolio was sold off to individual property groups, and these tenants, like others throughout the rest of Covent Garden, are in no way protected from the pressures of market forces. Within its broad mandate for most of the square mile, the CGAT reviews planning matters, opposes some licensing applications, and makes positive suggestions, but its only power is persuasion. The local authorities need only nod politely and do what they want to in any case. But the presence of four councillors as trustees at least ensures that the community view is made clear to the councils.

In practice the formal powers of the CGAT are restricted to three former GLC-owned parcels of property. These are the Central Market Building, the old Flower Market now housing the Theatre and Transport museums, and the lower James Street area, between the Piazza and Floral Street, which includes Bedford Chambers and Cubitts Yard, all of the buildings fronting James Street, and three on Floral Street. These freeholds, which the LRB had inherited from the GLC, were subject to commercial leases to shop and office tenants, and in a few cases residential leases to those who had exercised a right to buy. In 1988, the LRB invited sealed bids and sold this chunk of the heart of Covent Garden to GRE Properties Ltd, part of the Guardian Royal Exchange Group, one of Britain's largest and best known insurance companies, with roots going back to 1720, for £84.1 million.

A 150-year headlease was granted to the CGAT, giving it specific powers and duties in regard to these 'Protected Lands'. The Trust was sandwiched into the leasing structure of the 'core properties' as follows:

Freehold:	GRE
Headlease (150 years plus 1 day):	LRB (assigned to the CGAT)
Underlease (150 years):	GRE
Commercial sub-underleases:	Tenants

Where residential leases were involved, a further 150-year sub-underlease was granted back to the LRB which assigned it to the Housing Association. (Similar 150-year restrictive covenants in favour of the Trust were built into the sale of the freehold of the Jubilee Hall to Speyhawk, though in this case without the creation of a specific landed interest for the Trust.)

The Central Market Building is the key attraction of the area, and what happens here will largely determine the economic future of Covent Garden. It is supposed to provide speciality shops which can not readily be found elsewhere. The Trust must approve any change of lease, and exercises detailed control over the nature of retail outlets and the specific goods they are permitted to sell. Ladies' fashionwear, for example, is an activity which can generate high profits. Without restraint, the Central Market could easily be saturated with schmatter. Applying its change of use covenants, the CGAT acts to keep the types of trade in balance. Not only must its permission be sought for any retailing activity, but it can determine the specific goods allowed. Its litmus test is whether the intended use would improve or detract from the specialist nature of the shopping activity. Thus, it would perhaps look more favourably on a shop selling wedding dresses than one flogging denim or trainers, which are available everywhere.

Nevertheless, market forces can thwart this intention. Some of the original attractions of the Central Market Building, shops of special character such as the candle store and the Aladdin's cave of mechanical toy exhibits, can scarcely be expected to generate the high income which is necessary to pay the high cost of maintaining the listed building, now that it is owned by a public company which owes a profit responsibility to its shareholders. Also, some of the tenants which took the plunge in 1980 as small, unique businesses have been rewarded with great success and are now spread far and wide. *The Body Shop* is now a public company with branches in towns and cities all over Britain. *Thornton's* chocolate shops, then new at least to London, are now more commonplace. One High Street fashion multiple, *Monsoon*, challenged the letting policy in the High Court, and won, on the judge's logical, but perhaps commercially naïve, ruling that the existence of a chain of High Street clones did not preclude the possibility that this particular branch *might* stock unique goods.

IN LESS THAN 20 YEARS, massive change has been forced upon Covent Garden. A busy, untidy, wholesale fruit, vegetable and flower market surrounded by a traditional, run-down urban neighbourhood, it slumped suddenly into quiet decay in 1974. In this wasteland of warehouses, colourful community activities and quirky shops began to flourish, wild flowers and nettles amongst the paving stones. In the 1980s, much of this was swept away as the Central Market Building became a magnet for tourists and shoppers. Rentals sky-rocketed, and though Covent Garden entered the 1990s with many empty shopfronts and offices, the private landlords who now control most of the leases, perhaps affluent enough to weather the current recession, have resisted a softening of rent demands. High rents, the crushing new uniform business rate, and the indifferent attitude of the local authorities in comparison to the stringent application of planning regulations by the GLC, have set the scene for further change before the end of the century. What next, Covent Garden?

The fear of local community leaders is that rising rents could force out the eccentric and unusual in favour of the ordinary. Rumours surface periodically of large multiples and fast-food chains negotiating leases in the area. And there are three major redevelopment schemes in the pot which would have a massive influence.

In June 1991, GRE put about 10 per cent of its Covent Garden holdings up for sale. These were the properties fronting lower James Street which had been changed from residential to office use by the GLC Panel under Dr Mark Patterson, prompting Jim Monahan and the CGCA to launch an unsuccessful lawsuit against the GLC in 1979. The judge had ruled that, as the GLC owned the land, it could determine the use. The price tag was £13.5 million, but the properties sold eventually to the NatWest Pension Fund as a long-term investment for £10.2 million. GRE retained the courtyard behind these buildings – Cubitt's Yard, part of the 'Protected Lands' under the direct supervision of the CGAT – where it proposes to erect yet another shopping centre. The scheme would drive an arcade through from Bedford Chambers to Floral Street, at the point where an unfinished building has stood vacant since 1985, a forlorn monument to the National Jazz Centre, an ambitious GLC project which ran out of time and money.

Though Jim Monahan, for one, is disenchanted, the buildings affected are not of great historic merit and GRE marketed its ideas sensitively. Although there is only token housing provision – one flat which is likely to be occupied by a caretaker – the plan includes some light industrial or craft workshops to give vitality to the area, and a promise to preserve the exterior streetscape. At first there was little community opposition to the July 1991 GRE planning application for a mix of office, light industrial, and retail uses. After insisting on three drafts of the plan, the CGAT, goaded by Monahan, eventually decided that its conservation requirement had not been satisfied, and in May, 1992 decided to register an objection. Subtracting the current provision on this site, the Cubitt's Yard development will add 800 sq.m. of office space and 1,170 sq.m. for shops and restaurants to Covent Garden's already ample supply.

More contentious is the proposed redevelopment opposite the Covent Garden tube station, by the Worshipful Company of Mercers of the City of London, a medieval guild which has owned property in Covent Garden since Dick Whittington was a mercer. Its emblem of a saintly lady (which originally may have been a saintly boy), within a cartouche, may still be espied on buildings in the area. The intentions of the mercers for the large block on the north side of Long Acre, however, are purely inspired by Mammon. In 1987 this group gained planning permission for a large-scale development of the rectangle enclosed by Neal Street, Shelton Street and Langley Street. The intention is to punch a hole through a fine 1830s warehouse of the type which used to crowd Covent Garden, but which now lingers only in as yet untouched portions of Dockland, to create a shopping mall plus an office block and luxury flat complex of 23,455 sq.m. The recession stalled this ambition, but a revised application was made in September 1991 in time to prevent the permission lapsing. In its advisory capacity, the CGAT has put in a detailed list of objections against the proposed addition of another 2,710 sq.m. of unneeded retailing space and 3,595 sq.m. of office space.

The third scheme is the longest running and most prominent – the plan by the Royal Opera House to finance much-needed backstage facilities by raising another block of shop and office space on the Piazza. The ROH is not within the 'Protected Lands', and it can muster a powerful supporting chorus of the great and good.

The one-and-a-half acre site stands behind and on the side of the ROH. It borders Bow Street, Russell Street, the Piazza, and James Street, and includes the existing structures on the north side of Russell Street, the Floral Hall, and the tiny garden in the corner of the Piazza, which has won a certain affection from the locals. The redevelopment, designed by Jeremy Dixon, will produce three office buildings containing 12,250 sq.m. (an increase of 10,520 sq.m.), an additional 4,010 sq.m. of retail space, and a few flats and houses creating a residential gain of 1,285 sq.m. This is, of course, in addition to the extra 19,230 sq.m. of space devoted to ROH purposes, plus a 48-car garage for the use of ROH staff, businesses, and residents. The total usable area almost doubles, from 36,410 sq.m. to 70,995 sq.m.

This plan was vigorously but unsuccessfully resisted by the CGCA. But where community resources failed, market forces have achieved a temporary standstill. The ROH financial plan recognised that, even when the new property was fully let, there would be an £80 million shortfall which would have to be met by gifts. However, the valuation of potential commercial revenues was made in the boom years of the 1980s. There are, at the moment, no takers for expensive new retail property, even in the heart of Covent Garden, and few lavish donors can be espied on the horizon. The ROH redevelopment scheme is on hold.

However, prosperity is presumably around some corner or other, if not the next one. If they were to proceed, these three pending developments would provide in round figures an *increase* of 14,900 sq.m. of office space, 8,000 sq.m. of shop and restaurant space, and 1,300 sq.m. of housing. Can Covent Garden cope with it? Quite apart from the effect on the community, is the golden-egg-laying commercial goose committing a gluttonous form of hara-kiri?

The main argument, as it has always been, is about the character of the neighbourhood. English Heritage ensures that the historic listed buildings throughout Covent Garden are appropriately preserved by their owners, but today there is no single close-at-hand strategic planning authority for the area. The GLC had been forced by local initiative to adopt a policy of consultation with local people about the control of uses and character of the neighbourhood. With its abolition, responsibility was split between between Camden (north of Shelton Street) and Westminster Councils, both remote, and administering wide regions.

Most local residents and business people and the artistic community agree that, to continue to survive, Covent Garden must retain its individual character, with a sensible balance of uses, each developing in its own direction. In the words of Mike Pargiter, the last Leader of the Covent Garden Team, which attempted to supply both Conservative and Labour administrations with impartial property valuation advice, "This is not left-wing politics, but sound estate management. Keeping the rents within the capacity of the very attractions which give Covent Garden its special appeal to all comers will sustain the area's long-term capital investment value."

The burden of preserving this principle remains where it has always been, in the hands of a few people who love the area and have remained faithful to their own ideas of the community. People like Jim Monahan, who argues his corner honestly and vigorously and is extremely reluctant to accept compromise. He made it his mission to protect Covent Garden from the sledge-hammer, and in the grand tradition of the English eccentric dedicated himself with no personal reward to the task. People like Ray Green, who sometimes found himself on the other side of the argument from Jim Monahan, but learned from him that if you really want to change the way things are, and put in the time and the work, you can.

But the levers the local community used to press upon no longer exist. Big landowners like GRE have replaced the GLC, and the powers of the CGAT are circumscribed. Tony Earle runs its one-man secretariat in the remote passageways of the warren of offices in Bedford Chambers, and the Trust is amply funded by an annual levy of one day's rental on all the properties it oversees. In 1991 this amounted to £44,000, and it invests the surplus against the day when it may have to finance a court action against GRE, should the freeholder find an offer so tempting that it elects to challenge the Trust's rejection of a lessee as unreasonable.

But is the will still there? Although almost anyone can join the CGAT, its membership income is a pittance. There are only 120 or so members, including its 20 officers. And only 45 people bothered to attend the 1991 AGM. Jim Monahan, who helped start it, is scathing about the CGAT, "because it does not confront issues." He describes its activities as "tokenism." Grace Cook says "Today the battle lines are less obvious. It's very easy to stir people up when you can say, 'Look, this is where you live. It's going to be knocked down and there will be a great highway through here.' That can get people worked up. But if you say, 'If we don't follow this line, then the whole character of the place will change,' people will not get as passionate about it, and you can't have the same sort of success."

MEANWHILE, in the Jubilee Hall, the market traders, enjoying the benefit of 125-year sub-underleases at a peppercorn rent, with very reasonable service charges, occupy an island of economic stability in the centre of a sea of troubled waters, provided, of course, that they continue to elect able, responsible, and far-sighted executives from their own ranks, to make sensible decisions which will protect their interests over the many decades to come.

An early test occurred during the property boom before the collapse of the stock market in 1987, when some traders began to realise the immense potential value of the property they inhabited. They reckoned they could cash in by selling off the underlease, and distributing the profits amongst the shareholders. The market would continue, but the traders would lose their independence to a commercial operation. An attempt was launched to change the Articles of Association to enable this move.

To Ray Green and his colleagues who had fought so hard so that the traders could control their own destinies, this was a short-sighted sell-out of the traders of future generations, and they resisted it successfully. However, it showed that the traders were potentially vulnerable to a predatory takeover. To preserve the principle of ownership and a peppercorn rent, at the Annual General Meeting on 25 July 1991, it was agreed to issue a trustee or 'golden' share putting a controlling interest in the hands of two Trustees, Ray Green and the company solicitor, Keith Hudson. To sell the trustee share and the company now requires 95 per cent agreement by the traders. This resolution received a massive vote of approval

The Memorandum and Articles of JMHL were also amended in order to redistribute seats on the Board. One directorship is now allocated to the antique market, and three or four each to the crafts market and the general market, to make up a total of eight. During 1990, the first elections were held. Tony Sherman resigned from the Board, and co-Vice Chairman Malcolm Landaw passed away. (With the agreement of the WCC, a bench was erected to commemorate him on the side of the Jubilee Hall). Ray Green suffered another personal loss when his assistant, Tracey Allen, who had persevered with him through so many obstacles, left to join Labour Party headquarters in the Walworth Road. All of the other incumbents had to stand for re-election. In 1992 Jubilee Market Hall Ltd was still led by Ray Green as Chairman and Trustee Director, with Vice-Chairmen Mike Aldridge and Andy Graham representing, respectively, the crafts and general markets.

It is in the directors' trust to maintain with diligence the relationships which have been so carefully built up with the WCC, the police, GRE, the ROH, the CGAT, the CGCA, the JHRC, and other responsible organisations which share their concern for the future of Covent Garden. It is only because of this spirit of practical co-operation that, as Covent Garden enters the closing years of the twentieth century, it still provides a home for 400 or so traditional British market traders, who persevere in what they like to do, in happy disregard of modern mass marketing techniques, while huge retail chains collapse all around them like kites in a sudden calm. Thanks to Ray Green and his members, their future is secure, for them and their descendants, at least until 2109 – and perhaps another 25 years beyond that!

The directors and secretary of Jubilee Market Hall Ltd, 1992, (front row, l–r) Jean Robson, Ray Green (Chairman), Rochelle Anselm, Eric Wilkin, (back row) Mick Aldridge, Keith Hudson (secretary), Frank Ferris, George Armstrong, Andy Graham.

Photograph by Ketan Patel.

Where Are They Now ?

David Bieda runs the Seven Dials Conservation Trust, which raised funds to recreate the sundial monument at Seven Dials, Covent Garden, and improve the visual quality of the surrounding streets.

David Bond remains a partner of Weatherall, Green & Smith, the commercial property agents.

Long-term Covent Garden resident **Grace Cook** has retired from both the CGCA and the CGAT, but remains active in community affairs as chairman of the Central Westminster Police/Community Consultative Group.

Martin Dyke-Coomes and **Jim Monahan** parted company in 1989. Dyke-Coomes now runs his own architectural practice in Islington, while Monahan continues at CGHP, now located in Soho.

Frank Ferris runs Covent Garden Estates, a small estate agency which shares an office with the Jubilee Market Hall administration, where **Ray Green** continues to look after the market traders' interests as Chairman of Jubilee Market Hall Ltd. Since 1989 he has also acted in the capacity of Chief Executive.

Former Covent Garden Team leader **Geoffrey R. Holland OBE** was appointed chairman of the CGAT in 1992.

Alex Kazantsis remains Chairman of the Jubilee Hall Recreation Centre Ltd.

Ken Livingstone, former leader of the Greater London Council, was elected a Member of Parliament (Labour Brent East) in 1987. In 1992 he made an unsuccessful bid for the leadership of the national Labour Party.

Managing Director **Derek Parkes** left Speyhawk in 1988 and now runs his own development company, Parkes Incorporated Ltd, from an office just off Covent Garden.

The last leader of the Covent Garden Team, **Mike Pargiter**, is now a senior estate surveyor with the Royal Parks Division of the Department of National Heritage.

Charlie Rossi stood for election to the Inner London Education Authority after the demise of the GLC and represented Deptford until the ILEA, too, was abolished by the Thatcher government. He is now retired and lives in Camden.

Tony Sherman and **Cyril Waterman** continue to run fourteen of Britain's public markets from their headquarters in Henrietta Street, a few yards from the Jubilee Hall.

BIBLIOGRAPHY

Anson, Brian, *I'll Fight You For It!* (London 1981)

Architectural Design, *Covent Garden Carve-Up*, 41(7), July 1971, p.403

Biddle, Martin, *London on the Strand*, Popular Archaeology, July 1984, pp.23–7

Borer, Mary Cathcart, *Covent Garden* (London 1967)

Burford, E.J., *Wits, Wenchers and Wantons* (London 1986)

Christensen, Terry, *Neighbourhood Survival* (Dorchester 1979)

Commission for Local Administration in England, *Report of the Local Ombudsman on an Investigation into Complaint 329/Y/84 Against Greater London Council* (London 1985)

Cowie, Robert, *Lundenwic: "Unravelling the Strand"*, Archaeology Today, 8(5), June 1987, pp.30–4

Cowie, Robert and Whytehead, Robert, *Lundenwic: The Archeological Evidence for Middle Saxon London*, Antiquity, 63(241), 1989

Dent, Alan, *My Covent Garden* (London 1973)

Ford of Britain, *Every Day Except Xmas*, a documentary film from the 'Look at Britain' series, producers Leon Clore and Karel Reisz, director Lindsay Anderson (London 1954)

Greater London Council, *Covent Garden Action Area Plan, 1978*

Greater London Council, *Minutes of Proceedings, 1980*

Greater London Council, *Minutes of the Covent Garden Committee 1977–1981*

Greater London Council, *Minutes of the Planning Committee Covent Garden Panel 1981-1982* and *1982-1986*

Hillman, Judy, *The Rebirth of Covent Garden* (GLC, London 1986)

Long, Mary, *Covent Garden and her Craftsmen* (London 1975)

McKean, Charles, *Fight Blight* (London 1977)

Monahan, Jim, *Up Against the Planners in Covent Garden*, from *Community Politics*, ed. Peter Hain (London 1976)

Pargiter, M.L. (FRICS), *The Covent Garden Team's Involvement with the Jubilee Site*, an unpublished monograph by the last Leader of the Covent Garden Team (London 1992)

Richardson, John, *Covent Garden* (London 1979)

Shepard, G.H.W., ed., *Survey of London*, xxxvi: *The Parish of St Paul Covent Garden* (London 1970)

Thorne, Robert, *Covent Garden Market* (London 1980)

Vince, Alan G., *The Aldwych: Mid-Saxon London Discovered?*, Current Archaeology, 8(4), August 1984, pp.310–2

Walford, Edward, *Old London, Covent Garden and the Thames to Whitehall* (London 1987)

Woodiwiss, Audrey, *The History of Covent Garden* (London 1980)

Index

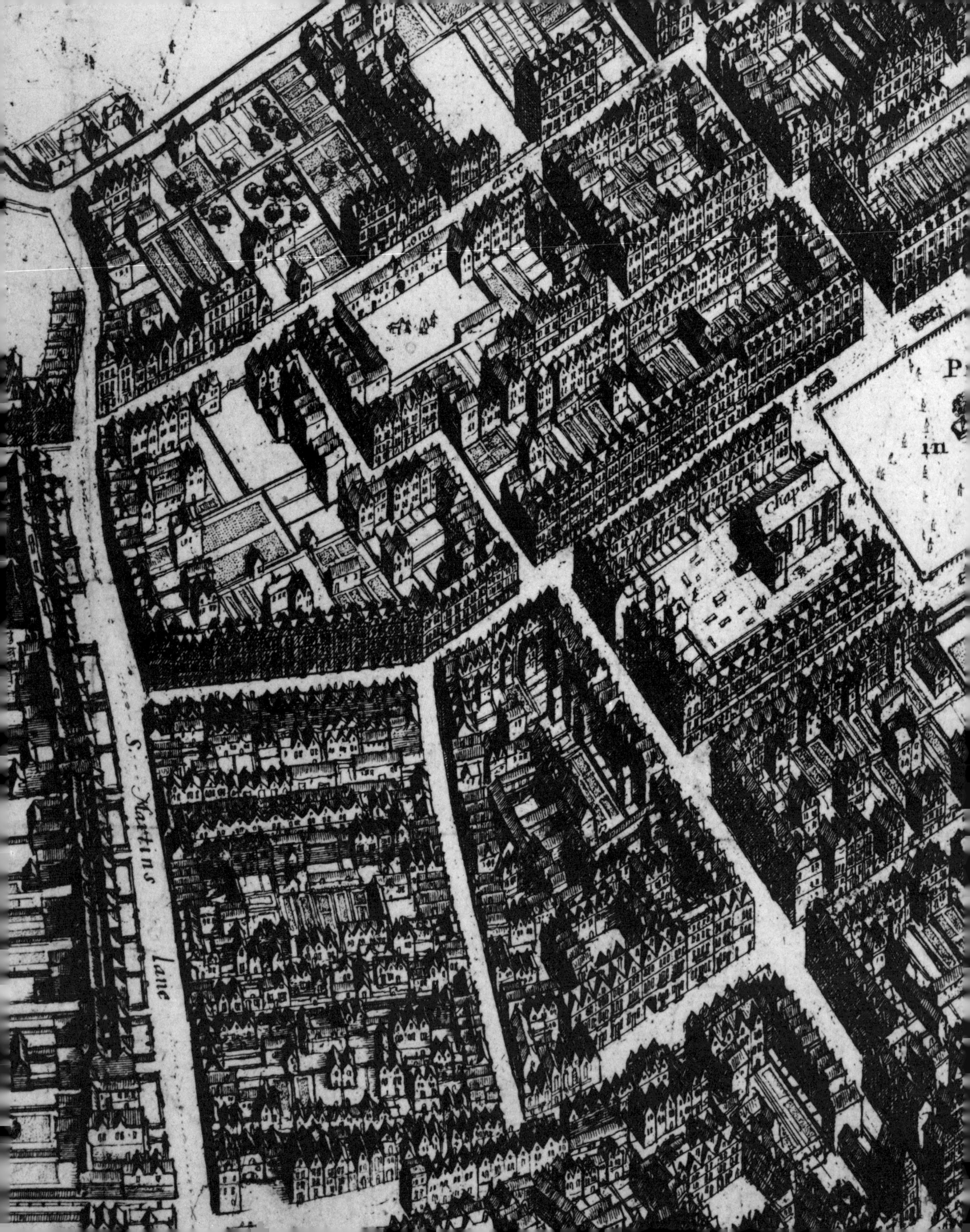